Erotic Surrender

Erotic Surrender

The Sensual Joys
of Female Submission

Claudia Varrin

CITADEL PRESS
KENSINGTON PUBLISHING CORP.
www.kensingtonbooks.com

To Meris

CITADEL PRESS books are published by

Kensington Publishing Corp.
850 Third Avenue
New York, NY 10022

All Kensington titles, imprints, and distributed lines are available at special quantity discounts for bulk purchases for sales promotions, premiums, fund raising, educational, or institutional use. Special book excerpts or customized printings can also be created to fit specific needs. For details, write or phone the office of the Kensington special sales manager: Kensington Publishing Corp., 850 Third Avenue, New York, NY 10022, attn: Special Sales Department, phone 1-800-221-2647.

Citadel Press logo Reg. U.S. Patent and Trademark Office
Citadel Press is a trademark of Kensington Publishing Corp.

First printing: March 2001

10 9 8 7 6 5 4 3 2 1

Printed in the United States of America

Library of Congress Cataloging-in-Publication Data
Varrin, Claudia.
    Erotic surrender : the sensual joys of female submission / Claudia Varrin.
        p.   cm.
    Includes bibliographical references.
    ISBN 0-8065-2181-3
    1. Sexual dominance and submission.   2. Sex instruction for women.
3. Women—Sexual behavior.   I. Title.
HQ79.V39   2001
306.77'5—dc21   99–14067
                                                                        CIP

Contents

Disclaimer

This book explores controversial and risky sexual activities. Neither the author of this book nor its publisher assume any responsibility for the exercise or misuse of practices described in this book.

As the cautions in the book make clear, practitioners of SM are keenly aware of the danger inherent in what they do. They take all care and precautions to reduce risk, anticipate problems, and understand them when they happen—but, most important—to avoid them. The author has provided only basic warnings and cautions in the appropriate chapters to remind the reader of the risks involved.

Practitioners of SM make a real and explicit distinction between consensual acts between adults for mutual pleasure, and any and all acts of violence against nonconsenting partners. Imposing any sexual activity upon a reluctant partner is immoral and offensive and, in some places, constitutes rape. Additionally, laws vary from state to state. In some jurisdictions, these activities are illegal, even between consenting adults.

Preface: Why I Switched

When I wrote *The Art of Sensual Female Dominance: A Guide for Women,* my intention was to give confidence and psychological insight, combined with practical instruction, to the budding domina and her newly submissive mate. In that book, I spoke of the power and fulfillment possible in an SM, or dominant/submissive, relationship with the female as the "top," or dominant partner. Although the submissive point of view was addressed, the book was written to the woman who wanted to be on top. The first book gave just a glimpse of the freedom, exhilaration, and pride of place a submissive can experience during consensual sexual surrender. It only hinted at the depths of emotion, the soaring passion, and spiritual exploration and fulfillment possible in erotic surrender. It gave no suggestions on becoming the best sexual submissive you can be.

I wanted to write this book to empower the nascent submissive female just as the first book empowered the budding dominant woman. I would like to tell you something about my life as a top and why I "switched."

One of the reasons I loved being a professional dominatrix was ultimately one of the reasons I retired. It saddened me that most of the men I saw were unable to continue to explore their submissive desires with their partners when the discoveries to be found there could be so valuable to their emotional health. Fortunately, I was able to combine that sadness with my own desire to be sexually submissive and to turn it into a deeply gratifying and emotionally enriching experience of my own. That inspired and encouraged me to write this book because I know there are many of you who will listen to me.

There is nothing politically incorrect about being sexually submissive, even in our world, because your sexuality is entirely a personal choice—*your* choice. I know that for some of you being sexually submissive in a romantic SM setting will heighten the intimacy, trust, and communication of your relationship. I know it will enrich your life and enhance your lovemaking. And it is to you I would like to speak.

When I first entered the world of professional domination, I was delighted and empowered by the men who requested me and the fantasies we enacted together. It was all new and different, each session a challenge, each role an opportunity for another Academy Award–caliber performance. After extensive training with my mentor, Ava Taurel, which continued even after I was seeing clients, I began to do the club and party scene to seek clients of my own. I modeled in fetish wear fashion shows, was seen at the clubs with the right people, got on private party lists, and attended fetish weekends. Finally, after years of only dreaming of a true SM love-style, not just my usual lucky but chance encounters, I had met others (many, many of them) with interests the same as or similar to my own.

In keeping with my voracious appetite for everything SM, I took on personal slaves on a regular basis. And just like when I was a child and, later, a teen dreaming of a sadomasochistic relationship, I read everything I could get my hands on. Only now I had the time to seek out books, the money to buy them, and, with my newly liberated spirit, the right eyes to read them with. I bought whips and crops and canes and paddles; I bought leather clothes galore, and latex, and PVC (a shiny, stretchy vinyl), too; I bought nipple clamps and cock cages and ball weights and blindfolds; I bought fetish stilettos and platform shoes; and I loved it all. I ate it up. Each time I was "requested," I inquired very carefully into the nature of the session: what type of clothing and demeanor the client envisioned. Each booking was its own little epic and I was the director.

It was at this time, in these early days, that I actually bore some sort of remote, distant love for these men who let me tie them up, discipline them, dress them up like women, walk on them, shower them with my golden nectar, torture and humiliate them in countless ways, some thought up by them, most thought up by me. But before all of that hap-

pened, the gentleman (95 percent of the men were exactly that) always
wanted to spend a few minutes of his hour talking to the mistress. Some
of that time was spent discussing a particular fantasy, but the rest was
not. First, the men wanted to "know" about me, then they wanted me
to "know" about them. These bookings were very much like therapy sessions.

Their questions were usually the same. Did I have another, or day,
job? Yes. Did I do this just for the money? No, I love to hear other people's fantasies—hearing and sharing theirs has made my own sex and
fantasy life so much richer, more exotic, more abandoned. Many told me
they thought my "enhanced love-style" was wonderful, then related their
fantasy with newfound confidence. A common question, either before or
after the session, was whether I had ever heard a fantasy such as theirs.
The need to validate fantasies of exotic sex is very strong in us. "Well,
I've heard similar themes," I'd say, "a common thread. But *your* fantasy
has your touch, your style to it, making it unique." I felt this was a win-
win answer. It validated the fantasy—similar themes—which is what
each man wanted, and needed, to hear. The plus was the second sentence: touch, style, unique. How nice to be validated *and* complimented
at the same time!

But with others, when I said that I enjoyed an SM love-style, their
sadness would creep into the dungeon on cat feet. I would then be told
that each wife or girlfriend had no idea what he was "into," and he had
no idea what would happen if she found out. Either the men didn't
think their mate would understand, or else the particular woman herself had never instigated anything. If that was the case, with no clue as
to its reception, he was loath to bring it up. The lack of trust and communication was sad enough, but what troubled me even more was the
mild nature of many of the fantasies that I enacted. If a hard-working,
educated man, and a good provider for his family cannot approach the
partner of his life with a fantasy about giving her an erotic foot massage,
I perceive a real problem. This is a common, mild, harmless fantasy. Entire vignettes in popular movies have been based on foot massage; others have foot fetish scenes, and still others treat foot fetishism with a
humorous, tongue-in-cheek air. If this is his fantasy, what would it really cost to fulfill it for him?

Perhaps, if the fantasy had been jointly enacted, it would have been the best foreplay the couple had ever had, leading to the greatest sex they had ever had in their lives! And yet this poor soul had to place his trust in a total stranger—a stranger who understood his dark side and dreamworld better than his partner! Many of the fantasies I have enacted have been just such mild and amusing foot worship sessions, cross-dressing sessions, light bondage and discipline, or naughty schoolboy scenarios. As a professional dominatrix, no session ever included any type of sexual service, although as a reward I may have allowed the man to relieve his "tension" (and I do mean by himself) before leaving. Many were scenarios that could have been shared and enacted with a loving partner for the betterment of the overall relationship, and could have included sex! Furthermore, these men had absolutely no desire to give up their lives or their wives; they were sincerely interested in preserving their marriages, and they loved their wives and families. They just wished . . .

After a while, these tales of noncommunication and lack of trust and intimacy began to wear on me. I found I had to close myself off from all but what I needed to hear to conduct the fantasy session. A while later, I found myself turning down bookings that were not exactly to my liking or when the submissive didn't know how he'd like to submit. I saw fewer and fewer clients and concentrated on personal slaves. I began to realize my love affair with professional domination was nearing its end. Apathy set in because I couldn't change their circumstances—only playact with them for an hour. I knew that once having had a taste of it, these men would think about sadomasochistic sex for the rest of their lives, and that saddened me. If they never sought the services of another professional, all they would have would be their dreams and a memory.

What had been a love/love relationship turned to apathy, which then turned to a cool anger. In the odd way the psyche works, I felt anger at what I perceived as the parasitic nature of the men's relationship with me. I began to think of them as psychosexual errand boys that came to my supra-sensual supermarket with grocery lists of fantasies they wanted fulfilled: the crook of a finger, the arch of a foot, the puff of a cigarette. The fantasies were so thought out and thought over that no ordinary human could possibly hope to fulfill them: It would have truly taken a divine or supernatural being. They wanted, I gave. They left rejuvenated, exhilarated; I left drained, tired. I took less and less "work" and spent more and more time fantasizing and writing about sado-masochistic sex.

At first I wrote as a domina dominating men. I churned out pieces about bondage, beatings, cross-dressing, foot worship, slave training, and humiliation—men in cages, men in stockades, men on auction blocks. Naughty schoolboys got the paddle; bad dogs got put in their cage; bad kitties got the spray bottle. Smart-asses got the cane. Police officers, postmen, drill sergeants, and peeping toms were punished with forced feminization. Butt plugs and ball gags, clamps and clothes pins, floggers and fetish wear paraded through my stories like well-loved, yet oft-hated, characters from an SM soap opera. My social life was pleasantly active: I was on a private party circuit, a member of the local SM society, and I went to two or three parties each month. There were SM meetings and on-off events in nearby cities that couldn't be missed. I made the rounds of the local fetish stores and called friends in the scene.

Life was enjoyable even if I was enjoying it alone. As far as sex in the traditional sense was concerned? I had been celibate for months! All of my sex had been dominant play with submissive friends which stopped well short of the sexual release I would have enjoyed if I had been with a regular *dominant* partner. Even as a child, I wanted to play SM games with a loving and supportive master, although I wouldn't have used quite those words. It was those sexually submissive fantasies that I had created ever since childhood that set me to explore my own submissive nature. After having explored the submissive fantasies of so many others, I decided it was time to do something more than just think about my own.

I began by defining my style of masochism and submission in short stories, written from my own submissive/masochistic point of view. By writing my fantasies, I began to distinguish between those things I *claimed* to fear, which were things I did want to happen at the right time with the right person, from those things I genuinely feared. I wanted to articulate the thrill of the downward emotional spiral of masochism and the cleansing effect of pain turned into pleasure and of being brought to the edge over and over in a trusting, caring relationship. In some of my masochistic and submissive fantasies, coercion and consent, turmoil and inner struggle became central elements of erotic pleasure. For me, resistance heightens my emotional pitch and intensifies physical sensation. Under the illusion of force, my master grants me license to enjoy my most debased sexual desires. By pretending that I have no choice, I can forget that I do. This pretense, combined with the orders of the master, permits me to explore my sexual nature and reach deeper for erotic intensity.

In other fantasies, I saw myself as "forced" to submit to ritualistic humiliation and to perform embarrassing acts. In the midst of these delicious degradations designed by me for me, I wanted to break down walls of resistance that had burdened me for too long. I wanted to attain a feeling of power and freedom because I had conceived my worst humiliation, confessed it to another, and then enacted it. I wanted to delve into the depths of my masochism and renew myself with voluntary suffering. Through humiliation and pain, I hoped to explore my potential for reduction of the self. Pain and humiliation are deconstructors of ego, and, via their magic, I wanted to explore those actions that, when the self is stripped naked and taken apart, ceased to be performed with reluctance. My body and soul would work together to submit in the chivalrous sense of the word; perfection was perceived as total obedience and loyalty to a higher power.

So there I was, being the top in public, but in private all my fantasies were still very masochistic and submissive. In the wee hours, I would lie in my bed or on my leather sofa and send myself to my own private subspace where I could be the submissive masochist once again. My masters have been a desert sheik and bandit, pirate, highwayman, the Marquis, Indian chief, a man in uniform, and so on, and I have scripted and window-dressed the set to match the master. In my fantasies, the prime erotic themes are humiliation and ritual, and coercion and consent. I come to adore my sadistic master who feeds me and takes care of me by day and sexually abuses me for his enjoyment at night. The master is the only person in my life, and I crave his attention; the pain he has given me has reconstructed my ego and I lose awareness of self. Through masochism, pain, and humiliation, I experience a spiritual rebirth when I subjugate myself totally to him.

Lovely ideals, beautiful dreams, hot fantasies all, but, like every bottom, I needed a top: a dom to my sub, a lord to my slave, a yin to my yang. The trials and tribulations I went through to find a suitable lord and master could be compared to the labors of Hercules. Quickly I realized that none of the men in my local SM scene were suitable. Same old story: All the good ones were taken; the rest were chaff blown in and out. One was so commitment phobic he thought the phone greeting, "Hi! What are you doing?" meant for the rest of his life. Another had a vomiting fetish and asked me if I had bulimia so I could throw up on him. Yet another required his slave to walk through SM clubs barefoot, where there are usually sticky spots on the floor which are better not thought about. Several were too old or too young, many were overweight, and others used SM sex as a quick thrill, like the one-night stands of the old days.

Sometimes, the male's lack of experience, "having only discovered his dominant nature," meant I would be topping from the bottom (if he would let me) until I could teach him enough to take over. In some cases, the scarier ones admitted they had no experience but didn't want to learn from me, they wanted to learn on me. But the real problem was that none of these men turned me on, none got my motor running, and none of them "blew my skirt up." Additionally, in the United States, I still had a reputation as a professional dominatrix to uphold and couldn't be led around clubs naked on a leash. My submission had to remain private for the time being, but my search continued.

One evening at the Gummi Club in London, where I was visiting a friend, I found myself sitting next to a man whose rugged handsomeness caught my attention. When he turned his sea-green eyes to meet mine, I noticed how strongly his dark side projected itself through his good looks. A strong, once broken nose divided his face; a deep dimple dotted his chin; and his sea monster green eyes twinkled merrily whenever he looked at me.

When he smiled, two deep dimples dented his cheeks, no doubt put there by some benevolent goddess to soften the jagged planes of his face. When he stood to get us drinks from the bar, I couldn't help but notice that he was the height and weight I like my men to be. As he walked away from me, I saw, delight of delights, a long ponytail streaming down his back, neatly controlled by a barrette with a black leather bow on it! I love long hair—something to grab ahold of, and long just like mine. His name was Niles, and he was a dom whose experience surpassed my own and whose tastes matched mine. He had a reputation as a creative, experienced top and was the most ruggedly handsome man I had ever met. Our personal electromagnetic fields blended beautifully, and, alone in a strange land, his warmth and friendliness made my inner light glow brighter when I was near him. I thought I had met the man who was to be my friend and lover, lord and master, and my equal.

Later that night, in the dungeon of a mansion in the English countryside, Niles sat me on a low stool across from his higher one; my knees were open and my arms folded behind my back to thrust my breasts out. He began by kissing me and he kissed divinely. After I grew wet from his extraordinary kisses, he began to pinch my nipples. Increasing the pressure ever so slowly, he made me come many times as he pinched and kissed me. Then he pushed my knees open wider with his legs and started to tease and gently torture my nether lips but he didn't penetrate me.

He played with me for over two hours before he moved us to the blankets and pillows we had piled on the floor. He pushed me onto my back and knelt between my legs; then he plunged two fingers into me and I had a cosmic orgasm. Exploring the inside of my quim (the British term for a woman's honey spot), he located my G-spot and began to wring one orgasm after another from my ecstatically tortured and ravenously hungry body. After an eternity had passed and I was weak and pliant from coming, he prepared to mount me, letting me see his large and lovely cock before he penetrated me. I watched in a welter of passion as the length of his cock disappeared inside of me. I opened to him like night-blooming jasmine under the luminescence of the moon. When I left England, it was with glowing memories of my experience with him.

Niles and I kept in touch by phone and through letters. I wanted to see him again and was in the process of making arrangements for the flight when a mutual friend called and told me Niles was very ill. I wanted to fly over right away to look after him, but I was told that his condition wasn't that bad and that the caller would tend to him. How-

ever, when I arrived I could see for myself that no one had been looking after this man. He was obviously in pain and was run-down from
taking a monthlong course of antibiotics. It took me less than two days
to sum up the situation and restrict his activities to hanging out on the
sofa, going to the bathroom, and sleeping. I did everything else. I
changed the bed and started on seven loads of laundry. I hit the supermarket with a vengeance, then learned how to cook what he liked. I
made daily trips to the local shops for fresh fruit and baked goods. The
trash went out. The mail came in. I fixed the vacuum and used it, repeatedly. The refrigerator, the cabinets, the floors, none were safe from
me and my sponge.

Before I knew it, I was on my hands and knees cleaning his toilet
bowl. I had on my big yellow cleaning gloves, with the toilet brush in
my hand, when I realized I was deliriously happy cleaning this man's
john! Because of his illness, we were being playful and affectionate but
not playing to a finish, so I knew I wasn't blinded by great sex. I felt
comfortable with this man, comfortable in his house. We talked often,
getting to know each other better. I learned he needed meat at every
meal and liked fresh fruit with his lunch. Our silences were comfortable,
and we knew how to give each other privacy in a small apartment.

I was happy because for the first time in my life, I felt I was giving
in the chivalrous sense of the word, without looking to see what I would
get back. I enjoyed being with this man; I felt good with him, better
than when I was alone; and it was a deep, trusting feeling. When I
looked at him, I saw someone who I liked exactly the way he was. I did-
n't want to change one thing about him (except maybe the carpet in the
living room!). I loved giving to him, and I was thrilled to be able to
repay his kindness to me in such a tangible way. How often does such
an opportunity come along? And how often do we turn away because it
isn't convenient for us just then? He needed something and I was able
to give it.

We played little games even during daylight task-time because he
needed to be amused and because I was certainly enjoying myself. Besides, a good friend would have been doing these household things and
homey chores for him anyway. We just added our SM flavor to it. We
had tea together every afternoon; I served his first, on a tray London-

style, and drank mine on the floor at his feet, nude. I had made it a practice to draw his bath and I became his bath attendant. I gave him manicures; I shampooed his hair and brushed it out. I mended ripped garments and sewed on buttons. I was a hive of activity, happy that I could be of great benefit to someone I really cared about. I was giving in a meaningful way and I was in heaven.

And he was a prince. At first he was concerned that I wasn't having a good time on my vacation. He realized what I was doing and tried to make me sit or stop or leave it. He even "ordered" me to sit and do nothing, but I "disobeyed" him. Just the fact that he saw and remarked on my efforts, thanking me for them in a way that made me think he didn't get or accept this type of care or kindness often, made me want to do more for him. I knew that under normal circumstances, he could cook a great meal, keep a neat place, and generally fend for himself. He felt badly that I was going to spend my holiday cooking and cleaning and looking after him. On the other hand, I was happy to do all that and more, plus getting to know him better as a person. Although the everyday intimacy of our relationship had been enhanced by our sado-masochistic sex, this was the first relationship I had ever had that was not based on sex. This man was first my friend and I never lost sight of that fact.

That's when I knew this was the first adult relationship I had ever had in my life. The feeling of being fulfilled from emptying myself of self, of using a downward spiral to raise myself up, and explore my deepest sexual fantasies was why I had switched and sought a master with whom to live out my submissive fantasies. It was my first step. I took it, kept walking, and I never looked back because I knew I was on the right path. I had gained a new understanding of myself and had become more comfortable with who and what I am. After having met someone with whom I could share and enact exotic masochistic and submissive fantasies, I have overcome a great deal of my natural shyness and am more at ease in the everyday world. When I left Niles that March, I was glowing from the way his personal energy blended with and enhanced mine. I felt great joy at having made a new friend and at having been chivalrously submissive to him.

He became my closest friend and confidante, my captor and my torturer, my hero, and my knight in shining armor. He became my muse and my mentor, my playmate and my lover, my archangel and my demon. And through all of that, we never lost sight of the fact that we were equals in a romantic, SM relationship. He took me where I most feared to go and showed me how to experience exquisite pleasure there. He was supportive of me, proud of me, and not the least bit intimidated by me. He knew my vulnerabilities, and didn't use them against me. I trusted him with my heart, soul, and body; I trusted his strength and his sensibility, and I knew that he cared for me. My playtimes with him were transcendental, and my only attachment to this earth was the invisible cord that kept me connected to him. When we are old and gray, he will still be as handsome to me as he was in the moment we met, because he carries his beauty in his heart.

Acknowledgments

To Ava Taurel, for being a soul mate; Andy Foley, for twenty-five years of it; Betsy Rochette, for patio days, hot tub nights, and cookies; Desire, for never forgetting her friends; Fizzy, for taking a chance, and darling, shall we dance?; Hazel, for her silly jokes and sweet laugh; Jennifer, for all she has given me; Julia, my tall friend, for her gentle soul; Keith, for showing me the man behind the master; Lori Perkins, my agent; Mulligan, for the artist in his soul; and to my Master, whose name is known only to the two of us, long may He reign.

To Paul Dinas, my editor, for his friendship and support above and beyond the call of duty; Ritza, for letting me take long, delicious baths at her house; Renee Orobello, for being herself; Ted and Diane, for being the couple to capture hearts; Tim Mullen, when on earth will he give me that bell?; Tim Woodward and Skin Two, for their help and support; Xena, for doubles in the dungeon; and, as always, Soft, Sweet Mary for our previous lives in a nunnery.

She

Dressed for passion in straps of softest leather
body held in delicate bondage by harness and tether
High-heeled boots give her a somnambulist's gait
as she walks slowly into the light, in love with her fate

Features enhanced by an angel's delicate paints
neck, wrists and ankles wrapped in love's leather restraints
Corsetted waist offers up breasts and plumps out hips
her pointy pink tongue moistens lush and trembling lips

Bound by a kiss and teased with joy
she has consented to be the master's toy
She opens her mind to explore her darkest desire
her power consumes her like liquid fire

Collared and cuffed and splayed on the rack
strangers' eyes launch their attack
Her glistening body a rare jewel, a treasure
her burning flesh fanning the flames of their pleasure

Quick flick of the wrist to flail the cane
double-dealing the cruelest of all pain
With religious fervor she makes herself wait
striving through pain to reach heaven's gate

Sweet scent of sex and the smell of fear
a muffled cry no one can hear
Rolling waves of desire beckoning
for the flesh to be tortured without reckoning

With each stroke more of her demons are slain
and her salty tears cool a steaming brain
Flooding a heart that beats hard and fast
filled with the hope that love and passion will last

—Claudia Varrin

Erotic Surrender

Introduction: The Dark Garden of Sex Magick

The exquisite sexual pleasure attainable from SM sex can be likened to a dark garden of erotic blooms. In the playground of your mind, there is a black lace veil separating you from this exotic landscape. Only glimpses of the garden can be seen through this veil; you can just barely make out the blooms bobbing dreamily on their stems on the other side. The veil flutters and you see the fantasy-flowers nodding their heads conspiratorially in the musk-scented breeze; it seems that they are beckoning you to enter the garden. "Come in," you hear them whisper, "come in." With a flutter, the veil drops back into place, obscuring your view. You reach out to pull the veil aside but your hand falls back to your side—the veil untouched. That's because the mind-set needed to draw aside this veil is located in a shadow land of the mind called "the dark side," and many are afraid of venturing there alone.

We walk in the light easily and unassisted. To deliberately cross over and step into the shadow land where the seat of your power resides can be a scary thing. It is when we look to tap into the power of our dark side, either as a top or a bottom, that we falter. But we should walk there with more assurance, because the power we will find in the dark garden is a very valuable and beautiful part of our character. The power located in our dark side gives us strength, helps us make decisions, and lets us see the difference between good and evil. If we do not know the faces of good and evil, how are we to recognize them? With the right partner, good communication, and trust, this shadow land can become your personal dark garden of erotic fantasies to be picked like fragrant blooms and enjoyed in their time. Your new power is the fertile soil of this delectable dark garden.

What draws some to this garden in the erotic shadows? Many who like playing in the dark garden enjoy the "taboo" factor involved in SM sex. Knowing they are "breaking" some societal no-no can be a very necessary part of their enjoyment. Because SM fantasies *are* located in a shadowy dark garden in the mind, no one has ever fully explained the phenomenon of SM. I personally hope no one ever does. The erotic garden of SM fantasies and sex (whether it be your garden or mine) needs to remain in the fertile soil of the shadows to keep its allure. It is my thought that exposing SM to the full light of day would incinerate it, like exposing a vampire to the sun.

Some are drawn to SM for the spirituality of the experience or relationship. They find SM to be a place where in public they are free to be the inner self they dream of being in private, to show their secret heart to a trusted partner without fear of reproach or rejection. In the SM arena, they are free to share the soaring beauty in their soul and by the sharing of it, expand and enrich the souls of both. It is a means of sexual expression that holds the promise of intense sharing on an almost spiritual level. Done with a loving, caring partner, SM can be a safe place to heal and grow, and to experience and explore your most exotic fantasies. The games SMers play are delicate exchanges of power; the scenes are crafted to fulfill the desires of both partners, to deconstruct and reconstruct their egos and to expand their potential as sexual beings. For some of you, SM can heighten and enhance the intimacy and trust of your relationship, in the bedroom and out.

Making Assumptions

Before proceeding, I am going to make two assumptions. The first assumption is that you are in an ongoing monogamous relationship. I feel this is the safest way to play at SM, because SM sex does carry some degree of physical and/or emotional risk. This risk is lessened when the partners do not change, or bear a meaningful responsibility for each other. Also, this assumption eliminates the need for constant reminders to engage in safe sex. Let's go over it once, for the record. In nonmonogamous relationships, SM-flavored or not, all protective safe-sex measures should be taken. Latex condoms should be worn during oral sex on the male, and during any and all forms of intercourse and penetration. Dental dams, or film wrap, from the kitchen should be used for oral sex with the woman. Gloves, surgical or fetish in latex, or finger-covers, should be worn during manual penetration or stimulation, especially if there are cuts or nicks on the hands. The proper nonoil-based lubricant should be used frequently to preserve the integrity of the latex according to the manufacturers' instructions. Enjoy!

The second assumption I will make is that the submissive partner is female, and she is the one reading this book. Doms and subs, tops and bottoms of either sex are welcomed, as are all others interested in SM, but to keep things consistent, here all bottoms are "she" and all tops are "he."

SM . . . all Talk

I think it would be a good idea to define the general terms I will be using in this book. Let's start with sadomasochism, which I will refer to as SM. Consensual, romantic, sadomasochistic sex (SM) is an erotic technique that can be used by anyone to enhance and embellish their regular lovemaking. "SM," for our purposes, will always silently include the phrase "among consensual individuals." Called by many other names, such as D&S (dominance and submission), B&D (bondage and discipline), R&P (restraint and pleasure), guidance and surrender, guidance and correction, role-playing, psychodrama, and fetishism, SM is the preferred moniker of those indulging in it. We also refer to SM as "Sex Magick" or "Sensual Magic," because the impact it has on the mind and body is magical. SM is the broad, all-encompassing term for all *consensual* acts of D&S, B&D, fetishism, and so on, which are aspects of sadomasochism.

Another term I will be using often is "scene." In SM play, a scene is a combination of mental, emotional, and physical components, as well as an exchange of power, which blend to produce an electrifying erotic event for both partners. A scene can be as short as five minutes; it can last for five days, five years, or five decades. SM scenes don't begin when the signal is given that playtime has begun; they begin in your mind long before the "action" does. SM sex is *sex* and sex starts in the mind. Your mind has to love it, to want it, before your body will respond to it. The first response is in the mind, not in the genitals. They benefit, indeed profit, by extension but are not the focal point. You could be sitting at a movie or the ballet, and the couple sitting right next to you could be engaged in an SM scene. At the direction of her master, that well-dressed woman might have a bare bottom under her evening gown or be decked out as a hooker underneath it. She could be in such a state of sexual arousal from what is happening in her mind that she may be ready to burst, and you wouldn't even know it!

Going bare bottomed for the master under your dress is an SM game. Some call it a master-slave scenario, others call it role-playing. But it makes no difference: It is all part and parcel of SM. Many people, both inside the scene and out, shy away from the term SM because of the unpleasant associations the words "sadomasochistic sex" can conjure up. We are not talking about you and your budding relationship with Torquemada (the head of the Spanish Inquisition) nor are we talking about someone like Ted Bundy, who announced that he was influenced by sadomasochistic pornography. What we are talking about is a romantic dominant-submissive relationship between two consenting adults.

The beauty of consensual SM is that both parties, top and bottom, giver and receiver, have planned the scene together and *want* to enact that fantasy with each other. Nothing is forced upon either party. Compromises are sought when fantasy-divergence occurs, and agreements are made and lived up to. Care and support, trust and communication, are the cornerstones of the loving SM relationship and safe, sane, and consensual fantasy enactment is a safe harbor from the stress of everyday life.

The Players

There are three basic players in SM: those who are dominants, or "tops," and those who are submissive, or "bottoms." These are the two players we will be concentrating on. The third group is called "switches," wonderfully greedy types who can be top or bottom: professional dominants who are privately submissive; masters who order their slaves to tie them up; slave-girls who are "commanded" to stay in bed while the lord puts the kettle on; and couples who switch roles part of the way through the scene.

Although there are more documented cases of males being submissive than of females, in the SM world the number of submissive males to submissive females is roughly even. Half the men are tops and half are bottoms; half the women are tops and half bottoms. SMers are a greedy bunch of sexual gourmands who sample from a large, groaning table of temptations. The temptations come later; first let's define the two players.

In SM, a bottom could be a submissive, slave, sex toy, masochist, harem girl, pony-girl, exhibitionist, the upstairs maid, or a footstool. I will use the word bottom to denote the partner who surrenders temporary control to a dominant during a romantic SM scene. A bottom, then, would be any person with the ability to eroticize and enjoy stimulation, such as pain and helplessness, which would be unpleasant and unwanted in a real-life situation. Holding your hands behind your back for a prenegotiated face-slapping of your own free will is very different from being hurt by the hand snaked out in anger that leaves behind its red print of shame on the cheek. A consensual sexual submissive has no desire to be abused for real, and can separate fantasy from reality.

The bottom's counterpart is, of course, the top. A top can be a dominant, dom, sadist, lord, fireman, Indian chief, centaur, alien, or whoever wields the crook and flail of authority. A top is a person who is willing to accept temporary control over another and turn an experience that would seem mean or disrespectful or otherwise unpleasant in real life into an erotic event. A good, caring dominant knows that being a dominant is a responsibility, and he looks upon the SM power exchange and the slave's submission as the precious gifts that they are. A good dom is creative and imaginative and is concerned with the emotional and physical well-being of his submissive. He can control his slave because he is able to control himself. A good top is never truly uncaring, mean, or abusive (unless it is upon your specific request!).

Definitions . . . by Gender

I would say that both men and women, whether top or bottom, would agree in some way with the definitions of top and bottom that I have given above. But now we come to what I perceive as a subtle difference in definitions based on gender. Under the general heading of bottom, male doms seem to have *two* subheads: slave/submissive (used interchangeably) and masochist. A woman, whether top or bottom, tends to have *three* subheads under bottom: slave, submissive, *and* masochist. Because we are women and I wrote this book for us, I'll talk about our definitions first. For countless women through the ages, being a slave-girl has been a hot fantasy. Bought, sold, and used like chattel, she is only useful to her master as long as her body continues to please him. Then he's free to trade her in for two 20-year-olds when she hits forty or even for a herd of goats, if that is his preference. Seeing herself as an object for the master's use and amusement and ultimate disposal when she no longer pleases is the mind-set of a slave.

There is absolutely, positively nothing wrong with this as a fantasy (it's one of my favorites, too!), but in reality do you want to be traded in for *anything* when you hit forty? Of course not! You are a submissive, or a masochist, with a slave-girl fantasy, not really and truly chattel.

Now for a woman's definition of a submissive. A submissive, in an action sense, can be someone who enjoys dressing up, serving the top in private or in public, and accepting humiliation and punishment; she sees all this as great fun. And it is; I personally vouch for it. To her delight, she has found her dark garden and entered it hand in hand with her lord. Emotionally, her character isn't reduced in any way; she is proud of who she is and what she does. She does this because she *chooses* to, because she enjoys it. She is valued for the beautiful and precious gift of submission she has given to her master. She wants to serve because she is serving the one she loves, the one she adores. Cherished and encouraged, she wants to please him above all else—her only reward may be a caress or a smile, but that will be enough.

Her joy comes from giving of herself, not looking for what she will receive in return. In serving her master, she frees herself from her ego and gives from her soul, from her heart. She believes that control, in a caring, trust-filled environment with a loving partner, can be exerted in such a way as to make her a better person. Her master shares her values and appreciates her worth; he respects her and takes pride in her achievements and accomplishments. Not given to mindless obedience, she is still a confident, contributing member of society who just happens to be exploring her sexuality. (And she has found it to be deliciously wicked and delightfully perverted!)

I have encountered too many male doms who don't value or understand a woman's concept of *submission in the chivalrous sense of the word,* and treat submission and slavery as one and the same state. You should be aware of this difference that exists in the minds of some, because it may affect you. A submissive may glory in her servitude, like the explorer described above, and think it is all wonderful fun and sexy games with a loving Master. A slave, however, may worry about the time her body no longer gives pleasure to the lord as her body is the only thing she has to offer him. A slave, like chattel, can be loaned out for the night, bartered in exchange for another, or shared with others. And although the need to serve seems genetically ingrained in some of us, we are not chattel and are not prepared to give up our self-esteem to serve. This thinking is primitive, and we have come too far in society (thank the goddess) to revert now.

Fortunately, more submissive men than women think of themselves as slave property. Unfortunately, many dominant men think of women as chattel-slaves rather than as valued submissives. Make sure your partner has the same understanding of bottom that you do and that you are clear how you define yourself. (See chapter 4, The Seeds of Desire.)

Topping From the Bottom

Some doms love it when the submissive acts up: They love the challenge these subs present and like putting them in their place. Other tops consider this sort of behavior unacceptable because they feel it is an insult, or affront, to their dignity and position. Not wanting to constantly defend their position as the top, this group regards informal, playful behavior in a bottom as undesirable. Those who consider acting up to be a challenge to their authority call these slaves or "SAS" (smart-assed slaves). I prefer to call these subs "frisky slaves," and I must confess that I have been frisky myself upon occasion.

Whereas the frisky slave is high spirited and really is just "acting up," the slave who is topping from the bottom is one who tries to out-top the top. This slave tells the top what to do and when to do it, tries to take over the scene without the top's consent, or totally loses interest when everything they want to happen isn't happening. Classically, behavior of this type is considered bad form and is referred to as "topping from the bottom." Under normal circumstances, it is not appreciated by any tops that I know. But because you are a submissive female hoping to teach your man how to be your master, top from the bottom you must. This is the one circumstance under which topping from the bottom can, and does, work: when the top is the novice and the bottom is the experienced player! Which is just your situation now, isn't it? Experience is given its due: As the "teacher," you will be walking him through his paces, training him to top you the way you want. This is a most benign and pleasant form of manipulation, and the top has consented to be instructed by the bottom for mutually agreed-upon purposes until he gains enough experience.

The Allure of Sensual Submission

Giving the gift of submission, or being a submissive, can mean many different things, depending on who you are talking to, where, and when. In general, the submissive exists to fulfill the wishes of the dominant in a prearranged scene. For the slave-girl, it can mean wearing only golden bracelets and anklets as her costume while curled on the floor, acting as her master's footstool, warming and cushioning his feet. For the masochist, it is a good beating interspersed with the brush of a hard cock against her thigh, and a large, warm hand crushing her breast. Those who dream of being sex-toys are used over and over, even awakened during the night to serve her master's needs. Sexual submission can be the thud of a lover's foot as he chases you into the apartment and knocks you to the floor. The rip of your secondhand clothes, bought especially for the occasion, becomes beautiful music as he forces your legs open and mounts you. He whispers your name and you know him to be your lover; safe in his arms, you are free to experience the heady adrenaline rush of rape without the danger.

Sexual submission is a provocative and alluring condition. The sexual slave lives in a constant state of sexual arousal and anticipation. In sexual submission there resides a deep seductiveness, an empowerment of the submissive that the uninitiated seldom see. The submissive is not powerless, not abused, not degraded, or downtrodden—that would be abuse and SM is not abuse. Consensual sexual submission is a joyous, wonderful state. The submissive is respected by the dominant, and vice versa, and theirs is an exchange of rare and precious gifts.

In SM culture, a sexual submissive is usually someone who has great responsibility in real life and uses SM to provide an outlet for tension and stress of the day. This would lead you to believe that all, or most, submissives are men. But the desire to escape responsibility and enjoy guilt-free sexual fantasies need not and is not limited to male empire buildings. Homemakers and secretaries need outlets, too, and SM can be easily molded to suit their purposes. The fantasy enactment can become a place where her good qualities, lost in the shuffle of the kids and the workday, are praised and appreciated in the context of "serving the master."

The time of submission is surreal time—no decisions, no distractions, no responsibilities. A separate time and space can be entered by the submissive (initially called subspace, at the advanced level it is called flying or floating), a certain spirituality is attained as she frees herself from her ego and gives herself over to the joy of giving to another to fulfill herself. Sexual submission can fulfill a temporary need to "honor" a person "higher" than oneself; it can be a deconstructor of ego, and a flight into the inner realms of the self. The power of the SM relationship is such that the dominant and submissive partners, when properly connected, can literally hold each other in thrall. The gift of love and trust you are about to bestow upon him is like a perfect prayer, given without thought of self.

Now that you are familiar with the some of reasons why one would want to pursue an SM love style and some of the general terms we will be using, we are ready to continue our exploration into the dark garden. In the following chapters, I will introduce you to the mind of SM, strip away some of the pervasive misconceptions about SM, and help you decide if sexual, sensual submission is for you.

~ 1 ~

The Hidden Beauty of Sensual Submission

The requirement that there be a single kind of sexual life for every-one disregards the dissimilarities, whether innate or acquired, in the sexual constitution of human beings; it cuts off a fair number of them from sexual enjoyment.

—Sigmund Freud, 1930

SM is fueled by fantasies and its goal is to turn those fantasies into an immensely pleasurable, erotic reality. To do this, an exchange of power must take place. SM *is* a delicate game about exchanging power; it is about erotic control and sensual surrender. Power, and the surrender of it, are very, very sexy. The submissive partner relinquishes control of her body and mind (to the negotiated point, of course, and perhaps just a little farther if she is ready) to the dominant who is skilled in SexMagick. The surrender is temporary and for an established amount of time. During this "surrender," we can explore feelings that would be too risky for us to experience otherwise. But to do this, a caring and supportive partner is necessary; someone who can be trusted with your emotional and physical safety and understands the person you are, whether this partner be a top or a bottom.

If SM is about command and authority for the dominant, it is about helplessness and vulnerability for the submissive. The lack of power experienced by the sub is as intoxicating as the heady dose of power surging through the dom. SM is the empowerment of the dom by the sub to act out sadomasochistic sexual fantasies to the fulfillment of both partners. It is always respectful of the body and mind of both top and bottom, and of their boundaries and limits.

That is a lot of official-sounding and serious language for a golden-twilight world filled with mystery and illusion, fantasy and delight. Sensual submission can be a luxurious pretend-captivity where one can indulge in sexual pleasure, and where each playtime is an opportunity for exploration into enhanced sexuality, communication, and deepened trust. It *is* romantic, fun, and sexy. It gets your heart pounding and your endorphins pumping; it kicks your love motor into high gear. It is sharing long-unspoken fantasies of sexual torment and anticipation, then making them live and breathe. SM can hold the promise of intense intimacy and profound gratification in one's chosen variety of sexuality. It can open your heart and free your soul, then make your spirit soar above the earth; your only attachment to our world is the invisible cord between you and your master.

A Position of Power

In SM, things are not always what they seem, so I'm going to clear up some common misconceptions about being a submissive or a slave. To the casual observer, the submissive's position on the floor, crouched perhaps at the feet of the master, is a lowly position, an inferior one. Or maybe the welts left by the cane appear to be stripes of shame on a smooth, otherwise milky-white ass. But neither is true.

SM can also mean smoke and mirrors and illusion—in this case, the illusion of power. Most tops agreed that, to some extent, the top is submissive to the will of the slave. Another way to express the sentiment would be to say that the submissive is the one who is really in control of the scene. SM players know the dominant only wields the illusion of power. All of the power the master has over the slave has been given to him by the slave herself, and it can be withdrawn at any time. Being a slave is sexy; the illusion of surrendering your power is sexy, but it is still only an illusion. The bottom, in making the *choice* to be submissive, is the one truly in control.

To the uninitiated and uninformed, submission can imply that a person has no power or self-esteem. I can assure you that *that* is not the case. These are SM sex games we are playing, and part of the game is a temporary exchange of power. You can't give up what you don't have—in this case power—so the more power you have, the more you have to give up. The more you give up, the more empowering, or liberating, the lack of it becomes. My lack of power then makes me feel fantastically powerful; my power is an important part of who I am and what I am. If I am able to give it, even temporarily, to someone else, I become more powerful.

When I was the top, I put a lot of time and energy into planning a scene. I planned loosely yet still strove for perfection. After all of that output, I wanted a worthy submissive who felt pride in his submission and was gracious in manner and service. I want my submissives to share my ideal of submission and to feel about submission as I do. And when I bottom, I want my submission to be a valuable gift. A bottom gives of herself, and generously, too, and any top worthy of their whip will be able to recognize the great selfless gift of submission.

The act of submission can help to build a person's power and raise her self-esteem. Through her submission, a woman can realize how much she has to give and the worth of that offering; she can realize that she has enough control over her power, and herself, to give it away—if and when she chooses. In her control, she realizes that she can give her power to her master the way the master wants it, not the way she thinks he should have it. The beautiful and powerful submissive realizes new levels of pride in her submission because her pride, like her humility, comes from the depth of her self-knowledge and her deconstructed ego.

The sexual-submissive woman is not a passive victim; she is in a consensual relationship. She has not given up her social, economic, or professional power or standing. I find the ability to surrender my control, to give up my power over my sexuality and enact delectably "dirty" fantasies with my master, to be an overwhelmingly empowering experience, not a degrading one. If the fantasy is wanted by both partners, and gratifies both partners, then what is degrading about it? Degradation only occurs when one party is an unwilling participant. Two willing participants make it a fun, romantic playtime.

An Exchange of Gifts

We have spoken of your submission to him as a rare and precious gift, and it is. You are giving life to your fantasies by speaking them aloud to him, and you are giving him your mind and body as his personal playground. By inviting him into your dark garden, you are trusting him not to tread on the exotic blooms you have nurtured in secret for so long. No one will deny the beauty of sensual submission; however, I like to think of SM as an *exchange* of gifts. Your gift to him is not one-sided; he, too, is giving you a gift: the gift of dominance. Too few see it this way, focusing more on the submissive's gift as perhaps one of greater value because submission includes the giving of one's body to another. But the gift of dominance includes the accepting of responsibility, and although the responsibility is temporary, that acceptance makes the gift of dominance as rare and special as that of submission and should not be undervalued.

The gift of dominance is as complex and multifaceted as the gift of submission, but the elements of dominance's gift are largely unrecognized. One part of the dom's gift is his ability to listen to and accept your sexual desires, as well as your need to explore your dark garden. Next is his willingness to enter the garden and enact your fantasies with you. Other facets of the dom's gift are his creativity and imagination and the time and energy he puts into the fantasy-enactment. Topping is usually some degree of work for the dom, and not all fun and games while waiting to be told what to do next. He has to keep you in a constant and increasing state of sexual arousal and to do that he must be clever indeed!

Another important facet of dominance is the dom's ability to understand the needs and limits of his submissive and to fulfill her needs and test her limits. Hand in hand with his capacity for understanding is his ability to give affection: to snuggle, cuddle, and caress; to nestle, nuzzle, and spoon; and to give emotional support before, during, and after a scene. Although the loving dominant enjoys his time at the top, he never forgets that *you* put him there.

When you make an exchange of these wonderful, sensual gifts, you are truly seeking to explore your own and each other's sexual natures in a meaningful and enlightening way. With each new exchange of gifts, you are both freed from perhaps another societal or self-imposed sexual taboo, allowing you to explore more paths next time you are in the garden.

Indulging in Fantasies

Romantic SM can be emotionally uplifting while allowing you to wallow in your sexual fantasies, free from guilt or harm. SM sex can be transcendental and mystical, a meeting of two minds and bodies joined together for a sublime sexual experience. And, if it pleases you, you can still be a feminist all the while you are being submissive. My definition of a feminist is a woman who is emotionally and physically independent. Behaving submissively for erotic pleasure can be a way to meet your sexual needs and enjoy yourself. The surrender of your control is voluntary, and it is control, not your self-esteem or your own personal power, that you have given up.

In the prearranged SM scene, the dominant and submissive are given permission to act in ways that are not acceptable in so-called "polite" company. In the SM scene, the nurturing mother can unloose the sex-toy locked up inside, the rock of Gibraltar can become the clinging vine, and the prim schoolteacher can turn into the voracious slut. In SM, the timid become bossy; the priggish, hedonistic; the quiet, aggressive. But remember that these playtime characteristics are just that— playtime, pretend, like a child's game to be put away when the mantle of adulthood and its responsibilities are again around your shoulders. Enjoy the playtime and the pretend world you and your partner create for yourselves. By all means enjoy the sexual rewards of adulthood when you are through. Although it is sometimes tempting to blur the line between fantasy and reality, the distinction must always be made.

Misconceptions about SM sex grow like weeds in an untended garden. Because of the intensity of a consensual SM scene, what the uninitiated fail to see is that these *are* prearranged scenes which are often scrupulously scripted out and planned for weeks in advance by *both* players. Some scenes may have been growing in the dark garden of the

mind for years. These SM scenes are passion plays written by the players for themselves. All things are done with permission; all scenes are
negotiated and planned; the best plans are flexible and leave room for
flights of fancy and expanding, exploring, and, finally, maybe, pushing
limits. The trust and communication involved in these scenes are rarely
visible to the outsider; what's visible are the gear and paraphernalia,
which make it all seem very strange indeed.

"Tis because I love you that I do these things with you," is a concept that the uninitiated are unfamiliar with. Open your mind and think
of your favorite SM fantasies. Imagine yourself sharing these flowers
from the garden with your partner; imagine your joy at his acceptance
of your fantasies and his at discovering this new sexual being inside you.
It is like rediscovering what made you fall in love with him the first
time, only this time you will be discovering your love as more mature
adults. The physical manifestation of our sexual preferences in a romantic SM relationship is not an abusive one but rather an enlightening and
uplifting experience for both partners, taking them to higher levels of
communication, trust, and passion.

Pain and the Submissive

A popular misconception about SM is that it is about pain and hurt. It
is not. For many submissives, it is the surrendering of control that is
highly erotic. In surrendering control to the dominant partner, she relinquishes responsibility for her actions and emotions. The protection and
support given by the dominant allows the submissive to abandon herself to her erotic nature without fear of harm, guilt, or reprisal. Sharing
the fantasy, and then allowing someone she trusts to direct her actions,
and perhaps even thoughts, for a short time, gives her permission to feel
the way she does and validates her sexuality. Sexual submission allows
her to be helpless, feel nurtured, release anger, or just send her blood
pressure skyrocketing. It can make her feel beautiful and desirable and
as if she were the most wanton woman in the world. *Everyone* is beautiful when they are turned on! This has nothing to do with pain.

There is also some confusion about the difference between a submissive and a masochist. A submissive is not necessarily a masochist, so

pain may not be a part of her fantasy mix. The submissive's desire is to serve, and she may not like pain in any form. As a good sub, she will "accept" the occasional beating for the pleasure of the master or as corporal punishment, but this need not be an integral part of the submissive's fantasy. A masochist enjoys pain for the sake of the pain itself, and is able to take pain and transform it into pleasure and to hell with serving the master!

For the nonmasochistic submissive, pain doesn't have to hurt. A beating can be "symbolic" and feel like a nice massage, or it can be short and "punitive" to correct the bottom for infractions or disobedience. Punishment can take many shapes, and the type preferred should be specified prior to enactment of the fantasy. In other words, when you tell him which way you prefer to submit, you can also tell him which type of punishment you prefer. The choices are endless and each submissive certainly has her favorites, but here is a short list of preferred "punishments" that do not involve physical pain: to be made to expose oneself to the dominant, to assume and hold a humiliating position, to perform oral sex or have intercourse on command, to perform household chores, to appear in a suitable setting scantily dressed, to allow oneself to be stripped or disciplined privately or publicly by the dominant, to have sexual favors withdrawn by the dominant, and so on.

The Joy in Giving

Emotional gratification, as well as the individual acts of service she performs, is of great importance to the submissive. The submissive *wants* to focus on the task at hand, execute it perfectly, and please the master. For the submissive, the joy is in the act of giving to the dominant, of performing service for another, of placing the will and comfort of another before her own. In doing so, she discovers a well of strength that comes from the relinquishing of her power and the deflation of her ego. She discovers herself in selflessly serving another and delves deep into the depths of her psyche to reinvent herself and her fantasy. She is not motivated by greed or the promise of reward; her joy is in giving. She knows that if she is devoted to her master and her duties, she *may* receive the romantic rewards that her loyalty, generosity, and selflessness have earned her, but the promise of reward is not what motivates her.

My definitions of submission and chivalry are almost interchange-
able in this context. Selfless service is the underlying ideal of chivalry;
chivalry itself is doing your very best for someone you respect and love
to bring them pleasure and honor. Notice there is no promise of, not
even a mention of, reward for the service. The service itself, and the
honor and pleasure that will be given to the other, the master, the higher
one, is the reward. Because many do not understand submission in the
chivalrous sense, the submissive woman may feel sexually adrift in a
world that does not value, or care to remember, the age-old qualities of
chivalry. They have forgotten, or perhaps never knew, that chivalry is
service to a higher purpose or person, and they have dismissed the gracious service, courtesy, and honesty that are implicit in chivalry. These
people would also be likely to overlook the responsive, almost telepathic
spirituality inherent in erotic surrender or being in submissive.

The sexual adventurers that we are, we know that sensual submission is a release of powerful, if unreasonable, emotions. This release can
give us great joy and fulfillment and help us discover new facets of our
psyche. The enhanced level of trust and communication necessary for
the SM relationship spreads tendrils through our daily lives, changing the
way we think and feel, making us more accepting of those around us
because we are more comfortable with ourselves.

A State of Mind, a Means of Expression

For some bottoms, the state of mind called submission is the ultimate
exposure, the most desirable form of nakedness. For others, submission
is a warm cloak of security for it is the master's care and skill that protects the slave from the intrusion of the outside world. In the world of
SM, the shy become outrageously extroverted, and the sexually timid
become sexually adventurous. I call submission a "state of mind" because
to me submission is not gender specific, unless it relates to how the top
plays with the submissive's anatomy. If the sub favors public exposure
as an act of humiliation, it hardly matters what is being exposed (cock
or breasts), or who it belongs to. I also call submission a state of mind
because of the wonderful, mystical, almost telepathic connection a slave
can make with her master. It is the freeing of the spirit for the shy, and
a means of expression for the inarticulate. Unable to express her love in

words, the submissive woman can make her feelings known with a thousand gestures. Perhaps at a future time she will be able to verbalize to her partner, under her guise as slave-girl, what she would not be able to say otherwise. And, having taken that step, perhaps she will be encouraged, empowered enough by the new confidence she has found in her dark side, to say those words in the bright, beautiful light of day.

While being submissive, I have experienced a soaring, heady delight, a great joy, and a freeing of my spirit. My soul has taken flight to circle our little planet, still blue when seen from high above; the scene I am in on earth imprinted in my mind. Tears of joy roll down my face, and in each tear the image of me and my master is crystallized and repeated over and over in their prismlike facets. Frozen in time like a firefly caught in amber and fossilized, the exquisite trust, the emotional satisfaction, and the beauty of sensual submission can be called up at will, its serenity tapped into as needed for the benefit of the submissive.

~ 2 ~

Are You a Sensual Submissive?

It is not a person's sweet and loving side that shapes a bond with an intimate; it is the talent for airing aggression that counts most.
—Psychologist George Bach, Bach and Wyden, 1968

SM sex is sex, and we all agree sex takes place in the dark garden of the mind. Fantasies of sexual submission and erotic surrender grow in its fertile soil like exotic flowers, their roots encircling the libido and then spreading to the heart. A million tendrils, as strong as leather and as delicate as lace, wind their way from the mind down the waiting and wanting body to the heart, and then to the secret gate. Directed by the mind, the tendrils become a key for the gate's lock and the lock falls away. The gate swings open, revealing the dainty opening and the tender pink petals the gate protects. Glistening with sweet nectar, the petals beckon as they unfold and hint at the untold joys to be found inside.

You have already decided that SM is a garden of erotic fantasies you would like to explore, but you are unsure if you are submissive or dominant, and don't know how to be good at either one. Earlier I called submission a state of mind rather than gender specific. The major difference between a female and male submissive is their individual body and, by extension, what can be done to that body. Female and male submissives often have the same desires: to be submissive in public, exposed in public, punished or corrected by the top, verbally humiliated, and so on. As this list demonstrates, it is the action, the fantasy, the desire, that makes one submissive, not the gender. And it is honesty that makes a good submissive.

Awakening Your Submissive Persona

Before you can be honest about being a sexual submissive, you have to decide *if* you *are* a submissive, and if you are, what is your particular brand of submission? Think back to the definitions in chapter 1. Are you a submissive in the chivalrous sense of the word? Are you a masochist with submissive tendencies? A submissive with masochistic tendencies? Or are you a straight-out don't-bother-with-all-the-bowing-and-scraping masochist? Perhaps being a slave-girl or a wanton sex-slave is your idea of romantic fun. Remember, no fantasy is politically incorrect, and your own submission can wear many faces.

To be honest about your style of submission, you will need to enter the dark garden and access your memories and fantasies, past and present, to set up scenes for future SM play. Let your most powerful erotic personas take shape in your mind. Be assured that the fantasies we are accessing are not rational, so you need not be embarrassed by them. Instead, look well at the personas you adopt in your fantasies, as they will give you important clues to your submissive turn-ons. Walk through the dark garden slowly, thinking about your preferences openly, giving time and space to aspects of yourself you have only glimpsed before, and then select the blooms that will make the most beautiful arrangement.

Looking for Clues . . . in Fantasies Past

Start by casting your mind back to your younger days—your childhood. Did you prefer to be a cowgirl, riding across the plain lickety-spilt on her broom-pony, shooting her water pistol at the Indians? Or did you prefer to be an Indian, especially when the little boy next door was the cowboy tying you to the tree? Did the sight of the fair maiden, struggling, bound and gagged on the railroad tracks while the evil villain leered on and the train approached, have you squirming with pleasure? Perhaps you dreamt, as I did (and do!) of rolling along the desert sands in the closed cart of a harem-woman, and being beset by desert bandits. The handsomest one selects you as his spoil-of-war, and, throwing you over the saddle of his prancing steed, carries you off into blissful sexual slavery under the black tents of his tribe.

For some of you, your earliest sexual desires may have been expressed by a character who embodied your secret desires. Did Nancy Drew have a special place in your heart? She had one in mine. Nancy got herself into some of the most interesting predicaments and always needed to be rescued. Or maybe Lois Lane is more to your liking—with Superman as your "lord," who could find fault with your taste? Some might have been influenced by the sweetly submissive Marianne on *Gilligan's Island,* and her devotion to the Professor. And who could forget Jeannie, with that harem outfit and ponytail, her enthusiasm to serve her "master," and that adorable little bottle she called home. I could go on in this vein but you get the point. All the above are scenarios where the woman is submissive to the man.

Clues From the Present

Now, take a good look at your fantasies, the fantasies you have today. What are your favorites? Although you may no longer want to be Nancy Drew, do your fantasies still have bondage, sensory deprivation, even kidnapping scenes, in them? Or maybe your fantasy is to serve the master his dinner, then be handcuffed to the table while he eats? Would he then feed you from his own plate, and force your head down on his cock between bites? Does your lover pin your hands down over your head when he digs in for his come-stroke? Does it send your needles into red? Does the thought of a low voice whispering in your ear to "spread your legs," then his knees prying them open, make you creamy?

Perhaps your fantasy is one that doesn't require you to think or serve, just be—the master's footstool. Think of his large feet on your soft, warm belly, feel the weight of them on you as you work harder to breathe. Focus on them, the feet from above, and make them the center of your universe. Release your ego into the nothingness and exist to serve and be used. Or, you may fancy yourself the sex-toy, with no other purpose in life than to satisfy the lust of the master and whichever lords it pleases him to give you to for the night. With permission to play the slut, or being "forced" to be the slut, the guilt is removed. You might fancy being a pet, in the dog or cat sense of the word. Or, more exotically, maybe you dream of being a pony-girl, your head plume aflutter, your arms bound behind your back, thrusting your breasts forward, and your waist tightly corsetted. High-stepping in your pony-girl pumps, you pull the chariot in which your master rides, in tandem with two other well-trained pony-girls.

Next, call to mind the best sex you have had in real life and try to remember if there was an SM flavor to it. Never mind if you or your partner didn't call it SM sex; lots of sexual techniques that many people do not think of as part of SM *are* part of SM. I had one lover who swore he had no interest in SM, yet he would bury his fingers deep inside me and tease me until I begged him to let me come. Another liked me to strip for him, sexily and to music, of course, and then, when I was completely naked, to follow the striptease with "floor work" (the term exotic dancers use to express lying on the floor and simulating sex). During the floor work, he would mount me in whatever position most appealed to him and shag me senseless right there on the carpet, giving me the occasional rug burn as a memento. But, no, he wasn't into SM either.

The binds that tie you—bondage—could be one of your sexual buttons. A very large number of people are into bondage and no other aspect of SM at all. Additionally, many of those people don't consider bondage to be an aspect of SM. They refer to their type of bondage as "love bondage." A lover of mine was a natural with ropes. He owned an auto body repair shop and was accustomed to doing somewhat intricate bondage on the mangled frames of cars, ostensibly to "straighten" them out. Although he thought SM was "silly," he would spend a considerable amount of time making sure his "rope tricks" looked lovely on me and worked perfectly. Worked perfect wonders on me, too, more than once!

Still Undecided?

At the beginning of this discussion, I said that honesty makes a good submissive. Perhaps what you have read so far makes you think you would rather handle the ropes than luxuriate helplessly in them. If you would rather learn intricate bondage than learn to relax into it, then perhaps the dominant role is for you. My book, *The Art of Sensual Female Dominance: A Guide for Women* (see recommended reading list), among others can teach you the basics of being a female dominant.

Alternatively, if all this *has* interested you, echoed your own feelings and fantasies, or made you breathe a sigh of relief that you are not alone, let us assume you are a sensual, sexual submissive. For some of you, it may be embarrassing to admit that you are submissive—even privately, in the shelter of the SM playground. Stop worrying—there's nothing to be embarrassed about! You are in very good company in your newly recognized state though some of you may still be uncertain of your preference.

Top, bottom, switch, or undecided, all of you may be wondering what's in it for you.

The Joys of Sex Magick

Although the dominant and submissive partners are playing in the same erotic garden, the blooms each gather differ greatly. Some people recognize the rewards and joys of SM instantly; others need more time and information to understand them, and yet others have great difficulty understanding SM at all. And, of course, there are responsibilities attached to SM sex, for both top and bottom. Perhaps you think SM sex is interesting and you would like to experiment with it. You think that you would like to experience stronger sexual sensations, but your yearnings and desires are far from concrete. Although you are interested, perhaps even intrigued by the first chapter, you need more information to articulate your desires. Since understanding the joys and rewards of submission seem to be more elusive, I will speak about the joys I get from being a beautiful, powerful, and sensible submissive first.

What's in It for the Bottom

If you are like me—independent, strong, and accustomed to taking care of and looking out for yourself—then the siren call of the world of the sensual submissive will be sweet music to your ears. In the first chapter, I spoke at length of the hidden beauty of sensual submission: that you can have pride in your submission, that you have a position of power, and that SM not only heightens and enhances sexual pleasure but also the trust and communication in the everyday relationship. What I told you in those pages is not information gleaned from others living the love style, nor is it information gathered from sexologists. I am able to speak to you so eloquently, so convincingly, about SM because I live this lifestyle. I believe in the magic of the SM relationship, so I have embraced the love style of SM as an essential and delightful part of my sexual makeup.

In sexual submission, I am able to shed my everyday persona of author and businesswoman and become his silent and willing servant. With joy, I can direct my energies toward fulfilling the wants and desires of another. The devotion of thought and self to him frees me from my ego and allows me to serve, humbly, yet with pride, in my submission. I submit because *I* want to, because *I* love it, and I love the way it makes me feel. When I am my master's slave, I feel looked after, cared for, and nurtured. He makes sure the room is warm enough and that I am physically comfortable. If a lock of hair falls in my face, he tucks it behind my ear for me; he brushes my bangs from my eyes. I'm allowed, *encouraged,* to be helpless, to let him do everything, and he is still there, he stays. I don't have to be a strong, knowledgeable woman of the world—he will be strong and protective enough for us both. Often I feel safer in the SM world with him than I feel alone in the real one because the power of love and giving cannot, will not, be denied.

Being on the bottom also gives me a safe place to release pent-up frustrations or rid myself of fear and anger. Sometimes when the world's weary ways have gotten to me and all my railings and rantings against *whatever* haven't cleansed me, I ask him for a different kind of beating; a beating that will allow me to release these feelings and let them dissipate into the air rather than keep them locked up inside. This beating has nothing to do with correction or discipline, or his pleasure, although he is pleased to give it to me. And it doesn't have a great deal to do with pain either, even though I know it will hurt and I want it to hurt. This is a cathartic beating, and it frees me of the irritants and the petulance bottled up inside. It has a wonderful effect that lasts for days, and the effect of his understanding lasts for eternity.

What's in It for the Top

Although this book is about how to be a sensual, sensible (and sought after, if that is your desire), submissive, that same submissive may want some insight into the mind of a top. Alternatively, a top looking for insight into a bottom's wants, fears, joys, and rewards might benefit from reading this, too. Or, you could be like me, a greedy-guts switch, and want it all. But because I am a switch, and did see many men in the capacity of a professional dominant, I can give you a look into the mind-set of the top from the top's point of view. As there are many types of tops, this will also help you to decide the "type" or "style" of top that best suits your bottom.

Power, and the exchange of it, is a main ingredient in SM play. Some tops get off on the raw power rush they experience during topping. This power rush can communicate itself to the bottom in a few ways: vibrations (yes, good old-fashioned vibes), a physical communique as in the brush of his hard member against the thigh, and, of course, verbally, if he is a talker. When a scene is really working for a top, he feels full of power and control. Some claim a "crystal clarity," that is, sensing that the last stroke was the *last* one that would give pleasure to the sub and stopping right before the utterance of the safe word. Others claim that upon seeing someone is "thinking" about walking into the scene-space, they can avert the mishap almost telepathically with a look and projected thought. Others feel filled with ability and competence and ultraheightened awareness.

Like bottoming, being dominant gives the top permission to explore feelings and energies that are not totally acceptable in the outside world. Cruelty, bossiness, haughtiness are all acceptable, even desirable, traits in the SM play world when they fit the fantasy. Having a safe place where one's dark side can be explored is an immensely freeing experience for anyone, top or bottom.

On a lighter level, some tops truly enjoy the services they receive from the bottom, or have a wonderful ability to eroticize ordinary services such as housework, cooking, errands, the laundry, or whatever. Just because he is a dominant doesn't mean he doesn't like to be pampered, appreciated, and tended to in personal ways. Massage therapy is one way for the top to feel appreciated and nurtured, but some don't like or need massage. If he is one of those, try giving him a bath instead. I love to bathe my lord and shampoo his long, straight hair. I love the selflessness and humility that allows me to perform this service for him in joy and with pride as I soap his limbs, his back, his chest, and the delicate and delicious area between his legs.

Then I shampoo his hair, giving his scalp a firm massage before I rinse out the shampoo and apply the conditioner. After thoroughly rinsing the conditioner out of his hair, then hosing the errant bubbles off him with the removable showerhead, I swathe him in towels and help him out of the tub. As he stands, I dry his upper body, his back, his chest, his arms, and even underneath them. Then he sits down comfortably on the toilet seat cover, accustomed to my adept service. I dry between his toes and between his legs and every other inch of skin before I brush his hair. When I am done, he rises, thanks me, and heads for his "throne" (his favorite corner of the sofa) in the living room. This small act of drawing and giving him a bath, something he could do ably for himself, gives me such joy that tears of happiness well up in my eyes in anticipation of the next time I can perform such a lovely, intimate service for him. Then I have the exquisite pleasure of washing myself in the remains of his bath!

What's in It for Both of You

After performing all these little rituals and services, and being taught how to do this and that according to the master's pleasure, your master may want to "move the earth" with you as part of your reward for good service, or just because he enjoys taking you. Lucky you! Sex, orgasm, coming, moving the earth, for at least one if not both of you, together or separately, is a wonderful addition to SM play. During your playtime, your master may have brought you to the brink of orgasm many times, and many a time he let you come. He has been working hard all night to keep increasing your level of arousal and desire, conditioning you with pleasure and pain until they become one and the same thing. He is as aroused as you are, filled with the power you have given him. You are wild for each other and cannot stand it another minute.

When my master fucks me *during* a scene, I know it is *part* of the scene and that he will probably mount me many times that evening without coming. However, if we fuck *after* a hot scene, I know he wants to come, so I exhort him, and beg with him and plead with him to come, so that he can experience the same smashing, ecstatic release that he has given me.

If what you have read in this chapter has appealed to you, if it spoke to your soul on a new level, if it made you want to know more, then I would assume that you have what it takes to be a sensual, sexual submissive. You have explored your submissive personae and have found some that you are fully comfortable with now, and others that you will ease your way into when you have gained confidence and the time is right. Being a sensual submissive is empowering and sexy; it can take you to places in your dark garden that you wouldn't have dared to go before. Once there, you can explore your deepest desires, and with your trusted partner, you can discuss your shadow land fantasies.

We know now you are a sensual submissive, but are you a sensible one as well? The next chapter, How to Be a Sensible Submissive, will add practical advice and instruction to the esoterics in this chapter to aid you in determining if sexual submission is a worthy addition to your present love style.

~ 3 ~

How to Be a Sensible Submissive

Safe, Sane, and Consensual

—The Motto of the TES Association

Just as vanilla sex or straight sex carries responsibilities, so does SM sex, although the responsibilities of SM sex are a little more complicated, because SM sex has an element of danger or risk to it that vanilla sex does not. This danger-risk factor can occur on two levels: psychologically and physically. The danger or risk factor cannot be eliminated—and SMers don't want it to be, danger seekers that we are, because the danger is also a strong part of its allure. But the risk factor can be reduced by education in safe and sane SM practices and by exercising good, old-fashioned common sense.

The Responsibilities of SM Sex

I would like to say that there are "rules" to SM. "Never put someone in bondage and leave the house," yet I do it often to run to the trash can and back, gone all of forty-five seconds. "Never put a rope around someone's neck"—yet if it isn't a slip knot or a noose but part of a halter rope dress, why not? And who can forget the top's Golden Rule: "Do not do

30

unto another what has not been done to you." But how practicable is that? I fisted someone even though I've never been fisted myself. (For someone of my size and build, that will always, and only, be a hot fantasy.) Why should that preclude me from giving the pleasure to someone else if I have the knowledge?

For fun and for safe SM sex, you need to think with your head, as well as your gonads. The rules will not work in every situation, especially because the desires in play in SM aren't rational. What is rational about wanting to become a footstool, to serve the master in naked silence, or to be owned and operated by another person? However powerful and sexy these desires or images are to you, what they are not is *rational*.

I don't want to burden you with a set of rules that may not work for you, or rules with lists of exceptions to them. Nevertheless, I feel there are three principles that are as close to rules as I care to get: Be as respectful of the wants and needs of your partner as you want him to be respectful of yours. (Real-world respect has a very *real* place in SM.) Acknowledge rather than deny your dark side; it is an integral and beautiful part of your psychological makeup. Claim the responsibilities of sexual freedom as you enjoy them.

The responsibilities of a sensible submissive are the flip sides of what makes a responsible top. A good top has limits of his own, his own personal standards, and knows them well. He knows and respects your limits and treats you with the dignity you deserve (even when he's pulling you across the floor by your hair!). He is creative, contributes to the fantasy-pool, and acts out his part with gusto. The terrific top will eventually become expert with his equipment, will maintain safety standards, and will listen to and watch his sub closely during a scene. His protective aura should engulf you and make you feel safe and secure in his care. He is in control of you and the scene because he is in control of himself. A good top does not press for agreement from a hesitant sub, nor does he engage in emotional blackmail. His manipulation is benign and with the consent of the submissive. The terrific top is communicative and open and understands the fine art of cuddling, snuggling, and nesting after a good scene. He also knows to have snacks in the house, so that even if you have to get up and make them, at least you don't have to go out and get them!

Other qualities for a terrific top? Honesty, warmth, and caring, just like we would want, and expect, from a "vanilla" lover. Does he know when you need to work instead of play? Does he pitch in and help get things done before and after playtime? Does he have a good grip on the difference between SM fantasy- and real-world time? If you would like to introduce something new into the scene, is he willing to listen to you? Is he flexible enough to adapt or adjust the scene to meet your needs and make the scene work? Or stop the scene, if necessary? Would he be willing to talk about the problem right then and there, whether it was physical or emotional, if that is what you wanted? Would he be understanding or dismissive?

I would also look for someone with whom you make a exceptionally good emotional connection as this invisible cord may be your only link to the earth in an intense scene. Over time, he should be able to read your body language, become more adept with his equipment, and plan out scenes with less and less help from you. Your repertoire of SM tricks will increase rapidly, and if he is in tune with you, less and less negotiation will be needed. He will know your likes and dislikes, how to mix and match them, and how far to "push" you. After time, only new additions to your screenplays will be thoroughly discussed, and through all of this, a terrific top will not only be concerned with your well-being and care about how you feel, but will let you *know* that he does.

Because you are topping from the bottom for the time being, it is important for you, as the teacher and mentor, to be as fully versed as possible in the proper use of the equipment and toys you will be playing with. Familiarizing yourself with the human anatomy is an excellent idea, especially if you would like to be flogged, caned, paddled, bound, and so on. (Chapter 13, Sensual Sensations, contains an anatomy lesson, and chapter 12, Erotic Discomfort, gives safety tips for romantic human bondage.) Additionally, since it is your body he will be playing with, keeping it safe and beautiful will be in his best interest, too. As you teach him the physical skills, speak to him about the value of your submission and about your feelings regarding SM. Let him see beyond what is visible to the eye. Believe in your glory, your beauty, and your radiance, because it is there just waiting to bloom in the dark garden. Make him aware of the special intimacy you are about to share with him.

Another responsibility of the bottom is to support her top, to see that her master's needs are met. On an emotional level, when I top I expect smooth, adept service, not sniveling or groveling or whining for what he wants to happen later on. This is not a true submissive mind-set. When any one of that terrible threesome occur, I am not a happy top; my needs are not being met. I need service that stems from pride in submission, to the selfish giving to a higher power, not from sniveling or unspoken demands for "later." On a practical level, let's say he has a severe head cold but has agreed to play as a top anyway. Under these circumstances, the sub should be appreciative of his condition and act accordingly. After all, he is sick! The submissive should use her head and realize that chicken soup for him would be better than the deerskin flogger for her. Look after your master's mind as well as his body: One cannot not be well without the other.

The Thinking Slave

Although I speak in glowing words of the allure of sensual submission, of the guiltless and mind-blowing passion of the SM sexual experience, and of the joy in selfless giving, I would not want to mislead you into thinking that being a sensual submissive also means being a brainless one. It is easy to think that while one lives in a state of sexual anticipation and heightened arousal, that is *all* one thinks about. That should not be the case. We know that the desires we are experiencing and exploring are "unreasonable," but becoming sexually submissive does not mean that one leaves common sense and intelligence on the floor along with recently shed clothes.

When I am dominant, I want my slave to use his reason—as in "think"—and exhibit some independent thought upon occasion, as long as it is not contrary to my wishes. And most other good dominants, male and female, would agree with me when I say that no one wants a brainless submissive who wants her top to do all of the thinking for her. If your master commands you to silence and then the draperies catch on fire, by all means, sister, sing right out! If you and your master are playing fetch in the park, and your ball goes out into the street, would you run out into the road without looking? Of course not—you're not really a dog and you may get hit by a car!

I have had slaves pledge their devotion to me by promising me that I can control their every move: when they eat, sleep, and go to the bathroom; what they wear and when and where they wear it; who they are allowed to associate with; what parties or clubs they could attend; and all of their other daily activities, including when they can have release. Others wanted me to have financial control over them by taking their pay and credit cards and putting them on an allowance. This kind of absolute control only works in stories, not in real life.

By all means be an obedient and joyful submissive, and revel in the newfound power and beauty of your sexual state, but be sensible as well as sensual as you explore new paths in your dark garden.

Word Up

Knowing your desires and limits is an excellent start to being the best and most sensual submissive you can be, but there are other elements you need to think about. One particularly important element is the "safe-word," and this should be picked out and decided upon with your partner. Once you know your desires and limits, you need a way to stop the scene or slow it down when those desires and limits are about to be "exceeded." In SM, this code word is called the safe-word (or "safe-signal," if the mouth is immobilized). We need this word because a lot of us really like to *pretend* that we don't want these wonderful things done to us and to help ourselves maintain this pretense during the scene, and add a realistic touch, we joyously shriek and scream, "Nooooo!" or "Stop!" at the top of our lungs. Of course, we don't really mean no or stop at all, so we need another word when we *really* want to stop. This other word is the safe-word. This is what you will say (or do) when you want to communicate to your master, quickly and easily, the true status of the scene.

Both male and female tops commonly complain of the uncommunicative sub who says nothing and gives no bodily indications right up until the moment she or he says the safe-word. The top is confused, because, after carefully looking at body language and other signs, the top proceeds as if all is well. Then—*bam!*—the safe-word is said, seemingly out of nowhere. Using the safe-word can be a difficult decision, even for an experienced submissive. The use of the word may spark temporary feelings of inadequacy in the submissive: Is the master disappointed in me? Have I failed him? Have I not lived up to my expectations of myself? The submissive may feel inadequate, or chagrined, at having to use her safe-word. Everyone's pain threshold works differently, so maybe she just "tilts" quickly, with little or no visible indication, or she may be struggling with herself over the use of her word.

Never feel embarrassed to use your safe-word. Its use is your decision and is not open to discussion or debate. Never allow anyone to reproach or ridicule you for using your safe-word. If you have said your safe-word, it could mean that you are having a hard time on one of many levels or are feeling disappointed or chagrined over the scene. The scene could have gotten too intense, or you are reacting in a way that you hadn't anticipated (or you may have to go to the bathroom before proceeding). And although you have given your consent in the pre-scene negotiations, you *are* entitled to withdraw your consent if the scene, or specific activity, isn't working for you. Your safe-word is now part of your self-defense mechanism, and you are never wrong to use it. If you or your top (tops have limits and sometimes say safe-words, too) feel the need to say the word, there is no reason for anger and reproach. This is the time for caring, support, and open communication to make for a better experience next time.

Safe-Word Styles

Safe-words and styles differ greatly from master to master and slave to slave, so you are free to choose what works best for you. Selecting the safe-word is a responsibility for the two of you to share, enhancing your communication skills and deepening your trust. Keep in mind as you work out your safe-word that you don't want it to be too complicated—simplicity is better. Recently, a piece of literature came to my attention that was a list of eleven (yes, eleven!) different colors that this top wanted the sub to memorize and spout out at the appropriate time. I couldn't even begin to remember the difference in the emotional connotation between "pink" and "mauve," let alone the remaining nine words which constitute a running technicolor commentary during a hot scene. In this case, less detail is better than more. But after reading this list several times, I realized that the rainbow list of safe-words was one sub's alternative to the use of "universal stop-light colors." A clever but hard-to-remember alternative: I envisioned eleven colors, with their corresponding emotions, written on my arm for easy reference. The top, of course, would have a slip of paper up his sleeve to refer to when I called out an unfamiliar color! It was too funny.

Stop-light colors are universal, so saying "red" when you want everything to stop right now means the same thing to everyone, and green always means more, harder, faster, pussycat, kill, kill! Next, depending on your geographic location, yellow, amber, pink, or orange all can mean slow down. In the rainbow system, orange and white communicate different levels of pain, whereas yellow means this is fun and flirtatious. Using different colors could get confusing.

The name-game is when you use either his name or your full name as your safe-word. If you *always* call him "master," "lord," or any other honorific during a scene, calling his first or full name will get his attention.

Other masters like to keep things more formal and elect to use "mercy" as the stop-word and "pity" as the slow-down word. The use of these two words is also universal, and saying one, even with a strange master or mistress, will produce the desired effect. They are my words of choice because I think a woman begging for mercy, for pity, is extremely sexy—much more so than one yelling out her own name. You can whisper "mercy, master, please," and revel in the sexy sound of it, even if you are stopping the scene. You can plead "pity, master, pity on your poor slave," and perhaps the sound of your own voice begging so eloquently will change your mind about slowing down. Sometimes the time it takes to say the word provides me with the necessary breather. This is much more appealing, and every bit as effective, as squawking out your name like some silly parrot.

If stoplights, names, and begging words are not your style, consider that *any* word can be your safe-word. Its only criteria is that it can't be a word you would say in the course of your play. So, "snowflake" would be a good safe-word, "candle" would not. (Hot waxing is a popular SM game.) Alternatively, if you are having a specific problem, just call it out:

"My hand is asleep," or, "I need a break now." These are acceptable as safe-words if your master doesn't mind the informality, because they clearly communicate the problem. If your master demands more ceremony, saying "Master, may I speak?" is a polite form of communication, as is "may I have a moment, please, Master?"

Speaking in Signs

Safe-words need not be verbal. If you are enacting a scene that requires silence or you are gagged, how do you speak? This is where the safe-signal enters the scene, and each master and slave have their preferences. Some masters like the submissive to make three loud grunts as the signal, others prefer a vigorous shaking of the head from left to right, signifying "no." I don't think either of these methods are reliable. What if you grunt and he doesn't hear you? Three grunts can get lost in the bass response from the stereo, then what do you do? Grunt some more and hope for the best? As for the head shake, well, I tend to thrash around a lot when certain deliciously painful things are happening to me, and shaking my head in a no gesture could get confusing. I know I make that very head-shake action (often accompanied by the verbal NO NO NO!) in a welter of passion—not resistance!

My master once decided to assign me a certain position to assume as my safe-signal. I was not gagged but had been ordered to silence; no words could pass my lips, only screams, moans, and groans. I was to crouch at his feet on the floor, my head on his foot, and caress his shoes, ankles, and calves. The position was very sexy. That night he caned me very hard. I broke the punishment position and crouched at his feet, and, of course, he stopped caning me immediately. Several months passed before I needed to use my signal again (but it was still my signal), but this time, things did not go so smoothly. He was caning me *in* the safe position, his ankles gripped firmly around my neck. I couldn't break away to reassume the "safe" position, and although I tried calling his name, saying mercy, and finally shouting "enough, stop right now," he didn't hear me and he didn't stop. With the strength of great anger, I managed to break his hold on my neck and get away from him. I can't describe to you how angry and upset I was, never mind how my bottom was hurting!

Hence, I prefer a signal that is more audible, visible, less esoteric, and less likely to be missed or mistaken for something else. I would recommend a bright-colored rubber ball you can hold in your hand and toss (literally!) at your master as your stop-sign, or a bandana or scarf of any color can be waved to signal distress. Alternatively, a ring full of keys can be jangled to get the master's attention. Signals like these are never mistaken for anything but what they are—stop-signs.

What else can you do to enhance your desirability as a submissive? Active participation in the creation and development of the scene is also partly your responsibility, not just that of the top. This is referred to as the "negotiation stage" where safe-words and signals, and length of playtime, as well as what will occur in the playtime itself, are settled. This is the time when you will communicate to each other what the scenario will be and what key elements will be included. Prescene negotiating is strongly recommended for all beginners. Less emphasis can be placed on this stage later on when both of you are more familiar and skilled with SM safe practices.

～ 4 ～

The Seeds of Desire

Mary, Mary, quite contrary, how does your garden grow?
—Children's Nursery Rhyme

You have realized that there's more to being submissive than just being a passive recipient of whatever the master dishes out. You recognize your power, beauty, and worth as a submissive and take pride in your submission. You have come to think of yourself as a vessel waiting to be filled with new sensations and experiences. You know you always have a *choice* as to whether you wish to start and continue with SM sex games. You have welcomed the powerful desires you set in motion when you entered the dark garden because these desires freed you. All the above is very lovely, but quite esoteric and mystical. Your responsibilities as a sensual, sensible submissive are actually more hands-on than the above prose would imply.

As the more experienced player, what you will be learning how to do is "topping from the bottom." Usually this is an unforgivable sin—to take control of the scene without the top's consent—but this is not our case. You will have his consent and cooperation, and as the more savvy partner, it will be your responsibility to teach him how to top you. Although this does involve some work, because you need to know how to do everything you want him to do to you, you will have the unique and wonderful opportunity to teach him exactly what you want to be done. How do you figure out how you would like to be done?

The first thing I would recommend you do is discover and explore your desires as we discussed in chapter 2, and then establish your limits. Your desires and limits should be written out into a simple list of definite "Yeses," definite "Nos," and a bunch of "Maybes." Start by writing down all of the SM and vanilla-sex things you have ever done (especially the ones you enjoyed or have fantasized about), or have seen, heard, or thought about. The Wish List on pages 42–43 will help you articulate your new SM desires and limits; use it to supplement your own. Give each "activity" a letter: Y for yes, N for no, or M for maybe. After that, write down any health problems you may have: low blood pressure, sensitivity to hot or cold, poor circulation, claustrophobia, even things like wearing contact lenses or if you have allergies to things like wool or grass. Before you go on to make your fantasy-fun lists, please do not forget that the life experiences and common sense that you bring to the dark garden of SM pleasures will not threaten or diminish the romance of your encounter, but enhance it.

Common Yeses

A good place to start is your Yes list. These are things you have done before and would like to do again, and things you know you would like to experiment with and experience. The things on your Yes list are what you consider *absolutely* necessary to the scene. Without these elements, the scene would not be worth doing. If you live on the plains, fantasies of pirates on the bounding main can only happen almost entirely in the mind for "set design," but with a real gag and rope bondage, a strategically located support pillar in your home, and some creative costuming (how does he look in a ruffled shirt and eye patch?), one can almost smell the salt sea air and feel the spray on one's face! Then you feel the chemical rush as the fantasy takes holds and carries you away, just like a tidal wave! This theme is a basic captor-captive fantasy, and the isolation, helplessness, and vulnerability of bondage and the deprivation of speech are scenes within the theme (see chapter 7, Living Out Fantasies). Hence, the basic captor-captive fantasy is the theme, bondage and sensory deprivation are scenes within the theme, and the "ship" is window dressing.

Single out those special elements that you *need* to make the fantasy an erotic event; items are essential to your fantasy and are not negotiable. Put a pretty star (☆) next to them. Need some examples? How about being blindfolded or put in leather wrist and ankle restraints? Would you like to wear a collar, be walked on a leash? Would you like to wear a favorite or empowering garment or a pair of shoes as a slave? For some submissives, a scene is not a scene unless a service has been rendered for the master; to others, not to be tied up would be terribly disappointing; and yet other submissives are so afraid that they will not receive their fair share of pain that they act up just to ensure that they do! And for many of us in a monogamous male dom/fem sub relationship, a scene must include some orgasmic activity for at least one of us!

Common Nos

Now your list needs fine tuning and you are concerned that you may have left some things off the No list. Here is a short list of common Nos among the players: no cuts, burns, tattoos, or breaks in the skin; no blood sport or playing with feces (some may extend this to golden showers as well); and parts of the body that you don't want touched (I *hate* anyone touching my ears) or hit or slapped (face-slapping can be a delicate issue) or put in bondage. For example, women with breast implants should not engage in breast bondage or tit torture, though limited nipple play may be OK. (Check with your doctor.) Submissives with sinus problems that flair up suddenly may want to stay away from gags. (By the way, do not allow anyone to gag you if you have a cough, cold, stuffy nose, bronchial problem, or respiratory problems.)

Other things on the No list? Well, that would be for you to decide, even if some of them appear silly. No to handcuffs, yes to leather restraints. No to a hood, but yes to a mask. No sex in a public club, but yes, yes, yes at a private party. No tickling with feathers, they make you sneeze. Yes to the crop, but not on your thighs. No furry or woolly lined blindfolds, the fibers mess with your contact lenses. Pull my hair but don't tickle me. Let me come . . . but not too often!

A Wish List

Age-play:
  child
  teen
Blindfold
Body Modification:
  Ritual Shaving
  Tattoos
  Piercing
  Branding
  Corset Training
Body Service
Body Worship:
  Ass
  Cock
  Balls
  Feet
  Chest
  Hair
  Armpit
Bondage:
  Mental Bondage
  Scarves
  Ropes
  Neckties
  Chains
  Leather Restraints
  Tender Tethers
  Velvet Cord
  Lace Restraints
  Steel Restraints
  Plastic Wrap
  Body Bag
  Arm Restraints
  Straight Jacket

Breast Bondage
Spreader Bar
Cages
Closets
Stockade
Cross
Slings and Swings
Spread Eagle
Bondage for Control
Bondage for Punishment
Bondage for Reward
Bondage/Suspension:
  Full Suspension
  On Toes
Boot Service
Break-in Fantasy
Collar, Wearing a
Crawling to the Master
Dirty Talk
Discipline:
  Hand spanking
  Flogging
  Paddling
  Caning
  Cropping
  Single Lash
Ear Plugs
Edge Play
Face Slapping
Foot Kissing
Gags:
  Ball
  Bar
  Scarf/panties

Hoods
Hostage Fantasy
Humiliation:
  Verbal
  Physical
  Kneeling at the Master's
  Feet
  Leash, Wearing a
Leather/Latex Service
Locations:
  Indoors
  Outdoors
  Semipublic
  Public
  Totally Private
Maid Service
Masks
Medical Scenes
Military Scenes
Nudity:
  Total Nudity
  Partial Nudity
  Stripped Publicly
Objectification:
  Dog
  Cat
  Other Pet
  Footstool
  Ashtray
  Table
  Art
Penetration:
  Cock
  Fingers

Hand

Dildo

Vibrator

Butt Plug

Multiple

Pet Training

Punishment Scenes

Sensation:

Nipple Clamps

Clothespins

Pin Wheel

Hair Pulling

Scratching

Biting

Ice

Oils

Lotions

Hot Wax

Abrasion

Clit Stimulation

Nipple Torture

Sensitizing:

Tickling

Teasing

Feathers

Fur

Sex:

Sex in Public

Secret Sex in
Public

Public Display

Vaginal Sex

Oral Sex

Anal Sex

Fingering

Fantasy Rape Fisting
(Anal)

Fisting (Vaginal)

Analingus
(rimming)

Masturbation

Bisexuality

Threesome

Group Sex

Shoes:

Boots

Spike Heels

Fetish Shoes

Styles of Dress:

Innocent

Corsetted

Slutty

Elegant

Ultrafeminine

French Maid

Slave Girl

Dance Hall Girl

Saloon Girl

Gangster's Moll

Latex

Leather

Lingerie

Costumes

Garters/Stockings

Pantyhose

Torture:

Cunt

Clit

Breast

Anal

Nipple

Vampire Scenes

Victorian Scenes

Water Sports:

Enemas

Golden Showers

Forced Retention

Wrestling Fantasy

The Maybe-Sos

Last but not least, we have the Maybes on your list. Do not dismiss them
lightly just because (or even if) you have a nice long list of yeses. The
maybe group is what you'll look to when you want a variation from your
usual set of yeses. Scan them carefully and reassess them for anything
that you *may* want to happen *if* the circumstances are right or you are
turned on enough or it feels safe. There is a wealth of buried sexual treasure here—don't let it go to waste.

Look over the remaining things on your list, and even reconsider some of those nos. Now, put a Cupid's arrow next to these maybe-so elements you have picked out, and use them as icing on your SM cake. Odd as it may sound, even sex magic can use a new infusion of ideas now and then, and the Maybe list is where they will come from!

Communicating Your Desires

Your personal exploration of the dark garden so far has crystallized your desire and given you the courage to call yourself a sensual, sexual submissive. You have an understanding of the benefits that can be obtained from erotic surrender and have given thought to the variety of submission that most appeals to you. But now that you know *you* are submissive, how do you go about interesting your future master in your plans? I wish there was a magic formula that worked on everyone at all times—a regular Love Potion No. 9, if you like—but there isn't, so practical advice is what I'll give you.

Your success in turning your current partner into your future master depends on several things: your communication skills, timing, your emotional states (yours and his) when you have your chat, how you read his reactions, and your ability to appreciate his feelings and still keep talking. That's a lot to take in, but it can easily be broken down into simpler steps.

A Sense of Timing

Often our receptiveness toward something depends on the mood we are in when we are first approached with it. A good mood usually makes us more willing to listen and a bad mood, impatient. Choose your time to broach this subject carefully, making sure he is not preoccupied with work, worried about a sick relative, or on his way out the door. If you alert him to your need to talk when he doesn't have the time to listen, it may cause him anxiety and make him less than receptive when you do speak. If he seems nonreceptive, or overly distracted, back off and wait for another opportunity—a better time when you can have his full attention. An adequate amount of time to discuss the subject leisurely is an absolute must so try to ensure that he doesn't have to tend to something else very soon.

If your man is one who prefers discussing sexual matters in a non-sexual setting, I would suggest you discuss this on neutral territory. For some, a sexual discussion that takes place in the bedroom implies a responsibility to accept the suggestion because of the setting. Be positive! Tell him you enjoy being in bed with him and would like to spice up your lovemaking, but tell him out in the living room. Or, having your talk over dinner in a lovely, softly lit restaurant with waiters who appear on cat feet and where neither of you have to cook, serve, and clean is always romantic, usually nonthreatening, and can be made to work to your advantage.

If you'd like a definite, positive sign from him before you approach him outright about your plan, I would recommend you test the waters first. Do you remember that earlier we agreed if your partner had no, or less, experience at SM than you, you would be topping from the bottom for a while? Well, consider topping from the bottom as the most benign form of manipulation, because right now you know more about this than he does (unless he's been holding out on you!).

Try some little service on him and see if he responds positively. And I do mean a *service*—do *not* present him with a bullwhip-out-of-the-blue and ask for a beating! Suggestions? After a hard day, help take his boots off and give him a little foot massage. Or, if he is unusually tired, offer to do a task that he usually does. If he is agreeable, continue to serve him, then curl up on the floor, leaning back against his chair. Observe his reactions. Did he like it in more than a thank-you-honey sense? Would he have liked it more if you had on something different, something a little sexier? Heels and stockings, perhaps? Don't push or overdo it, but perform the same services again the next day, even if he isn't tired! If his response is positive, wait a day or two and "serve" him again. Maybe this will put him in the right mood and help your cause.

You may already have some positive signs from him and that is why you are reading this—to find out how to get more of it! Positive signs: he likes to pin your hands down, or to cover your eyes or your mouth with his hand. He calls you his slut and makes you strip for him. He likes to pinch your nipples; he gives you an occasional spanking. He whispers lovely lewd things in your ear as he fucks you, and makes you beg him to make you come. Although many people do exactly what

I have described above, very few of them think of it as SM. Well, SMers know that those little scenarios are all part of SM! As I said in the first chapter, calling it SM may turn him off—labels, tags, and stereotyping can do that, but anything along these lines could mean he is harboring secret SM desires!

A Clear Message

Sending a clear message about his desires could be difficult because he probably has only the vaguest idea of what you are talking about. Perhaps he doesn't have enough information to be specific. (Or perhaps he has been harboring secret desires about SM play all along but has been embarrassed about verbalizing his secret desires to dominate you and be your lord and master!) When you tested the waters, he didn't respond to your service, and he hasn't shown any previous interest in SM. Now what? I can make some suggestions but because you know him, only you can decide which one he will respond to. You may need to come up with your own idea if none of these work.

Love Lists for Two

Let's go back to the Yes-No-Maybe lists idea. Instead of doing yours separately, suggest that you both do lists, either separately to be compared when you are finished or created together. Explain that everything sexual he ever thought of, heard of, or did, whether he liked it, whether it was SM-flavored, should go on the list. Tell him you will be doing the same thing. Then compose your lists, together or separately; then read over or exchange the lists. Hope there are lots of things in common on your two lists. Start with the Yes list, then move on to the Maybe list, and finally go to the No list. Use the list idea and make up combinations of your own. Use the "Wish List" and the "Roles to Play" list in chapter 8, Role-Playing, to help give you ideas.

If you don't think he is a writer, or would be embarrassed writing his "chauvinistic" desires down, leave out some tasteful, and I do mean *tasteful,* reading material (*The Topping Book* and *The Compleat Spanker* [see Recommended Reading] seem to attract a lot of men in bookstores), and see if he takes the bait. If he is a photography buff or fancies himself an amateur photographer, a fetish-photo anthology by Doris Kloster, or some of Helmut Newton's fetishy stuff, might attract his interest. If he is comfortable with the idea, why don't you look at it together? Then make your lists, separately or together, of the photos that interested each of you. If only part of the fantasy depicted is of interest to you, be sure to note that, too. Then, compare or exchange the lists, and hope for lots of matches!

The Siren Approach

The siren approach differs for each of us—we have to search our fantasy personas and find the siren among them. Your siren could be a nameless exotic dancer, or Hot Honey Harlow; a librarian or Cicciolina, a former porn star and now a member of the Italian Parliament. Or your siren could be the sensual submissive you have just awakened inside of you—not a character or role, but a hidden facet of your sexual make-up that is now ready to be explored. But how do you interest him in exploring with you?

There's my old favorite: dress up (see chapter 5, Cultivating Your New Sensuality). I dress up in something he will absolutely drool over, or nothing at all except spike-heeled shoes, then I wait for him to come into the bedroom. (My master has a special affection for a corset that pushes my breasts up and leaves my bottom exposed, which I wear with platform shoes.) There he finds me attractively arranged on the bed (of course), awaiting his pleasure. A variation on this is to tie yourself—one wrist will do—to the headboard, or bed frame, with an old scarf or piece of lace. If you have leather wrist restraints or tender tethers from a previous excursion into the dark garden, dig them out. I envy you if you have a four-poster bed or brass headboard!

Good storytellers can whisper fabulously filthy ideas in his ear as he does the deed—then observe and remember which ones get his motor running faster! If he loosely holds your wrists down as he does you, move them up over your head first, and then beg him to hold you down. If he does this, next time add on another little request—would you cover my eyes with your hand? If he still agrees, get bold and add a third item.

The Oblique Technique

If the "service" tests were inconclusive, you couldn't get him to sit still for the lists, and the siren approach didn't lure him in, but you still think he is interested, perhaps we are overlooking something about him. Perhaps he's *shy* of letting you know of his SM interests before he's even sure if he has any interests, or what they are! He'll want to appear competent and confident when you have your discussion, and he has no basis, experience, or information from which to conduct this conversation. Maybe he didn't think of SM as part of your love style until you brought it up. And now maybe he needs some private time with reliable, more male-oriented material (not the "Crazed Whip-Masters from Hell!") to take it all in and see what he likes. All you need to do in this case is help select the reading material for him. (The Recommended Reading list has a brief description of each nonfiction book which will aid you in selecting the most appropriate for your man and situation.) You can give it to him as a gift for a designated holiday, or as result of your talk, or as a present for no other reason than to express your love for him. (I gave my master little gifts as often as he would let me.)

Or, you could give him the TVSF (Television Submissive Female) test. He won't even realize what you are asking, but it may give you some insight and probably a good laugh along the way. It goes something like this: Think of all the old TV shows that featured submissive women that he would have watched, and maybe liked. Then, make up a mental process-of-elimination questionnaire. Ask him this: "Ginger or Marianne?" (from *Gilligan's Island*). If he said, "Ginger," stop here and try another method. However, if he says, "Marianne," ask "Marianne or Samantha?" (from *Bewitched*). If he still says, "Marianne," ask him, "Marianne or Yeoman Janice?" (from *Star Trek*). If he says, "Janice," ask him, "Janice or Jeannie?" (from *I Dream of Jeannie*). If he now picks Jeannie, the pattern indicates that he keeps preferring the more submissive of the two.

This is helpful at least in that you already know something about the character in question. Then, you can dress up as one of these characters and try to spark his interest that way. (Let me know if you find any of those wonderful bottles like Jeannie lived in. They never wash up on my beach.)

Message Received

After you "confess" your secret desires to him, he will need to let you know whether your message has been received. He should let you know that he has heard what you have said about your wants and needs, and he is ready, willing, and able to respond to your desires. Hopefully, he is supportive of you and interested in exploring with you. Let him speak without interrupting him; you will have your chance to respond. Give him a chance to express his feelings without pushing him. Listen to him, really listen, and not just long enough to start talking again. After he is through speaking, repeat back to him your understanding of what he said. Paraphrasing is a useful technique in making sure your desires, and his, are clearly expressed. Later on, it may be easy to exaggerate, or downplay, what you have heard, or to claim a misunderstanding, if each of you don't repeat it back in your own words. For example, make sure he knows you are looking for a limited exploration of SM and not a full twenty-four hour day, seven day a week lifestyle relationship.

As you communicate your thoughts and desires to him, it is important to express your feelings and emotions also. Be passionate but in control. Do not make your fantasy scenario sound like a dry recitation of facts or some computer program. And no matter what his response, be sure to let him know how much you trust him and respect him for listening to you so openly and with such acceptance. Thank him for allowing you to share a piece of your inner self and to give voice to these desires, whether he accepts the invitation. Avoid statements such as, "I thought every man would want to dominate a woman," which keeps the focus off the real topic.

If he is disapproving of or ignores your needs, if he ridicules your desires or labels you, then, I am sorry to say, your relationship is ailing and will not be helped by SM. Please seek help in a therapist's office, not a dungeon.

Lastly, you get to assume a more passive role (just what you've been waiting for!) and let him talk. At this point, he will either close the door to the dark garden, or hold his hand out so you may enter it side by side. Or, he may simply let you know that he is interested and there is more to talk about—later. Maybe he needs time alone to absorb and digest all of this hopefully wonderful fantasy information you have related to him. If he is sincere, "later" won't be too long. If you feel he isn't being honest with himself, or he is trying to deny his new feelings, or is trying to stop the discussion prematurely, don't let that be the end of it. Approach him and ask him to set some time aside to discuss the matter again. Tell him this is important to you.

The Prevailing Climate

What, if after trying all of the above suggestions and then some ideas of your own, the prevailing climate around your home is hostile to openness about sexuality? What if there is no adventurous nature to discover and explore? What can you do to turn your bedroom into an erotic oasis?

First, you need to look at yourself. If you are reading this to appease him, stop right here. It is the wrong reason and will probably make you resentful. If this is for yourself, ask yourself if you are comfortable exploring SM in your sexuality, *really* comfortable. If you are not, this could be communicating itself to him. Reexamine your reasons and try again, approaching it from a more honest angle. How are your communication skills? If you feel you communicate well, perhaps in this matter you need to be less assertive and more like a therapist to encourage him to express his feelings. Do you need help in overcoming a painful experience, sexual trauma, or childhood abuse? After discussing his desires, are you uncomfortable with them?

Consider this: Perhaps it is difficult for him to deal with this new information you have given him. Does he feel that you have been keeping something from him all this time? Is he angry or upset that you have been "deceiving" him about your lovemaking? A man can feel very threatened when he finds out you would like him to change his lovemaking style. And why should he change? You've deceived him! Unfortunately, many couples who find themselves in this situation break up. But that is only *one* option. Help him see these revelations not as betrayals, but as invitations to deepen the trust and intimacy of your relationship. Assure him that neither of you are different people just because you know more about each other. If you think pointing out that his negative attitude is part of the reason why you felt motivated to conceal these needs in the first place will help, please do so but with as much compassion as you can. If he is more receptive, invite him to explore the dark garden with you.

If he is unreceptive and you find you can't let go of your anger or resentment, or would just like to talk with a supportive, nonjudgmental person about sexual issues, see if there is an SM support group in your area. Sometimes they will speak with you or they may be able to recommend an SM-friendly therapist, if you think you need professional help. Alternatively, if you have a friend you think you can talk to, start by bringing up sex-related topics on a social level, not a personal one. Their initial response will let you gauge how much you would be comfortable telling them.

Lastly, after deciding what you need to be comfortable with your sexuality, go read about it! Read books, magazines, and articles that present alternative love styles, such as SM, in a favorable light. Concentrate on having good feelings about your first SM adventure, and then start planning your first SM scene!

~ 5 ~

Cultivating Your New Sensuality

Mirror, mirror, on the wall,
Who is the fairest of them all?

—The Wicked Queen, *Snow White and the Seven Dwarfs*

In our adventures in the dark garden so far, we have been on a mission to define terms, to dispel misconceptions, to discover your erotic personas and his, and to learn how to craft our scenes to fulfill the desires and needs of both. Seeds of desire have been planted for cultivation later, some fantasies are blooms ready to be picked now. Limits have been established and the safe word memorized. In chapter 6 you will learn how to ready your play space, amass props, and create an atmosphere with candles, incense, and music. But what about *you*? You can hardly show off the new erotic personas you have discovered if you are not feeling erotic. If you are like me, sometimes I feel more erotic, other times less. Sometimes it takes very little to get me going, but at other times I need more time and preparation to get my fires burning!

For those times that I am starting out at a lower level of arousal, I find that there are many things I can do that help to heighten my excitement and anticipation. Some are things that I do before each encounter;

others are things that I do when I am alone or when I have a lot of time prior to the erotic event. Some of the preparations I am going to suggest give you a physical uplifting and others give an emotional one. Because the intention of each is to clear the mind, free the soul, and relax the body, give yourself plenty of time to complete them without rushing. As you perform each personal ritual, say to yourself that you are making yourself into a receptive vessel for the passion play about to be enacted, and remember that your mind has to love it before your body will want it!

Your Personal Preparations

What do you normally do to enhance your attractiveness, your desirability, when you get ready for a vanilla-romantic encounter? Your beauty and feel-good ritual for an SM evening will probably be no different from your vanilla one. For most women, a shower is a must. Sometimes a bath is preferable to a shower, but some sort of all-over body wash is imperative to wash away the stress of the day. If you need shaving, this is when to do it. Next, shampoo and condition your hair. After you step out of the tub, a full body moisturizing might be absolutely necessary to your clean routine. Then blow-dry your hair and brush your teeth. Take special care with your makeup. The makeup I wear at night, and especially for playtime, is darker and more intense than what I wear during the day. I am sure all of this sounds very familiar to you because I believe these simple steps are a part of every woman's feel-good routine. Your routine may also include a manicure and pedicure, a facial and a massage.

You really don't need me to tell you to bathe and brush your teeth, but these personal preparations are an important part of readying yourself for any romantic encounter. They help you feel terrific about yourself and heighten your anticipation of what is to come. Heightened anticipation is an essential ingredient in any fantasy scenario. How can you actively heighten your anticipation on an emotional level? As you go about your preparations, think about the erotic event that is about to happen. While you are in the tub, relax and let your mind dwell on the intimacy you are going to share with him. Let your mind open and expand; let it become receptive to the things you are about to experience.

As you select your wardrobe, imagine what you will be feeling later, when you are in persona and wearing that outfit. Try not to think of what you have to do at the job on Monday but instead think of the beauty and sensuality at hand.

As you make your preparations, explore your emotional state. If you are anxious, locate the source of the anxiety and try to turn it into a feeling of security. You can feel secure because you have come this far, and your master wants to come with you. Each one of us, top or bottom, male or female, requires validation of our sexual desires and acceptance of our alternate erotic persona; his willingness to play SM games with you is definite validation. Focus on the fact that what you once may have perceived as a weakness, your desire to be sexually submissive, with his validation and acceptance of your desire, has been turned into a new strength. If you are holding onto anger at outside influences, release the anger into the air and turn it into appreciation of your good fortune to have a playmate, a life mate, who is accepting of your fantasies and embraces them as his own. Turn anger at the outside world into appreciation of his understanding of your needs. Begin to appreciate the cleansing effect playing SM games will have on your spirit.

Most of all, as you make your outer self as beautiful as the inner one, turn any lingering feelings of guilt about being sexually submissive into a new freedom that will let you explore and experience a rich yet undiscovered garden of pleasure without fear of reprisal, ridicule, or rejection. The sexual adventurer will find that exploring her erotic fascinations can greatly intensify the pleasure of sex and, by extension, enhance her entire life. While you make your preparations, let your mind embrace the potential for personal growth that is possible in an SM relationship. Think of yourself as an exotic flower, or as a tall and graceful willow tree, or a rare and fragile butterfly; bring your womanhood alive and let it glow. In each encounter, give him lessons in what is in the soul of a woman, then let your love take wing like a dove of hope.

The Empowerment of a Name

Would a rose by any other name still smell as sweet? It certainly would, but would we be likely to get as close if its name conjured up something other than a sweet scent? A name, in part, represents the personality of the life force. It expresses imagination (on someone's part), and often people will remember an unusual name and the face that goes with it before a more common one. I noticed this myself at an early age when my mother cursed me with a common name. This practice's continued existence was confirmed recently by my friend's five-year-old. She and three other little girls in her class are invited to all the parties, and no one would ever miss theirs; they start little fads and the other kids follow their lead. Jamie, Hailey, Stephanie, and Aspasia are their names, and they are *the* kids everyone wants to hang out with. This is a "name-prejudice," and it demonstrates that a name can be empowering or disempowering.

Your name is an integral part of the person you are and an important part of the first impression you leave on someone. It should be the most comfortable garment in your wardrobe and should fit you, inside and out, like your favorite slipper. Your name should express something of who and what you are. Unfortunately, this is not always, or even usually, the case. The name bestowed on us by our parents usually reflects their taste, not ours, or else, the child is named after a favorite grandparent or relative. In some regions, tradition dictates that babies are bestowed with the last name of the maternal grandmother. Hence, your first name could be Pier or Truly. Additionally, names go in and out of style, sometimes dating the wearer/bearer more effectively than an ID check. Mary, Linda, and Nancy have been replaced by Jennifer, Ashley, and Tiffany. Some names carry their own expectations: What if your name is Aretha and you can't squeak out a note? Or you are five feet tall and carrying around a name like Sigourney?

When you explored your alternate sexual personae, you may have found that in your dreams you were called by another name, or by different names in different fantasies. Some names are old-fashioned and others are old and reliable; some are androgynous, others are ultrafeminine. Some names express the warrior, others express the poet; some impart an artistic flair, others, the tone of the accountant. And while balancing the warrior with the poet in your soul is a very good thing, perhaps the warrior's name is not so sexy, and a more poetic name would better express your inner radiance as a sensual submissive. I think it is a wonderful idea to have a slave name: a name that makes your heart triphammer when he says it, a name that makes your spirit smile, and your inner light glow more brightly. During playtime, he can address you by this name just as you add master to his.

Whether you want to negotiate this one with him is up to you. You don't want to pick a name he dislikes for obvious reasons. I didn't even think of discussing this with anyone because I believe a new name is an entirely personal choice—what if he sticks me with a name I don't like? I already *had* one of those. (I changed it.) *I* tell people what to call me: I chose my name because I love the way it sounds and how it expresses the elegance inside of me. The story of the name's original bearer enthralls me, and his spirit of giving and his strength inspires me. The name I choose for myself expresses my idea of who I am. Your new name should empower you; you should respond to it like a flower turns its face to the sun.

If you are truly unhappy with your real name, first and surname, you can have it legally changed. In some states, if you want to change only your first name, all you need do is begin to use the new first name with the same last name and the change is legal. Changing your name to express the flower of beauty inside of you can help raise your power and self-confidence.

The Voice of Sweet Submission

We all have a variety of voices we use on a daily basis: one voice for family, another for friends; one to show the kids you mean business, one voice to answer the phone and another to deal with telemarketers who call during dinner. We have a business voice and a voice for telling jokes. We have one voice for cajoling and another for driving home a point. And then there is the voice we use to speak sexily with our lover, the voice we use to call our lover to bed, and the voice we use to urge him on. Some of these voices we have cultivated, and others come to us naturally. Anyone can learn to cultivate an erotic voice—or several.

When fantasizing of being submissive or when playing the submissive, your voice could become pleading or breathy, husky or urgent. Your speech could become peppered with "please," or "I beg you," and other worshipful and submissive phrases. When addressing him, "master" or maybe even "lord" may be your words of choice. Your tone will be dependent on the role you are playing or the persona you are assuming. It will depend on your frame of mind and the actual position you are in. If you are feeling feisty, this is bound to show in your voice. If you are kneeling with your head down, it will be very hard to make your voice loud and strident—the head-down position naturally lowers your voice and makes you sound more submissive.

How do you find, and fine tune, this voice of sweet surrender? If you talk when you masturbate, isolate and cultivate that tone, or tones. Now try to talk like that out loud and with purpose, without masturbating. It really doesn't matter what you say, but give it all the erotic nuance and inflection you can. If you speak in different tones, explore which ones make you feel more erotic. Begin training yourself to notice and use these variations to express your sexuality. Try and make sure that each tone you cultivate matches the way you are feeling and the role you are enacting at that time; it is totally possible for you to have different voices for different personae. To help you flesh out your persona's verbal personality, think about what attracted you to that erotic persona in the first place. This will help guide you to the right tone of voice and help you decide what that character would say. What in that character's personality or behavior makes you able to eroticize it? Is it her insatiability? Her tolerance for pain? Is she obedient or mischievous?

The final factor to be considered is the response of your partner. Does he fantasize about a matching character? Is he a seducer for your virgin, a rescuing knight for your damsel in distress, a rapist for your tease-next-door, a libertine professor for your shy college student? Even if you go no further than to voice the character or persona of the submissive inside, it is important that he is on the same wavelength as you are and that he responds erotically to your voice of sweet surrender.

Image

What if, after all your preparations, you don't like what you see when you look in the mirror? Few of us have bodies that belong in a *Penthouse* or *Playboy* centerfold or on stage at a strip club; few of us are blessed with faces that would grace the cover of *Vogue* or *Elle*. But that is absolutely okay because each and every one of us is beautiful (trite as it sounds) in our own way. And the one time everyone is beautiful is when they are turned on (guaranteed). Furthermore, it may surprise you to know that even those women who are regarded as paragons of beauty and grace by the rest of us consider their looks to be flawed in some way. And if that is the lament of the "ideal" woman, then perhaps we ordinary people are more beautiful than we perceive ourselves to be.

Not only are social standards of beauty foolishly narrow but they can change from era to era. The Reubensesque figure may be fashionable one decade, and a Twiggy-like figure the next. Also, what a man admires in a woman can be different from what a woman admires in another woman or in herself. These problems are compounded by a prevailing concern that only the beautiful, or talented, or gifted, or thin can attract love and sexual attention. As if all of that isn't enough, in our culture we find youth to be beautiful while age is not. This weighs more heavily on a woman, although men are not unaffected by it. Panic sets in when the aging process becomes evident, and we begin to see ourselves as less sexually desirable. A common lament of an older woman is "What am I going to do when I am too old to attract the kind of man I like?" One survey in the 1980s purported to show that a woman in her forties had a better chance of being hijacked by a terrorist than she had of getting married! And although we can't do much to change that way of thinking on a large-scale basis, there is plenty we can do at home, starting right now.

Let's consider when we feel the most beautiful. Some of us feel good after a day at the salon; others are physically and emotionally refreshed after a good massage or workout at the gym or a dance class. (Exercise releases feel-good chemicals in the brain.) When you feel good inside, it is reflected on the outside and vice versa. So when else do you feel that you are radiating inner beauty? The answer is when you are in love, when you are really turned on, and when both of those things are happening simultaneously! All of us have noticed how much better we look to ourselves when someone else is in love with us! When we are in love, nothing can distract us from the beautiful exotic creature that has come to life within us. And if that is true, how can we duplicate the glow of love whenever we want, or all the time?

Mirror, Mirror

Do you remember the wicked queen and her magic mirror in the tale of *Snow White?* If you were the top in the relationship, you may choose to play the wicked queen; as the bottom, perhaps Snow White is more to your liking. But no matter, it's the magic mirror we are interested in. Imagine having a mirror that told you each and every night that you were the fairest in all the land! Imagine the boost to your self-confidence and imagine the feeling of being in love all the time because you have constant reassurance that you were beautiful! Any mirror in your home can be your magic mirror if you learn to look at yourself with new eyes.

Let's start by creating a little atmosphere before we begin looking in the mirror. Go to "Lights, Flowers, Incense" and "Setting the Tone" in chapter 6 and use some of those ideas to make your play space feel sexier. First, kill the halogen lamp and light the candles instead. A little incense would be nice, too. When I want to boost my body image, or play "dress-up" as I call it, I create a personal play space right in front of the mirror by tossing my black quilt on the floor and strewing leopard print pillows around it. I bring in whatever "toys" and wardrobe please me that night: several pairs of shoes, lingerie, a sexy sheer robe, a mask, body oils. My music is all cued up, and when all of my toys are in place, I hit the remote control and lovely melodies fill the air.

Then I nest in the quilt, trying on this and that, admiring myself in the mirror as a whole or in parts. I admire my long legs and slender ankles; my long, shiny straight hair, my muscular curvy arms; and my perfect little pot belly. I admire the dimples at the bottom of my back, one on either side of my spine. I loll around on the quilt, pretending I am a cat, lithe and graceful, without a care in the world. Or, I play with the toys I have amassed, change my shoes, my outfit, darken my makeup, and strike poses in the mirror. I readily admit that, upon occasion, I have taken pictures of myself dressed in my favorite outfits for the viewing pleasure of myself and my master.

Dress up sometimes includes a fantasy that I am an exotic dancer so I do sexy dances in front of the mirror. Sometimes I dance for the many, sometimes I dance only for eyes of The One. I roll my stockings up and down my leg in the sexy, old-fashioned way and point my toe to accentuate the muscles in my legs. I play with a boa or fan, and take off little bits of my clothing, one piece at a time. I tease and flirt, encourage and deny, seduce and pout. (Suggestions on how to strip for your master are next.) Other times, I dance solely for myself, for the sheer joy of movement and freedom of expression I find in the dance.

When you play the dress up game, the rules are very simple: You are not allowed to look at yourself critically, and you must banish every negative thought like "I'm too old to play dress up," or "I must look ridiculous doing this." Disconnect your head from the narrow standards of beauty dictated by society and concentrate on the beauty you carry in your heart. As you look at yourself, do not allow yourself to find fault with your appearance—that would distract you from the higher erotic purpose playing dress up serves. Let the beautiful, erotic sylph inside of you get the upper hand and luxuriate in the sensuality of her. I don't think anyone is ever too old to express the soft, sensuous side of her nature, and it is never ridiculous to find your inner beauty and make it visible to all.

The Art of the Strip

If you enjoyed playing dress up and would like to experiment with something you can share with him, let me suggest you learn the art of the strip. Can't strip? Who told you that? Of course you can, you just don't know it yet. I can teach how to strip sexily—did it myself for years! There is a science to the art of the striptease: It's in the order in which you remove your clothes. You always want to look sexy and alluring. I know you can dance. And the music you choose can help or hinder you, so make your selection carefully and practice stripping to it in front of a mirror. Listen up.

You can begin your striptease in any state of dress or undress, so let's start with the fully dressed state to give you the whole picture. Let's assume you are wearing a blouse and skirt (or pants), a bra and panties, and stockings (not pantyhose) and high-heeled pumps. The order of the strip that I prefer is as follows.

First, you are going to take off your blouse. Unbutton it slowly, to the music. Now turn around and present him with your back. Turn slowly, trying one of those hip rolls you see the dancers on TV do. Look at him sexily, your chin dipped over one shoulder. Now slip your blouse down over your shoulders, revealing one shoulder at a time. You can either drop it to the floor in one motion, or let it slide down to your wrists and linger there for a second or two before letting it fall to the floor and pool at your feet. Pretend you are one of those dancers on TV—you can do it every bit as well as they can! Then turn around and face him, showing off your bra and breasts. You can play this knowingly or coyly, depending on your personal style. And, if you look in the mirror, you will see that you still look sexy dressed as you are. If you had taken off your skirt first, your blouse would have been hanging down messily, maybe even wrinkled from being stuffed in your skirt. A wrinkled shirt would make you look, and feel, like an rumpled frump, not like the alluring creature of the night and sister to the moon that you truly are.

Yes, I know that in one of the dance scenes that Demi Moore performed oh-so-wonderfully in the movie *Striptease,* she wore a suit and took off the shorts first. Certainly try it that way because for some body types bottoms off first is better. See which way looks better on you and adjust these suggestions to suit your personal style.

Now that you are shirtless, you can remove your skirt or pants. Wiggle your backside a little as you slide them down over your hips, then turn around and show him your back. Look at him over your shoulder, and beckon to him with your eyes. Lower your bottoms a little more, then stop their progress right above the crack of your cheeks. Another wiggle will help slide them down to below the cheeks of your ass, on the smile line. Turn sexily to face him and make more eye contact, smiling seductively. Take your time, following the music. This is easier than it sounds, especially if you practice in the mirror. Holding the garment you're using to cover up in place, turn around again and show him your back. Drop the garment to the floor and gracefully, or playfully, step out of it. Stretch your arms over your head as if you are luxuriating in the feel of being almost naked. Bend over at the waist and look at him from between your spread legs. Run your hand up your leg to the thigh and then buttock, holding his gaze in yours the whole time. He'll still see what the rest of you is doing, believe me!

Taking It All Off . . .

Now you are wearing your bra and panties, stockings and shoes. Look in the mirror. You look pretty damn good, don't you? At this point, you can opt for any number of things: remove the bra, or not; keep the panties, or lose them, too; hose on, shoes off; bra, hose, and shoes, no panties; hose and shoes, no bra or panties. And remember this is just the beginning of the game. The initial striptease is just that: a tease for both of you that should not last more than one or two songs. The point is to get him to sex you, not tip you!

I would take the bra off next. Choices for removal: one strap at a time, then unhook in back, and hold up in the front to cover the breasts. Flirt with him as you slowly reveal yourself to him. Or, unhook it and bend over at the waist facing him, letting the bra slide down slowly over your arms, revealing a bit of breast at a time. Now look at yourself in the mirror! All you are wearing is your panties, hose, and shoes. Just like an exotic dancer! And it gets better. Hotter. More submissive. Right now you have more of the illusion of control because his full attention is on you as you strip for his pleasure and amusement.

Another decision: Will he find you more enticing with your hose and pumps on or off? If the answer is "on," skip directly to taking off your panties. If the answer is "off," the shoes and hose are the next items to go. But then another choice presents itself: to remove a pump and a pump then a stocking and a stocking; or a pump and a stocking and a pump and a stocking? The latter, to be sure. Slip off one shoe then place your foot on the edge of the bed. Roll the stocking down your leg in the sexy, old-fashioned way men don't see anymore. Then repeat the process on the other leg. Remember to point your toe, take your time, and make eye contact. Flirt with him—you are trying to entice, lure, seduce him into sexing you! You may want to consider putting your pumps back on: members of both sexes find this to be visually appealing because the heels give a great line to your leg.

Last but not least, remove your panties. Slither them down over your hips and don't be in a hurry. Push them down to the top of your mons Venus (hairline) then turn around. Roll them down over your butt cheeks, and leave them there while you slither and dance to ensnare him. Keeping your legs closed, bend at the waist, and ease your panties down over your thighs. Speak to him with your eyes. Tell him without words that this is just for him. He's tired, you're in a welter of passion—convince him it's worth staying up for!

Of course the variations are infinite: a G-string or thong can replace the panties; a teddy or camisole will easily and sexily replace the bra and panties. A slip, half or whole, would come off after the skirt or pants, and before the bra and panties. A dress should be taken off by stepping out of it, if possible, rather than pulling it over your head. Sweaters or pullovers should be pulled off slowly, maximizing the elongated torso effect this action is famous for. Arch your back slightly as you remove the pullover, and then give your hair a sexy shake or finger-brush when you are uncovered. If you would like to experiment with floor work, you need a graceful way of getting down there. There's a trick to it: transfer all of your weight to one leg, let's say the left leg. Cross your right leg behind the left and behind the left knee, turn your right ankle to the side, and in a controlled slide on the right leg, sit down. Improvise, make it your own, and do it!

Fashion for Passion

I have said that fetish dress establishes the group identity, and that is true. Most clubs have a dress code and enforce it. But at a party held in a private home, people can indulge their erotic personas by wearing out-fits that they feel would be unsuitable in public. Your manner of dress sends out signals about who you are, your interests, and your sexuality. What we wear and how we wear it relates directly to our self-image. Like your name, your garb should fit you and the persona you are enacting; it should be appropriate for where you are going and what you are doing.

But if you aren't leaving your house, the dress code doesn't apply and you are free to dress as you please. So what I wear when a dress code is enforced, I call fetish wear, but what I wear at home I call *play clothes*. What are play clothes? The good news is anything you like and that makes you feel sexy when you put it on. In "Mirror, Mirror," I described to you how I play dress up and what my favorite bits and pieces were. Dress up is the most common variation of visual exhibitionism and a desire that is easily satisfied. But before you go on a search-and-seize mission in the closet, ask yourself a few questions.

What response do you want your outfit to evoke? If you want different responses in different scenarios, which one do you want to elicit tonight? What are his preferences? If you wear a black lace G-string with a push-up lace bra and lace-topped thigh-highs, his response, and yours, are bound to be very different than if you had on white cotton panties and a pleated skirt. If you are unsure about what you will feel sexy in, pick a time when you know you will be alone and undisturbed and try on things from your closet or dresser. Look at that white full slip with the lace bodice with new eyes: Try it without a bra, and add the highest heeled shoes you can walk in gracefully. If you have always avoided ultrafeminine lingerie, try wearing a well-cut blazer with lace-topped thigh-highs and pumps. Or give the lingerie another try—maybe you will feel differently about it now that you are further exploring your sexuality.

If your body image is good and you are happy with what you see, try exploring nudity, or partial nudity, in the safety of your home. Try a lace bra with high-heeled pumps, and nothing else. Try a garter belt, hose, and shoes, and nothing else. One of my favorite states of undressed-dress is to wear opera gloves, lace topped thigh-highs, a waist cincher, collar, and pumps. All my limbs are covered and I actually feel quite dressed, but everything the master may want to play with is accessible to him. Another favorite of mine is a floor-length sheer jacquard print robe, loosely tied at the waist, and high-heeled pumps. Crotchless pantyhose worn with pumps makes me feel sexy; so does a corset and crinoline with lace-up boots.

While you are searching out the closet for play clothes, don't forget your footwear! Many types of shoes carry an erotic message: pumps, high-heeled strappy sandals, and boots all convey their own sentiments.

Shoes and the Submissive

Ah, shoes! What woman does not harbor a secret passion for shoes—a passion that has nothing to do with a fetish? My passion is for pointy-toed pumps with high, thin heels, decorated or plain, leather or not.

Additionally, the vamp, the amount of toe cleavage, the cut and placement of the heel—all these must blend together to become a work of art befitting my foot and leg. But what I am describing is a woman's passion for shoes—not shoes, or the lack of them, as they relate to an SM setting. To be, or not to be shod? And what impact each has on the submissive is more ground to be explored in the dark garden.

Reasons for the barefoot slave and the shod one abound. Of course, in SM one is free to choose one or opt for both. Opting for both, dependent on the will of the master, makes playtime much more interesting because two paths of exploration are open to you. Those who prefer the barefoot slave point out that stripping the slave of her shoes, as she was stripped of her clothes, further impresses upon the slave her inferior position. Shoes, and their high heels, lend an air of authority that as a slave she has no right to claim. The totally nude slave is a startling contrast to her partially or fully clothed and shod master. In this setting, her reduction is furthered by her barefoot state. Some of the doms who prefer the barefoot slave also require that their slave wears no makeup or perfume, and uses no artifice at all, to further strip her in the eyes of the dom and reduce her more. Shoes, perfume, clothes, makeup are all privileges to be given and taken away by her master to aid in the deconstruction of her ego. Proponents of the naked and barefoot slave say that the inner glow the submissive attains through the SM relationship is all the artifice a beautiful, sensual submissive needs.

I agree with their point of view wholeheartedly: stripping the submissive of her clothes is a basic right of the master in a romantic relationship. And I agree just as wholeheartedly with those who prefer their slave to wear some ornamentation, and I agree with those who use shoes as a tool to control the slave. On the shoe as body decoration, well, volumes could be written so let's try a simple demonstration instead. Stand in front of a mirror barefoot and naked—remember what you see. Now, remain nude and put on your highest heels—look again. Standing in heels gives you an elegance of posture not possible when standing barefoot. Walking in heels makes your hips sway back and forth, drawing the attention of male eyes and keeping it. A long, ground-eating stride is not possible in a high heeled shoe, so the dainty steps necessary to walk in heels adds to the overall helplessness and femininity of the wearer. Look in the mirror again. High heels are a potent weapon in a woman's sexual arsenal! The high heel, or stiletto, will be explored as an aspect of bondage in chapter 12, Erotic Discomfort.

Now that you have picked out a selection of things that you like as play clothes (including shoes!), go back to your magic mirror and try them all on. Don't be overly critical of how each one looks; concentrate instead on how each one makes you *feel*. If you feel sexy and comfortable in more than one outfit, ask yourself if your arousal levels and sexual feelings differ from one outfit to the next. Then, sort the outfits by scenario: What would the blushing virgin, the sex slave, or the kidnaped maiden be wearing? What would work for a consensual rape scene? But the most important thing about the outfits you pick out is that they must make *you* feel sexy, and they turn your master on!

～ 6 ～

The Landscape of Dreams

Being poor, all I have is my dreams, which I lay trustfully at your
feet. Step gently, lest you tread on my dreams.
                                                    —Claudia Varrin

You have devoured the previous chapters and were delighted, excited,
and intrigued by what you read. Your initial sojourn into the dark garden of SM has left you titillated and hungry for more. Erotic surrender,
sexual submission, bottoming, masochism, or whatever variety of SM
you have chosen to embrace, you have decided this love style is for you!
And your partner has decided that he would like to experiment with
SM, too. You are out of your mind with joy at the prospect of the enhanced communication and trust, and the heightened intimacy possible
in an SM relationship—to say nothing about SM games sending your
rockets into red-glare!

From the information you have digested so far, you have realized
that you need more than just definitions, enthusiasm, and a willing partner—especially because you will be topping from the bottom for the
time being. What you need is a plan. A plan is how you will get what
you want; a plan is how you will fulfill all of the wicked little wishes
on your list. A plan is like a screenplay or a short story, and all good

screenplays and stories have a plot. The plot has a beginning, a middle, and an ending. Don't panic, this is easier than it sounds. You have the plot already: your fantasy!

Planning the Scene

In *The Art of Sensual Female Dominance,* I spoke of the three Ps of SM: Prior Proper Planning. Although you are the bottom, the three Ps will work for you, because you will be acting like the top. Planning is one of the things that sets SM sex above and apart from straight sex. Straight sex may have planned "romance" as part of the foreplay, like a candlelight dinner or flowers, but the sex itself just sort of happens, then rolls along on its own. There may be a few slaps, or a little hair pulling or restraint thrown in here and there, but there is no plan, no plot, and it is still straight sex. SM sex has some degree of planning and forethought even for a casual evening scene.

Your plan begins with your plot, which is your fantasy and his. I think of my fantasy as a play in three acts. Act 1 is how you would like your fantasy enactment to begin. Master and slave scenes could start with a collar-donning or other symbolic ritual; an objectification game could commence with a vow of silence; a flogging could begin with the submissive kissing the whip to be used on her. Other scenes, like a "break-in," could start with a simple word or a nod to signal that you are now in role, or by an actual departure from the premises. Anal scenes could start with an enema. The opening act could be different for each fantasy you have and scene you enact, but remember that the opening you choose directs the rest of the play. I often call Act 1 "the set-up," because it sets the tone and action for the evening's entertainment.

Act 2 is when the heaviest playing occurs in my sex-screenplays and is the longest running of the three acts, lasting from hours to days. If I am to be interrogated, put in bondage, flogged, caned, turned into an object, or made to serve, Act 2 is when we write it in. If we are going to do any improvising or pushing of limits, the flexible nature of Act 2 will nicely accommodate plot twists and additions, or sudden flashes of inspiration. Sex during my second act is usually in the context of the scene-screenplay: servicing and pleasuring the master and being used by him as a sex object. Act 2 sex differs from Act 3 sex in that third-act sex with us is lover-to-lover rather than master and slave.

My closing act, Act 3, always contains the same elements. If we began with a ritual collar or whip kissing, the same action manumits me from service. Interrogation and kidnap scenes, plus other scenes I consider to be consenting to the nonconsensual, end with my consent to his coercion and wild, passionate love making. Then comes another favorite part: my head nestled in the crook of his shoulder, luxuriating in the scent of him; my body pressed full length down the side of his, and the physical closeness we share after our play. Then perhaps we'll have a cup of tea and smoke a cigarette together and after that, some more sex, more penetration, and another merging of our spirits as we soar the heavens entwined as one.

But what happens if your fantasy and his have taken entirely different turns, or each of you start out wanting different scenes that evening? "Fantasy-divergence" is what I call it when he wants to enact one scenario that bears no resemblance to what I am interested in that evening. Hopefully, this will have come up during the initial negotiations, and not during the scene. If it does come up, this may be the time for one of life's little compromises. So discuss everything—if he wants silent service from a slave whose naked beauty burns more brightly than the exotic objets d'art in the room, and you want a kidnap scene complete with blindfolded car ride, you might end up as a stolen statue! Either you can play it his way one night and your way the next, or think up a new scene entirely. Alternatively, you could reenact an old favorite and go on from there. Even if there is no fantasy divergence, some adjustments to the combined fantasy may be in order to make it gratifying for both of you. Other than that, your fantasy already has all the magic ingredients it needs.

The Screenplay

The captor/captive theme (see chapter 8, Role-Playing) has been a very popular fantasy with many slaves and their masters for centuries. Although you *could* fantasize about being abducted, then taken and held hostage right there in your own living room, often the fantasy works better when you are abducted and then taken elsewhere: from the wagon bouncing across the plains to the ship on the high seas, or from the arid desert to the impregnable fortress. We realize, of course, that the living room or bedroom is exactly where we will be, but, with a little imagination and prior proper planning, any home can be turned into the torture chamber or pleasure palace of voluptuous captivity of which you have dreamt.

Let's say your fantasy is that you are a beautiful, aristocratic virgin who has been kidnaped from the castle stronghold by a low-down but dashingly handsome and sexy pirate for purposes that your fair head just cannot bear thinking about. He breaks into your tower room, ties you hand and foot, and maybe then he blindfolds or gags you. After you are tied up securely, he absconds to the ship with you tossed carelessly over his shoulder. Up the gangplank he goes, across the deck and down the stairs. He flings open a door and dumps you on the berth in his cabin for safe keeping on the rough high seas, and for his use and amusement later.

What can you do to make this work? Here's one idea. With both of you dressed for the part, you can be lounging in the living room reading or with your head bent over your needlepoint when he bursts in. You show panic and fear at the sight of him, he radiates wicked delight at finding such a suitable piece of "loot." (How did womankind become spoils of war? Who decided that? And, can I return the favor in kind?) After a little friendly chase and capture, he can execute simple wrist and ankle rope bondage on the appropriate appendages. The hallway from the living room to the bedroom, or playroom, could suffice for the run to the ship. Besides, too long a "run" could zap his energies, or strain his back, and that could cut the evening's pleasures short.

Once in the new location (I like the new place to be in total darkness so that he is in complete control), perhaps some rough handling would be pleasurable before he dumps you on the "berth." After jamming a pillow under your head, he leaves the berth and closes the door behind him. The ten minutes he leaves you there alone could be an eternity or an instant—the darkness has robbed you of your sense of time.

Your dress is flatteringly torn to ribbons, your hair is becomingly disheveled, and the ropes tying your wrists and ankles have become strangely comforting as the minutes drift by in the dark "cabin." You find you have learned to "relax" into the ropes, just like a member of the Perverati. Then suddenly, he flings back the small door of the cabin. You gasp in delicious fear. (Scared is sexy; terrified is very sexy.) He is backlit from the light in the hall, and his face is in darkness. As he approaches, his shadow looms large and menacingly before him. A lust-filled chuckle fills the room as he considers the pleasures that lie before him. You begin to plead and beg, whimpering in the back of your throat. You are loving this—he *is* the handsome and wicked pirate of the high seas and of your dreams, and your thighs are creamy. He grabs your wrists by their ropes and secures you to the headboard. Again, you hear yourself plead with him, "Please don't, sir, please, I beg you. Please! What are you going to do to me?" And you can't wait for it to happen.

You feel him unloosen your ankles and pull your legs open. You fight but give up quickly, realizing your struggle against his superior strength is useless. He ties your legs open, one ankle to each leg of the bed. Then he begins to remove what remains of your clothes, or he could leave you partially dressed. (Sometimes a small inconsequential garment is sexier than total nudity.) And then—whatever you have talked about happening, happens. To the great emotional joy and sexual satisfaction of both of you, I might add.

Then I highly recommend some nice cuddling and snuggling, followed perhaps by a snack or a cigarette (if such things are still allowed in America). And there you have it: your first screenplay or SM scenario! Starting with a basic fantasy, you were able to plan out a scene, with a beginning, a middle, and an ending, just as easily as that. With a few props and the right wardrobe, your home did turn into the ship of shameless delight. But just because you are planning the scene as the bottom doesn't mean that *you* have to plan everything. He needs to have a plan, too, but his plan can evolve and revolve off yours. As the "hapless victim," you need to plan only so much. He should be creative and imaginative, and get into the role he has agreed to play.

To make your fantasy enactment more realistic, there are other ingredients you may want to add. Props, wardrobe, music, and set dressing can be used to establish and maintain the theme. Additionally, if your man needs or likes a lot of visual assistance, then attention to these details will make the experience more enjoyable for both of you. Second-hand shops, thrift stores, kitchen-gadget shops, and hardware stores are great places to find things that can be "perverted" for your pleasure. Be creative, and let your imagination run wild.

Props

A prop can be just about anything ranging from an expensive, custom-made flogger to a flyswatter from the garage and everything in between. SM toys are considered props: The crop is a visible symbol of his author-ity; the collar is a visible symbol of your submission. Props can be formal or informal, like the case of the flogger versus the flyswatter; they can be symbolic, like the case of the crop and the collar. In the case of props, the number you have, and their quality, depend on your level of in-volvement in SM, the discretionary income you have to spend on your toys, and your personal preference. Besides, all any good dom needs is his own two hands, his imagination, and your consent, but for now you will have to teach him how to be imaginative!

The newcomer doesn't have to spend two hundred dollars on a deer-skin flogger—ladies' leather gloves have a very similar effect for a frac-tion of the price. You may even have a pair, or a lone glove, in the closet. These won't cost anything at all. The eight-button length, or longer, is recommended so that the arm of the glove can serve as a "handle" (see chapter 13, Sensual Sensations). There are many items in your home that, when looked at through your SM eyes, can be used as toys. You can search them out, imagine their possible use, and definitely experi-ment on yourself to ensure that you will like them. Then, when the time comes to teach him his skills as a master, present it to him as an instru-ment of discipline, bondage item, or sensitizer.

I personally would recommend that you do this search alone, and strongly recommend that you try each item on yourself before present-ing it to your master for his use on you. The first case, the solo search, will allow you to leave out any item that you don't like or may cause you a problem. This could be a belt (a leftover from childhood), a fly-swatter (you don't want to be hit with something that kills bugs), a bunny cloth (an animal died), or a feather (it makes you sneeze), and so on. The second recommendation, to try it on yourself, will ensure that you like it before you give it to him to use on you. Because you are topping from the bottom, it is absolutely necessary that you know how to use the item in case you need to help him!

Let's open up those SM eyes I spoke of earlier and go on a sex-toy shopping spree, and you don't even have to leave the house. You may have some things from a previous excursion into SM. You probably have lots of toys around the house, you just never looked at them as things that could be perverted into toys before now. Because they are many of them, I will try to group them into categories. This is the general information you will need to conduct your treasure hunt. More specific and detailed information, including safety tips where needed, can be found in later chapters.

Bound and Deprived

Items for human bondage and sensory deprivation abound; many lurk in your closet disguised as scarves, hosiery, and sleep masks. I also love scraps of lace, velvet ribbons and cords, and gros-grain ribbons as bondage items; I find it so romantic to be tied with these delicate-looking restraints. My master and I both favor them, so we have many varieties in different lengths. Some have been sewn into a circle and are very interesting to play with. These are good bondage items and easily available at the fabric store for an inexpensive price. Velvet cords, or black lace, make soft, lovely restraints and are deceptively strong, but be very careful not to tie these too tightly because thin cords and lace can cut the skin. Loosely tied scarves and hose can be used for simple wrist and ankle bondage. The use of scarves and hosiery, cords and lace, also requires that you have a pair of surgical or other very sharp scissors close at hand in case you need to be freed in a hurry. It will be easier for him to cut through the knots rather than fuss with untying them. Just don't hand over your favorite!

Another interesting and versatile item that is totally innocuous when viewed by a vanilla person is a large square of cloth, or a bandanna. When properly knotted, scarves and bandannas can be used as gags; properly folded, as blindfolds. Unfolded, a bandanna can be used as a beginner's hood because one can easily breathe and sort of see through it. The same square of cloth, rolled tight and thin, can be used as a gag. Folded flat, it suffices as a blindfold. Dark-colored fabrics work better than light ones as blindfolds and hoods. If you are hesitant about being totally sightless, use a two- to four-inch band of light-colored fabric joined in back of the head with Velcro instead. This will disrupt your vision but not block it off entirely. Sleep masks are perfect blindfolds just as they are.

An ordinary pillowcase is an excellent toy for bondage, objectification, and sensory deprivation. When your upper body and arms are tucked neatly inside, your lower body is accessible to the master for his pleasure. The pillowcase also makes a loose-fitting hood/blindfold depriving you of your sight. When I have been put "in the pillowcase," I have found it to have a very calming and very arousing effect. I am calmed as I imagine myself to be a falcon, hooded by my master until ready for his use. As I lay quietly under my hood, I become more excited, more eager for his touch. I try to imagine actions to accompany the sounds I hear in the room. Exposed from the waist down, sightless and without the use of my arms and hands, excited by the humiliation of being used as a faceless sex object, I eagerly await his pleasure. I am very aware of being exposed to him but being anonymous at the same time. As he spreads my legs and holds them open, I feel his eyes burning into my flesh. He speaks my name and I feel a warm wet rush between my legs. Now, where do you keep the linens?

Other items suitable for bondage are hiding out in that bastion of maleness, the garage. Things to look for are ropes, old "snow" chains, and duct tape. If you are handy around the house yourself, keep an eye out for eye hooks and old wooden closet poles. The ropes will be for bondage and the old snow chains, once cut into manageable lengths, will be nice to clip to the bed frame to restrain wrists and ankles. Double-clip hooks on each end of the chain will keep them securely attached to the bed and to you. Your local hardware store should be able to cut the chains for you, or perhaps you have a bolt cutter out there in the garage. Duct tape is useful for bondage, but never allow anyone to apply it directly to your skin. First wrap the wrists, or wherever, in plastic wrap or multiple layers of cheesecloth, and then apply the tape over the wrap. Duct tape *must* always be cut off, never pulled off, so have those scissors handy.

For the handywoman, a twenty-four- to thirty-inch length of wooden closet pole and two screw-in eye bolts can be made into an inexpensive and very effective spreader bar. If there is nothing suitable in the garage to press into service for this, consider making a trip to the local hardware store. Inexpensive SM toys abound there and most of the salespeople don't even realize it. (While you are there, pick up the chains, cut to size, and double-clip hooks!) They sell one-inch diameter wooden closet poles and will cut them to the length you specify. Then, simply screw one eye bolt into each end of the closet pole. Rough ends can be smoothed with some sandpaper and a coat of spray paint in glossy black gives your new spreader bar a sleek, sexy appearance.

The kitchen also yields a bondage item of great SM interest: plastic wrap. Clear, designer-tinted, or shiny black, plastic wrap is a favorite with masters and slaves as a sexy alternative bondage device. It's strong, cheap, and readily available, as well as being a surprisingly seductive restraint. See chapter 12, Erotic Discomfort, for more on human bondage.

Good Beginnings

For the sensation sluts among us (I don't mean that as an insult and I *do* include myself in their numbers), the home can yield quite a few items that are "pervertable," hence suitable for our purposes. Instruments of sensation include a wide range of items, from tickling and sensitizing toys to implements of discipline that are meant to hurt. Some, like a feather, require no skill to wield; others require considerably more. Your search for these items will take you from attic to basement and all rooms in between!

Mild sensations, or warm-up techniques, are the start of a good beating, even if the beating never progresses beyond the symbolic. The purpose of a warm-up is to the bring the blood to the surface of the skin, warming it up, readying it for more sensation, or moving you on to a higher level. Long-length leather gloves, a fur mitt, wool gloves, feather or feather duster, chamois cloth, a rolled-up bandanna, velvet cord or a strip of lace, a braided leather belt, a smooth leather belt—

all of these (and then some) will give you a variety of mild, warm-up sensations.

A good beating starts with sensitizing and caressing, not hitting, and the millinery feather or feather duster, fur mitt, and chamois cloth like the one he uses to dry the car are excellent for this. The feather or feather duster can be trailed back and forth over your prone body with varying degrees of firmness, from tickling to lightly scratchy. The fur mitt can feel silken or softly spiked, depending on how it is used and the lay of the fur. (A massage through the fur feels absolutely lovely and is very relaxing.) The chamois cloth is used like the mitt, only it is a bit rougher, more abrasive, but still well in the warm-up range.

Abrasion is often used as a step in the sensitizing process, and wool gloves, a strip of lace, an emery board, loofah washcloth (a wet one definitely feels better than a dry one but that is my personal taste), and braided leather belt can be used for abrasion. The gloves are a sexy kind of scratchy, and, as an added treat, you will feel the warmth and strength of his hands through the gloves as they glide over you. The strip of lace can be pulled tight between his hands and rubbed on or across your skin. The lace scratches more than the wool, but it *is* lace and that feels good in your mind, too. The use of the emery board is obvious but it should be used gently on your delicate protrusions. The loofah washcloth is big and soft-rough and can be used wet or dry. The braided leather belt can be wrapped around his hand, and then rubbed on your skin for a nice, scaly sensation.

Leather gloves, particularly good kidskin ones, have much the same effect as a deerskin flogger. Both are made of soft, supple hides; both have a lovely feel on the skin. As instruments of sensation, both make a nice big smacking sound on impact but actually pack little to no wallop. The marks left by either are negligible and disappear quickly. The deerskin flogger, although definitely a worthwhile investment later on, will run you about one hundred and fifty dollars now; alternatively, you may have a pair of gloves, or at least half a pair, in the closet (next to the sleep mask) that you can experiment with for free.

Other items that can be used for flogging are a rolled-up bandanna, a velvet cord, and a smooth leather belt. The bandanna is fun and sensual as a flogger as it allows your master to "hit" you very hard without hurting you at all. The cloth gives you a mild, thudding sensation *that is very arousing.* The velvet cord can be rolled up boat-rope style, and the looped-around ends used as a flogger. This delivers a little more sting than thud, but it is very pleasant all the same and a nice contrast to the bandanna. The smooth leather belt is the most severe item and does take some practice at wielding correctly. Swack it at your bottom a few times to see if you enjoy the belt before you hand it over to your master.

Pain: Part One

You enjoyed experimenting with the sensitizing items and the slightly abrasive ones, too, and now you'd like to experiment with a little pain. You'd like to find something in the house that packed a little more wallop. Not much—just a little. There's the flyswatter, a wooden ruler or yardstick, a sports paddle, his belt (again!), leather strop (for sharpening razors), and his slipper. The kitchen will cough up things like a wooden spoon, spatula, and egg flipper, but, I confess, the mental image of my master wielding a wooden spoon as he admonishes me cripples me with laughter. I would be wondering where his big poofy hat was and *what* did he have under that apron? I think this item works better with fem doms.

The ruler, yardstick, and sports paddle require a little anatomy knowledge to be used safely (see chapter 13, Sensual Sensations), or else he could bruise your butt. The flyswatter will sting like hell for a little while, but I find that it is more humiliating than painful to be hit with a flyswatter, like I was some annoying bug buzzing around his head. The leather strop works in a similar way but hurts more. His slipper (especially a leather soft-soled, slip-on, mule-type slipper) is my favorite if no formal piece of equipment is at hand. Then there is his hand itself. Almost anyone can give a spanking; however, a good spanking takes a little skill and a lot of listening to the person being spanked—you!

Items of Sensual Discomfort

Your home has an endless supply of items that can cause you the most delicious discomfort, making you squirm and squeal in feigned agony while you beg for more. Candles, ice, clothespins, chop sticks, toothbrush, skirt hanger—all are there waiting for you to discover them. Some items cause more discomfort than others so, again, try everything you can on yourself before handing it over to the master.

A personal favorite of mine, hot waxing, is an erotic extravaganza for the body and mind. The best candles are available in tall or medium glass jars. These candles allow the wax to collect in the jar, giving him a nice lava flow to pour on me. Alternatively, beeswax or paraffin tapers drip one hot drop at a time, providing countless tiny tortures. But beeswax and paraffin candles burn very hot and can cause second-degree burns. Ice can be used to harden the wax and/or cool the skin. Ice is also quite pleasant on the buttocks after a spanking, and feels lovely when trailed over your prone body randomly.

Clothespins and the skirt hanger are items for nipple torture but some can really hurt, so test them on yourself first, or loosen them up by keeping them clipped to something to stretch them. Look for clothes-pins with a spring action, and I particularly like the small plastic ones with the flat ends. The wooden ones can be too brutal unless they have been loosened up from use. The skirt hanger could be a sweet surprise. Mine is a metal rod with two grippers; the grippers have red insulating plastic on the ends. The grippers can be slid back and forth on the pole and the hanger hook makes a good handle for the lord to pull you around by and for other things to be attached to. Also, a pair of pliers will loosen the grippers if they are too tight.

The chopsticks and the toothbrush are both small, innocuous items that everyone has around the house. For the master who has had fan-tasies of being a drummer, the chopsticks can be used as "tapping" de-vices. A constant light tapping of chopsticks on certain body parts is a delightfully excruciating sensation. The toothbrush can be used as an abrasion device on almost any part of the body, and if your toothbrush has a rubber end . . . ! This too can be used for delicious teasing and various tiny tortures.

Preparing Your Home

Having collected what you think is a suitable group of starter toys, you now need somewhere appropriate to play with them. In many large cities, there are professional houses of domination that will rent you a dungeon or specialty room. This will be a wonderful idea when both of you have more experience and would like to venture out into the SM world to play. In the meantime, your home can be made suitably dungeonlike if that is your fantasy, or dressed up just enough to give the illusion of a dungeon, or anywhere else your fancy takes you. Let's start with the basics.

Creating a Play-Space

The first thing you will want to turn your attention to is the actual place where you will be playing. Although SM can happen anywhere (first and foremost, in your mind!), in the beginning you may feel more secure knowing that you *will* be playing in the living room and needn't plan on any forays out into the yard.

SM play can get noisy (all of that yelling "NO NO NO!!!" that turns us on so much!), so consider how soundproof your house is, then look at its layout. Pick the room farthest from your neighbors or the room most surrounded by other rooms of your house. Can anyone see into the room from outside? Are you comfortable playing in there? Usually the playroom would be the living room or bedroom, or if you are lucky, a spare bedroom. If you have a particular setting necessary for your fantasy, can your space be made to look like that setting easily? If you have a medical fantasy, white sheets can look like hospital room separators, and a shiny tray with some "medical" instruments will complete the illusion; if you have a military fantasy, perhaps a thin, hard cot can be found. If he is to be the sheik, squares of cloth can be used to cover the sofa, pillows can be tossed on the floor, and the living room made to emulate a tent pitched on the desert sands.

There are other things in your home that when looked at *improperly* are wickedly suitable for SM use. Perhaps you have an ottoman or a bench in your living room; these are lovely things to pervert for playtime. Betty Page–style bondage over the ottoman would thrill those who like to be tied; the bench becomes a "display" table for the slave to show the lord her attributes, or something to lean over for a disciplining. A chin-up bar in a doorway will make an inconspicuous overhead bondage device; a director's chair or ice cream parlor chair can be turned into a torture or bondage seat. And a four-poster bed or brass headboard is the constant delight of the SMer!

Of course, when he gets into the love style, he, too, should be looking around the house for suitable pervertables and perfecting their use for your erotic pleasure, and his.

Before You Get Dirty, Clean Up

"A" is for ambience and now that you have created a play-space in your home you will need to create atmosphere. Most men appreciate a clean home but know little or nothing about getting one that way, so before you turn the lights down, turn them up. Are there fuzzies in the corners that will cling to your hair (or other places!) when he throws you to the floor in a welter of passion? Is the mirror in which you are going to admire your submissive self streaked with smoke? Are there old dirty dishes in the sink or containers in the refrigerator that look like science projects? Is there a stack of newspapers molding in the corner just waiting to go out for recycling? Are there bras and panties drying on the shower curtain pole? If you are into a little instant gratification, this would be the perfect time to tend to these chores. Clean the house and free the psyche!

I never look at these types of tasks as housework; I prefer to consider them part of my preparations for playtime. While cleaning the mirror, I think of what my reflection will look like later on when I am glowing from love and submission. As I vacuum up the fuzzies, I think of how wonderful it would be if he were to sex me on that very spot in just a few hours!

Lights, Flowers, Incense

Now I would recommend that you turn the lights down, way down, and use a few candles to illuminate to room. Candlelight is flattering and very sexy, taking years off anyone's age, and it will make you feel sexier, too. If you have a dimmer or variable lighting switch, set it to the lowest illumination. If you don't, consider installing one—you could probably put it in yourself (shut off the electricity first!). Now, how does the room look? Inviting? Cozy like a nest? Would some flowers, arranged by you, help? How does the room smell? Like dinner? Cigarettes? Open the windows and air it out. Burning incense will help eliminate the odor and add an exotic flavor to the evening.

Next, check the temperature in the room. If it's the dead of winter, will you be warm enough if you are naked? If not, turn the thermostat up in sufficient time to make the room the right temperature for you. Because your master will be at least partially dressed, he may have to shed his shirt to be comfortable, but remember you are a sensual, sensible submissive, not a potential ice cube. It is unlikely that you will enjoy your romantic encounter as his slave if you are shivering with cold. In summer, the air conditioner may be necessary to keep both of you comfortable (but it may also blow out your candles).

Setting the Tone

Music can be a very important part of your life, and it can play an important role in your scene. On a practical level, having the music going helps to cover up whatever noise you may be making, or at least helps to confuse the issue by providing a distraction from your sounds. If your house has not been soundproofed, or you live in an apartment, noise can be a big consideration. On an aesthetic level, music can help free your mind and unburden your heart. One note, beautifully sung, can send your spirit soaring or call you back to earth.

Your choice of music is entirely personal but SMers do have preferences. Songs with loud or catchy vocals are a distraction for top and bottom alike. One gets caught up in the music instead of the scene as one sings along with the chorus. Trip-hop and trance-hop are popular music styles for dungeon parties in London, and this style is (finally!) catching on in the United States. Don't be fooled by the use of the word "hop": This music is dreamy and romantic, with Middle Eastern flairs and echoes, sexy rhythms and drumming, and vocalizings, but no discernible lyrics. Other current favorites of mine are the CDs *Dummy* by Portishead, *Karma* by Delirium, *Junk Science* by Deep Dish, and *Sex Fetish* by the League of Hedonists. Classical music by any composer is very popular, especially with older players who don't understand today's trance-dance music. Movie scores can provide another source for SM background music; also, traditional Middle Eastern, Indian, and Arabic music add an exotic, sexy element.

~ 7 ~

Living Out Fantasies

Thou shall not ridicule another's fetish or fantasy.

—The Prime Directive of SM

What are the essential ingredients needed to enact the fantasies growing in the dark garden of your erotic mind? On an emotional level, communication, trust, and caring, plus the will to discover, explore, and accept your sexual nature are essential ingredients. What makes a good fantasy good in the physical world? The active and joyful participation by you and your partner in cowriting the script for the fantasy is an excellent start. Planning the scene together will help stop fantasy-divergence before it begins. The assemblage of the props and the preparation of the inner and outer self and the play-space, as we discussed in earlier chapters, are also prime ingredients for a romantic and gratifying SM encounter. Afterward, the nestling and cuddling, the sharing of the feelings and emotions, the giving of encouragement and support, and the closeness between you and your master are additional essential ingredients.

The Elements of Fantasies

Mystery, emotion, and eroticism are also essential and magical ingredients, or the emotional aphrodisiacs, that direct SM fantasies. This trio of mind-magic wins out over logic and reason because our desires, the fantasies in our erotic mind, are not reasonable. We cannot use logic to delve into them, so we must surrender to them and experience them before we can begin to understand them. As you continue to explore your sexuality, you will find that without surrender there can be no knowing of the self and true merging with another. To surrender to one's desires, one must be accepting of them. Developing a comfortable acceptance of your SM-flavored fantasies may let you feel and express a wider range of emotions toward your partner. If in the safety of the fantasy you are able to express more facets of your erotic personality and show him your secret heart, might not that same trust carry over into your everyday life? Having trusted him to walk with you in the dark garden, couldn't you walk together more boldly in the light?

The fantasies you create are made of certain prime elements, and these elements are your emotional aphrodisiacs. Emotional aphrodisiacs refuse to follow any rules or be restricted by reason. The erotic feelings they invoke exist to be felt, and explored, by the sexual adventurer. Once you locate those elements, you can begin to direct, or orchestrate, your fantasies. These prime elements are always in our fantasies because they are conceived with little or no prodding from us in the subconscious mind, but maybe you haven't gone looking for them before. As you are still topping from the bottom, you need more information on how to find those elements, so that you can start to enact your fantasy and his.

Glance over your wish lists and let your mind linger on one of your favorite fantasies. Fast forward the fantasy in your mind, and search for its prime element. Now select another favorite and run through that fantasy too, searching out this one's prime element. If at first these two fantasies seem dissimilar, try taking a closer look at them. In the first fantasy, let's say that you want to be kidnapped by a masked invader who ties you to the bed and ravishes you. In this fantasy, you will see that you have an overall plan: You want to be kidnapped. Second, you want your kidnapper to be masked. Then, you want him to tie you to the bed and ravish you. In the second fantasy, the overall plan is that you are the consensual slave of the master, and you are there to service and please him in bed. His preferred position this night is to bend you over the bed, tie your hands behind the small of your back and gag you, then shag you from behind, in both openings. What one is your prime erotic theme and what is mere window dressing?

Although certain physical actions go with kidnapping, like being blindfolded or gagged, and, most likely, some form of bondage, some of those details also fit in very well with the second, consensual fantasy. Those are the small but essential and sometimes tangible things necessary to make a good realization of your fantasy. I call these details—the blindfold, the gag, the rope—window dressing. Strip them away and what is left? Your script: kidnapped in the first fantasy, the slave girl in the second. You may think that these are dissimilar fantasies: In the first, the theme is that you are forced to accept sex against your will; in the second, you consent to be the master's slave.

But upon further exploration, you may find that your scripts are window dressing also! The two seemingly dissimilar fantasies may, in fact, both be expressions of a desire to surrender to your own primal sexual urges without fear of guilt or reprisal. In one, you are taken by a masked invader, in the other, by a randy master who owns you. In both fantasies, you are in a position of helplessness, where your life is dependent on the whims and will of another. Perhaps *this* is your prime erotic theme. Being kidnapped is a way to ultimately surrender control and experience helplessness and heightened sexual arousal without guilt, and so is being a slave-girl. Many submissives have more than one prime erotic theme, preferring different fantasies to suit their frame of mind, as well as their need and desire for exploration.

Your Prime Erotic Themes . . . Your "Pets"

I call the essence of a fantasy its prime erotic theme (Pet). Your prime erotic theme occupies a special place at the heart of your erotic mind. All those who fantasize have a Pet although you may have not thought of it that way before. Themes are usually simple and can sometimes be described in a sentence or two, or even in a phrase. Your Pet can be inspired by a single yet profound and meaningful fantasy. In the fantasies above, my Pet could have been the helplessness of the captive, willing or not, and the sweet knowledge that one is still cherished and desired. Or the Pet could be my desire to surrender guiltlessly and totally to my sexual desires. In either case, my theme is the core of the fantasy I want to enact; scenes are the separate little vignettes I enact inside of my Pet; and the window dressing are the props and the wardrobe. If you are like me, as you explored your alternate sexual personae, you found recurring themes in your fantasies.

Different fantasies, SM or not, come to life under certain circumstances. In an ongoing committed relationship, as trust and communication deepen, you may find you are willing to go beyond what your original Yes List included and begin enacting fantasies from the Maybe List. Your willingness to play out more fantasies will increase in time, just as your willingness to accept more pain (see chapter 13, Sensual Sensations) will increase as you become more aroused. Pets in play in casual encounters may disappear when a relationship turns serious. Pets created in lust and those created in trust may be played out differently.

Remember, too, the levels of fantasies we spoke of: Those things we really want to happen to us, those we think we'd like to happen, and those we love to imagine but never would want to happen, which I call "bathtub fantasies." Your Pets grow quite nicely in all three categories, including the last. Enacting different scenarios allows you to explore issues and challenges, sexual and emotional, and heal wounds from the past. If you do explore your Pet, you may find that it is like a coded message that reveals which people (or characters), situations, or images will light your erotic fire. Some of your Pet's extraordinary power stems from the link it creates with today's turn-ons and yesterday's difficulties. Your adulthood concept of eroticism can reflect the challenges you experienced in childhood, and could be an attempt to deal with them. Inside of your prime erotic theme is a blueprint for turning unfinished emotional business from your childhood and teenage years into excitement and pleasure as a responsible adult.

On a basic level, your prime erotic theme is one that will elicit the most physical and psychic excitement. Much more than a list of what turns you on and off, it expresses your individual eroticism and empowers you with a new self-knowledge. As we said earlier, it is not unusual for the sexual explorer to respond to more than one Pet, and lucky you if you have more than one. Your Pets are the fertile soil where your special turn-ons grow.

Exploring Your Pet

When, and how, did your Pet start? Our eroticism is always evolving; it seeks to write new arousing scripts that settle dilemmas and crises started in our earliest life. A prime erotic theme begins its evolution during childhood, and some of your early fantasies probably stemmed from the veil of secrecy that surrounded those impulses and interests considered inappropriate for children. Other fantasies stem from societal mores and the breaking of taboos.

Over the years, our life experience has contributed to the choices we make in our Pets. There are some Pets that even as adults we keep to ourselves, deeming that fantasy too sacred or too personal to share with another. Fantasies on this level might be bathtub fantasies. When I create new bathtub fantasies, they are always created with my current lover in the role of master. Although he is my master in reality and we share many secrets, in the fantasy he does things with me that I enjoy thinking about yet don't care to tell him about, never mind allow him to do!

Each of us may wish to keep one or more aspects of our Pets to ourselves. I feel this reaction is very natural and hardly consider it a breaking of trust. Some things need not be spoken of; in fantasy land, you can both arrive at the same place even if you begin at different starting points. Does he really need to know that you are solving a childhood trauma in this fantasy or that? Would he understand? This is a very personal decision to make and a difficult one too. When acting out a scene that echoes an early trauma, the scene may trigger strong emotions in the submissive. Although informed consent is a byword of SM play, it can be very hard to explain to your master what may happen to you emotionally if he, say, slaps your face. You may not even know what the aftermath of the slap will be, so how can you explain it to him? Then there is always the possibility that he will not want to enact the scene because he is afraid of the emotional fallout. You can choose not to tell him and have your safe-word on the tip of your tongue, or you can choose to tell him about it so as to ensure his support throughout the experience.

During SM play, and any kind of sex, we are in a heightened state of awareness that makes us very conscious of ourselves and of how we are relating to our partner. There is an intense interplay between you and what you perceive your partner to be thinking or feeling. Discussions and dialogues about our prime erotic themes are rarely as satisfying as our mental enactments and this unintentional interplay could divert you from the undiluted version of your Pet. Furthermore, some thoughts and fantasies don't need to be shared. Your Pet can be most freely explored if unhampered by the need to negotiate it and make it mesh with another's needs. You can decide *if and when* you want to discuss your Pet with him. By all means let him know what turns you on, but you needn't tell him the extremely personal details, just what feels right and comfortable to you.

When you think about one of your best sexual experiences, look beyond the deliciously wicked details and flesh-tingling sensations and try to see why this experience was so exciting. Could it be because it dealt with one of your life's unresolved struggles? Irrational as it seems, high sexual excitement can flow from the tension between emotional problems and their joyous solutions. (Remember we said earlier that our desires during these times are anything but rational.) While we are caught up in our increasing arousal, we aren't consciously aware that we are thinking about any of our problems because we are riveted on the pleasure at hand. This is a good thing because the fact that we are that excited shows that our Pet is working. Part of our Pet's purpose is to turn old wounds and concerns into aphrodisiacs, as well as resolving conflicts of days gone by. But instead of resolving hurtful problems in a subtle way, SM turns the klieg lights on the pain and provides a strategy for mastering it by playing top and bottom, master and slave, sadist and masochist. As we discussed earlier, both top and bottom feel validated and powerful after a scene because the scene played to the needs of both.

Exploring this fantasy on your own is highly recommended, to whatever degree you are comfortable, because even a small discovery about it can be a useful revelation. Once you know what your Pet is, how it began, and what challenges it is meeting or what conflicts it addresses, you can start to "work with it." You can consciously direct the Pet where you want it to go. Exploring your Pet can, in some ways, set you free because choices, and freedom, increase with consciousness. A prime erotic theme is a strategy for turning pain into pleasure and excitation; it is also a search for validation and fulfillment. Many of us, including myself, tend to search out partners who fill in aspects of our own personalities that we feel we may be missing or lacking. I am an emotional, introspective person whereas my lord was as solid as the Rock of Gibraltar, as calm as the Sea of Tranquility, and not a self-searcher. His calm balanced my storm, and provided a safe harbor for me.

Of course, billions of people have perfectly good sex lives without giving one moment's thought to their prime erotic themes. These sexy scripts are written by us subconsciously and require little to no effort on our part. If you are not comfortable exploring this deep into the garden, then definitely don't. Only you can know how far into the dark garden you are ready to venture, and some people prefer not to know the reason behind their Pets. Others study their Pets closely because they feel this exploration has given them a deeper respect for their eroticism and a greater understanding of their sexual choices.

Sexy Scripts

Sexy scripts are twofold: the first part is the plot (the masked invader takes you captive), and the second is the details or the window dressing for our Pets. We spoke of possible props in chapter 6, The Landscape of Dreams and appropriate wardrobe in chapter 5, Cultivating Your New Sensuality, so all you need to do is match those to your scene. The first component, the sexy script, has been researched by sociologists William Simon and John Gagnon. They have separated the central themes of erotic fantasies, what we have been calling Pets, into three basic types: cultural scripts, interpersonal scripts, and intrapsychic (within the mind) scripts. Just as many of us have more than one Pet, some evenings preferring to enact one theme rather than another, so too can we have fantasies about each of the three script types.

Cultural scripts are about the societal mores so ingrained in us that we don't question their existence, or even notice them. A script contra to cultural mores wouldn't necessarily be a "fetish," like desiring to worship the foot; a cultural script usually breaks some taboo or ethic of the individual's society. Let's say there was an ancient tribe where some of the people had long ears and others, short. In this tribe, from time immemorial, long-eared men were proscribed from marrying short-eared women. No one even remembered why; it was just accepted as part of their culture. Indubitably, some of the men would have fantasies about the short-eared women simply because, in their culture, these women were forbidden to them. The neighboring tribe, however, had no proscriptions about ear size; small ears were no more or less preferable than long ones, so no cultural taboo existed. In short, a cultural script is imposed on us only by the society we live in.

The intrapersonal script is highly colored by our personality and early environment, and obviously varies greatly from one person to another. The intrapersonal script, thankfully, can exist in even the most erotically restrictive cultures. Starting in childhood, this script develops gradually as we learn the rules of our immediate society, first within our family and then from our peers in the world. Some change quickly, influenced by the times swirling around us; others stay with us a long time. An intrapersonal script could be one imparted to us by our family. For example, if you were always made to wear panties under your clothes, going bare bottomed under your dress could be a very exciting fantasy. To put it succinctly, the intrapersonal script is imposed on us by the people we are in direct contact with from the beginning of our lives: family, friends, teachers, and so on.

The intrapsychic scripts are the most fascinating scripts of the three. These are mind scripts, and they express the *individual's* responses to her own life experience even more than the first two. Although intrapsychic scripts are certainly influenced by and contain elements of both cultural and intrapersonal scripts, these scripts are as totally and wonderfully unique as are we who fantasize them. The Pets for mind scripts can begin in childhood and are as varied and numerous as the people who create them. Other Pets can start in adulthood, triggered or brought on by a specific experience. Mind scripts are the most compelling, as they reflect the erotic mind of the individual, the shadow land mind we are exploring in the dark garden, not built-in cultural or societal scripts. Intra-psychic scripts depend solely on the dreamer's preference and taste. They can be based on past experiences or unspoken desires. And because erotic minds and the fantasies conceived within them are so voluminous, it is difficult to find any connections among them.

The Devil Is in the Details

Scripts tend to be very detailed whereas themes can be expressed in a single thought. In the details of our script, our flights of fantasy come in and express the different facets of our erotic mind. The clothes we choose for the scene, the way we style our hair and apply our makeup, the voice we speak in, where we do the scene, and the props we use are the details of our sexual script that make the fantasy, our Pet, come to life. If the Pet is the helplessness of bondage, it makes it more fun and romantic to play the unwilling maiden (tied to the bed) one evening and the hot slut (tied to the bed) begging her master for it the next. This is the integration of a prime erotic theme (the helplessness of bondage) with a sexy script (how you came to be in bondage).

Think of it this way. Hundreds of murder mysteries have been made where the viewer is shown the perpetrator committing the crime at the beginning of the movie. Now that we know who did it, what becomes interesting to us is the way the crime is solved, the way each clue is uncovered, and how the other suspects are eliminated. This same theme occurs again and again because it works so well; what changes in each movie is merely the details: the location, characters, methods, motives, and mistakes.

Let's apply that thought to an SM script. You are enacting the part of a virginal young woman visiting her doctor. Although embarrassed by the examination, you decide to confide in the doctor, telling him about the problems you are having with a randy boyfriend. The doctor tells you that if you do exactly as he directs, he will teach you how to deal with your boyfriend. You accept, whereupon he ties you to the examination table and slowly caresses you until your protests turn into moans of pleasure. He touches you everywhere, doing things with you that no ethical doctor would do with a patient. Realizing that your struggles are useless, you surrender to him completely. He has become your teacher in the ways of pleasure, and you come alive under his expert hands.

The fantasy of being defiled, being taken, is probably as old as womankind. There is something about innocence in a fantasy that screams out to be trampled underfoot, and those screams are heard by women and men. There is a reciprocity between the defiler and the defiled as reluctance is turned into compliance and then into an exchange of erotic energy. The scenario is a classic example of being freed from the guilt of enjoying the loss of what was once so highly valued: virginity. Beginning with the purity that so fascinates and repels us, through the fantasy we are able to corrupt innocence without damaging its heart (the virgin comes to like sex) and release passion in both partners. The doctor and examination is stage dressing, part of the sexy script for our prime erotic theme.

Some people feel no need or desire to explore their Pets because they fear that overdissecting their fantasy will take away the fantasy's erotic power. If this is your fear, you needn't worry about your exploration, or lack of, affecting the beauty and eroticism of your fantasies. Pets operate, if not completely unconsciously, at the very edge of our awareness. Some Pets are very subtle and get lost in the sexy scripts we devise. If your Pets gratify you sexually without further delving, and do not harm you or make you feel inadequate, just enjoy them!

The Origin of SM Fantasies

Where do SM fantasies come from? We know they don't come from the stork or the cabbage patch. Freud said in 1919 that SM fantasies, especially of masochism, start in early childhood. He found a reference point for masochism in the Oedipus complex, so-called after the Greek mythological figure who fell in love with his mother and murdered his father. Disdaining Greek mythology, Krafft-Ebing, after having had Leopold von Sacher-Masoch as a patient, stated that masochism was a pathological growth of specific feminine psychical characteristics. Was it his use of the word "pathological" that changed the world's perceptions of SM and masochism? Did this statement cast SM into the shadow land of the mind, where our erotic dark garden is located? Too many have sought to explain the indefinable, because the meaning of masochism and SM in the romantic and spiritual sense of the words defies definition. The definition of sadomasochism is different for each one of us.

Having said that, I think it would also be fair to say that we don't really know why some people have SM fantasies and others don't. Adult survivors of childhood abuse dream of erotic beatings and consensual

rape; adults who do not recall anything other than the occasional dis-
ciplinary spank on the bottom dream of the same things. Every time
someone is ready to put forth a generalization, yet another exception to
the rule pops up and blows the theory. Psychiatrists and psychologists,
activists and armchair adventurers, SM's proponents and its antagonists,
all have their theories. As I have mine and you have yours. But because
no one has ever performed an autopsy on a brain and found a small,
large, or any lobe generating sadomasochistic fantasies, your guess is as
good as mine, or Freud's, for that matter.

A Slap in the Face

Do you really care why your favorite dessert *is* your favorite? No, you
simply like it. Just so, the origin of your fantasy is only as important
as you make it or as important as what demons it sets to rest or what
angels it invokes. For me, as an adult survivor of childhood abuse, the
origins of some fantasies are very important. My father physically abused
me in a variety of ways, but what I hated most was having my face
slapped. His hand would snake out and smash into my face, sometimes
knocking me down or off my chair. I didn't know why I was being hit.
Often there was no reason, or my mother had fought with him and he
took it out on me. I resented it deeply. Until recently, I pulled away from
anyone who reached out for my face, even to caress it, unless I "saw it
coming," and knowing that this person meant well, willed myself to
stand still.

All that began to change when one night, in a deliciously filthy, very
sexy, sadomasochistic, trans-Atlantic phone call lasting until dawn *his*
time, my master said, "Do you know that when I see you, Claudia, I am
going to make you put your hands behind your back and then I'm going
to slap your face?" I inhaled audibly, and didn't know what to say. At
this time, he knew very little of my childhood and early abuse, and not
that part. "I know that now, master," was all I could think of to say that
wouldn't break the mood. I didn't want to discuss such a traumatic time
of my life over the phone, especially not in the middle of an unusually
hot phone session. Besides, I thought it was a noncommittal answer—
more of an acknowledgment of his remark than an outright "yes."

I would bring it up when we were face to face; he wasn't much of a phone person in the psychological area.

But a wonderful thing happened. In SM, dominants speak of a training technique called "planting the seed." I don't know if my lord meant to plant this seed in my fertile mind (and at first I didn't realize I had been "seeded," accidentally or not), but the seed took root and grew. First I let myself focus on his massive, strong hands. For all of their size and strength, his hands are delicate and fine boned. His fingers are long and straight and his nails well formed and shiny. He is very deft, good at quick knots and bondage with ropes, ribbons, and lace. I love his hands, often asked him for pictures of them, and treasured the few photos where his lovely, long-fingered hands could be seen clearly.

I let my thoughts dwell lovingly on his hands. I knew how they felt on me; knew their size and strength and warmth. I knew the feel of them when they spanked my bare bottom or slapped my breasts. Then I imagined his right hand on my face, caressing it first, like he was sensitizing me for a beating. With my head cradled in his left hand, the right hand pulls back and cuts through the air, landing squarely on my cheek. After that, I began to think up fantasy scenarios that I could work the face slap into: I favored the fantasies where the slap was punishment for talking back or service that was not fast enough.

"Claudia . . .," he called my name in the tone of voice he reserved for correction time. "Yes, milord?" "How much sugar did you put in my tea?" "Two, milord." "*One* teaspoon in tea, Claudia, *two* in coffee," my lord said softly. "Have I told you this before?" "Yes, milord." "Kneel, please, Claudia, and rest your buttocks on your heels. Cross your arms behind your back." I obey each softly spoken command, wonderfully at peace with him and myself and eagerly anticipating the erotic adventures to come.

His large warm left hand braces my head and neck and holds me just a little too tightly. I revel in it. His right hand, a little larger and just as warm as the left, brushes my face. Breathless, my chest heaving, I stare at the carpet until he commands me to look at him, to look into his eyes. We smile. He withdraws the right hand from my face and pulls it back out of my sight as he continues to hold my gaze. Then, I feel his hand coming, feel it parting the air in its rush to my face. Although

I whimper and moan in the back of my throat and my stomach turns somersaults, I hold my kneeling position. His hand crashes into my face—a perfectly landed blow, square across the padded part of the cheek.

The shock of his hand radiates from my cheek to my brain and then straight to my garden gate, blasting it off its hinges by a tidal wave. His right hand travels between my parted thighs—I hurry to open them further—and he smiles at the wetness. "Now, Claudia, how much sugar in my tea?" "One in your tea, Master, thank you," I whispered with all my heart. I bent my head, breaking his gaze for the first time, and placed a reverent kiss on the arm that disappeared between my legs.

When we next saw each other, I was ready for my first face slapping. Although the scenario was his, I was totally in favor it, hardly discussing the setup at all. Not only was it cosmically orgasmic, but it knocked an old cobweb right out of my mind. I haven't winced when someone has lifted their hand in greeting since that first cosmic, orgasmic, consensual slap in the face delivered in love from my lord.

～ 8 ～

Role-Playing

In the dark garden of our minds, the erotic exchange of power during SM games is a romantic, fun, and enriching part of sex and fantasy. Often this erotic power exchange includes a lot of role-playing, which is probably part of one of your sexy scripts that expresses your prime erotic theme (Pet). Role-playing has been with us, vanilla person or kook-a-maniac, for centuries. Some SMers have a decided preference for elaborate role-playing and go to great lengths to design and stage their fantasies. This could include a penchant for dressing up in the appropriate costumes; for example, the "professor" wears a jacket with suede on the elbows, and his "student" has an armful of books. Some tops get into "decorating" the play area so that it reflects the Pet: a "medical" examination table, a tray of "medical instruments," and an overhead light. Other imaginative tops plan the arrival and departure of the bottom, so that it enforces the illusion: a woman "hired" to be a submissive could arrive in a cab and leave the same way. It is part of the smoke-and-mirror illusions SMers love so well because they feel their ability to experiment in different roles enriches their erotic relationship.

When you explored your alternate sexual persona, you probably found some characters or fantasies more appealing than others. This would be because the role "spoke to you": it exuded a familiarity that you were comfortable with, or it represented some sense of your preferred sexual personae. For example, if you fantasize that you are a virgin, then you would be able to express, or act out, your variety of "virgin." You may be an eager, hot virgin, just breathless to lose your cherry, or you may be a shy and fearful virgin. Maybe you are a virgin who tries to "fight" off her rapist and resists the whole time. In Jungian psychology, this "virgin," hot or resisting, is one of many "erotic archetypes."

You will find that the roles you assume affect your romantic encounter in many ways, on many levels. The role could affect you emotionally; suddenly you feel like the teenager you are pretending to be, or you start to speak like a teenager. Your tone of voice changes and so does your vocabulary. Additionally, the way you and your master relate to each other during sex may be very different when you are in role. The role affects you physically in that sex feels different in that role, or you feel more aroused. You may find yourself (and your master) saying and doing things that are new to both of you. You and the master may discover new and exciting facets of your sexual personalities to explore on other occasions. Things on the No list suddenly turn into, "YES, YES, YES!" The truly blessed, and those very in touch with each other, will experience two or more of these feelings.

Roles come in pairs, and like the slender linden tree and the mighty oak, should grow well in the same soil. The professor and the student, the rogue and the virgin, the lord and the maidservant are compatible scenes and persona, and have been popular pairings for eons. If you consider the above pairings, you will see that there are three general categories of role-playing that the pairs fall into: authority figure or age-play, captor-captive, and master-slave. See page 97 for a list of roles you and your partner may want to play.

Authority Figures and Age-Play

It has been said by many, professional and layman, straight and kinky, that an inner child dwells within each of us. I would like to add to that the idea that we cannot free the child inside of us until we become adults. Inside of us grown-ups lurks a child waiting for the right moment, the right opportunity, to burst free. Those who like age-play, or authority figures, are seeking to reinvent part of their childhood, or younger days, in an erotic setting. This erotic reinvention is intensely

Roles

Alien and Earthling	Master and Maid
Biker and Slut	Master and Slave
Boss and Secretary	Pimp and Hooker
Burglar and Housewife	Pirate and Virgin
Casting Agent and Starlet	Priest and Nun
Caveman and Cavewoman	Priest and Penitent
Centaur and Vestal Virgin	Prince and Castle Servant
City Slicker and Country Girl	Professor and College Student
Cop and Robber or Speeder	Rapist and Victim
Cowboy and Indian Maid	Repairman and Housewife
Doctor and Patient	Satrap and Concubine
Fireman and Rescuee	Satyr and Nymph
Forest Faun and Village Maiden	Scientist and Experiment
Gangster and Moll	Sergeant and Private
God and Offering-Sacrifice	Sheik and Belly Dancer
Hunter and Prey	Soldier and POW
Indian Chief or Brave and Plainswoman	Sultan and Harem Woman
Interrogator and Prisoner	Tarzan and Jane
Jailer and Prisoner	Torturer and Victim
Kidnapper and Hostage	Trainer and Pet
King and Subject	U.S. Marshall and Saloon Girl
Knight and Damsel	Vampire and Victim
Libertine and Maiden	Viking and Captive
Lord and Wench-Tavern Girl	Voyeur and Exhibitionist
Man of the House and Au Pair	Wolf and Red Riding Hood

personal and each person brings specific needs into the scene. Shy teenagers, blushing virgins, tomboys, and students all gather in the playground in the dark garden of SM fantasies.

For an age-play scene to work, there are a few essential ingredients. Authority figures and age-playing are ubiquitous in the dark garden of SM, but some degree of sensitivity, or genuine perception of the role to be assumed is required by both partners. Another important ingredient of an age-play scenario or authority figure fantasy is the aura of authenticity and sincerity that is created.

What writers call "suspension of disbelief" is another prerequisite for this type of SM game. Suspension of disbelief is what screenwriters rely on to make a movie exciting. We know that when Arnold Schwarzenegger takes six bullets to the chest he should be dead. But that would end the movie; instead he gets up and runs after the villain. Without suspension of disbelief, this would not be possible. This wonderful ability allows you and your partner to get into the role and really act out your fantasies. If you are fifteen years old in your fantasy and in reality you are thirty-five, suspension of disbelief will knock twenty years off your age, just like that! It will allow you to adopt, or reenact, the way you walked, spoke, and acted when you were a teenager. You may suddenly find yourself feeling all elbows and knees, like a gawky girl, or speaking in a younger, different voice, and using words from your wild youth. Role-playing fulfills our need for fantasy production, theater, and drama.

Some roles are very harsh and others are nurturing. The women I have spoken to (myself included) tend to prefer nurturing scenes over harsh ones. Not one woman wanted to be "G.I. Jane" to his drill sergeant or prisoner to his warden. This is not to say that they did not want some form of punishment or discipline in the scene; discipline from an authority figure gives erotic pleasure. A standing favorite age-play scenario for female submissives is for "daddy's naughty little girl" to be given an over-the-knee (OTK) spanking with her white cotton panties pulled down to her knees.

Age-play and authority figures are SM favorites, but playing this type of game can be dangerous if the submissive is an adult survivor of childhood abuse, whether physical, sexual, or both. In this area it is very important to know your limits and honor them, whether they make sense to you and your master. Also, psychological limits are hard to predict and can change drastically depending on your mood and the particular circumstances. You may not discover your limits until you happen upon them, fall over them, or fall into them. If you think that there may be a problem age-playing because of a psychological boundary, be sure to fully inform your master. This is not the type of thing you want to spring on him without his knowledge and full consent beforehand. Then you can decide together if you would like to play this type of game.

Consensual Captivity

The captor-captive scenario is a central SM theme, and one of the most popular for both men and women. Although at first glance, a captor-captive scenario may seem little different from playing master and slave, the difference is great. Your captor may be a terrorist to your stewardess, a highwayman to your Victorian virgin, or an official torturer to your caught-in-the-act spy. While playing master and slave, however, neither of you adopts a new character, but instead lets submerged dominant or submissive personae come to the fore. In a captor-captive scenario, adopting the role and really trying to get into the character are essential ingredients for making the fantasy enactment work. Props and wardrobe become more important in a hostage scenario than in the master-and-slave scene, because as window dressing, they can be essential for writing a somewhat realistic scene. But if his patch eye makes both of you giggle uncontrollably, then maybe an eye-patched pirate is not a role either of you can pull off.

Master and Slave

As discussed earlier, at first glance the roles of captor-captive and master-slave bear a resemblance to each other. But we insiders know that they are very different. When you play master and slave, you are freeing your inherent dominant and submissive proclivities without adopting or taking on another character or playing a role. In master and slave, both of you are still playing yourselves but are allowing submerged top and bottom characteristics to direct your fantasy. Master and slave scenarios are less intimidating for the beginner because the "roles" are an extension of your natural self. Additionally, you will need to sort out what type of master and slave you want to enact.

Is your master a sadist to your masochist? A masochistic woman would be very disappointed indeed if her master used the whip to simply point to where he wanted her to kneel. Is he a dominant to your submissive? If a submissive woman with no masochistic urges received a whipping, she may feel she is being punished for some infraction and for not pleasing her master. This could crush her newly blooming desires of submission without pain. Remember, the submissive's pleasure lies in service and serving the master, not necessarily in pain.

If you want to play master and slave, you will need to discuss whether the focus of your scene is a dominant master with a submissive female or a sadistic master with a masochistic female. The dominant master may want silent, naked service from his slave-girl: Make and bring him refreshment, massage his feet, give him a bath or a manicure, become his footstool, or "service" him sexually. The sadistic master may be more interested in increasing his slave's tolerance for pain than in receiving any sort of service, sexual or not. Of course, masochists have submissive tendencies and submissives can be masochistic, and all of this should be discussed in your negotiations. If you are more submissive than masochistic but you do enjoy being disciplined for infractions, let it be clear that the occasional beating for being "bad" is part of your fantasy.

Everyone has the right to create the fantasy that works best for them, and you can mix in as many ingredients as you can handle. There is no job description stating the requirements for a perfect top and a perfect bottom, so feel free to create your own! Since my prime erotic themes, my Pets, are the helplessness of the captive and the desire to be wanton without guilt, I have had many "captors" in my fantasy life. In the thirty-five years plus that I have been having these fantasies, I have been captured by a desert bandit, a pirate, a highwayman, a marquis, an Indian chief, a sheik, a man in the street, a man in a uniform, and others. I redecorate the set to match the man and add to my ever-growing repertoire of sublime tortures and delicious humiliations. Because my father used to tell me tales of Scheherazade from the *Arabian Nights*, my first captor was a tall, dark, and handsome desert sheik.

The Wadi of Desire

The wagon rattled along a trail only the horses could see. The stifling heat of the desert and swaying of the wagon put me in a delightfully dreamy state. Suddenly, thundering hooves, the clash of steel on steel, and the agonized cries of men and horses wrenched me from my reverie. People were screaming, but from inside the enclosed wagon I couldn't see what was happening. I heard the roar and crackle of fire but was too terrified to move. Hands grabbed me by the hair and pulled me from my hiding place in the wagon. I stood quaking in fear, waiting to be run through by my captors. They were talking and gesturing heatedly but I couldn't understand what was said. I tried to control my fear with little success. When one of them approached me, I bolted in fright. Strong arms caught me before I had gone but a few feet. They laughed as I struggled and kicked and fought, but I couldn't break free.

One of them, young and darkly handsome, stepped forward and spoke to the others. They nodded to him, then remounted their steeds. The young one swooped by on his mount, and bending, lifted me off the ground and tossed me across his saddle. Kicking his horse into a gallop, we pounded off to rejoin the rest of the raiding party. It seemed like we rode an entire day, but it was only a few hours. I bounced along upside down, sometimes crying, sometimes silent, always miserable. At last, the horses slowed their pace and I knew they were home. My captor stopped his mount and placed me on my feet next to his stirrup. He tied a rope around my wrists and attached it to his pommel. I understood I was to walk next to his horse, like the spoils of a raid, along with the silk, spices, and camels these men had killed my companions to get.

We entered a wadi dotted with the black tents they called home. My captor handed me over to a much older woman and gestured for me to be taken away. She led me to one of the black tents. The door flap was lifted and my eyes flew open in surprise. The inside of the barbarian's tent was much more lavish than my own wagon. Thick carpets, silk panels, and fat cushions were in abundance; soft light came from brass lamps, and incense perfumed the air. There were other women in the tent, dark like their men, with veils covering half their faces and gazelle-like grace in their movements. They seemed to be fascinated by my dark red hair, light brown eyes, and pale skin. I was quiescent under their hands as they started to remove my clothes. How ridiculous my clothes must have seemed to them.

Layer after layer of pantaloons, petticoats, crinolines, slips, and hosiery covered my corset; the whole tumble of garments was further covered by my dress with its tiers of taffeta and long sleeves. One by one, each of my garments was stripped from me by the rough desert women until I stood naked in the middle of the tent. I was deeply embarrassed. I had never been seen naked before and I rarely looked at my own body. Normally, even my legs and arms were covered in layer after layer of clothing, and my waist was usually constricted by my corset. Without them, I felt free, and uncaring, and this feeling humiliated and fascinated me.

Overcome, I thought to leave the tent and run away. But where could I go? My body went limp with the realization of my situation. They gently forced me into the sleeping area of the tent and pushed me onto my back. I struggled feebly but there were too many of them. Strong hands positioned me on the edge of the bed. Other hands wrenched my knees open and held them apart. A blush of shame flooded my face. I flinched when fingers touched between my legs. I screamed when those same fingers spread my nether lips and examined me. Something was said to the other women and they laughed. They were pleased I was a virgin. Suddenly, I was released and helped to dress in the garments they had brought me.

After several quiet but fearful nights in the women's tent, one twilight there was a burst of activity. A new tent was being set up. When I returned to the women's tent and found a large brass tub filled with hot soapy water and things to wash and comb my hair, I became curious and afraid. A brightly colored square of silk was draped over a small stool; a cool drink was nearby. I grabbed it and gulped it down. I began to feel lightheaded and dreamy—the drink was drugged. I wasn't at all upset when the women entered, stripped me, then began to bathe me. As they dried me, I lifted my arms to admire myself in the brass mirror. Giggling, I realized I was nude. I laughed when the women tossed the brightly colored silk around me and hustled me outside to the new tent.

Once my eyes had adjusted to the dim light, I saw the darkly handsome man who had captured me watching me closely. I just stood there, not knowing what to do or what was expected of me. He rose from his cushions in one fluid motion and came toward me. When he tried to remove my covering, I fought him. Grabbing my wrists in one of his hands, he pulled me to the tall tent pole, secured my wrists over my head, and ripped the covering from me. A whistling sound split the air and a red hot pain sliced across my buttocks and radiated outward. I felt his fingers between my legs. I fought and kicked until he stepped away. I screamed as another lick of the lash brought a fresh wave of pain. This time when he touched me, I tried to stand still. He beat me and touched me until I stood quietly, then he made me come.

He released me from the pole and led me to a pile of cushions. I became very nervous when he lay down next to me but, he gentled me, talking softly in his gutteral tone. I relaxed a little and compassion flickered in him. He touched my face and kissed me; his lips were warm and firmly full. I responded as best I could, hindered by fear and lack of experience. He gently increased his ardor when he realized I was trying to reciprocate. The passion of my response surprised and humiliated me. I writhed and moaned under his touch, and to my shame, I opened myself to him. I laid there, the property of a stranger, nude and spread, and to my shame, gave myself over to his touch. When his fingers parted my nether lips and found the wetness there, his groan of lust announced his pleasure at my responsiveness. He continued to touch me, play with me, and teach me to pleasure him. When I disobeyed or resisted, he beat me; when I pleased him, he rewarded me with pleasure. At night, as I gazed upon his sleeping form, I trailed my fingers over his belly and wondered what my new life would be like.

I could go on endlessly about his use of me and how he trained me to be his toy. I have been having this fantasy for a very long time! But you get the general idea: I was cherished and cared for by my master but I wasn't human. I was meant to be played with, kept naked, and beaten and sexually tortured and tormented for his amusement and pleasure. I was never allowed to speak words; only moans and sighs and screams could pass my lips. I understood that my master hurt me because it gave him pleasure to do so, and I was there for his pleasure. I adored my master and came to love him and all the humiliations and punishments he heaped upon me. And, ultimately, my master fell in love with me. Romance in chains—love conquers all.

Perfect.

As we discussed earlier, the captive-captor theme is a basic one. In my fantasy, at first there is coercion and then there is consent: I come to adore my sadistic master who feeds me and looks after me by day then sexually abuses me for his enjoyment at night. The master is the only person in my life, and I crave his attention. The pain he has given me has reconstructed my ego, and I lose self-awareness. I experience a spiritual rebirth when I subjugate myself totally to him.

~ 9 ~

Masochism . . . Still Defying Definition

The way the public at large uses the term masochism makes the word live in a constant state of abuse and misuse, overloaded with meanings and innuendos, connotations and associations. Yet this usage only refers to the negative side of the experience: negative, as in "sick," which is the way SMers would perceive a nonconsensual, or abusive, relationship. Consensual romantic masochism can be considered a metaphor through which your psyche, or alternate persona, speaks of its passion and suffering. It can tell a tale of pain born in childhood or simply release the pent-up frustrations and passions we feel as adults. But even as a metaphor, there is no single understanding or definition of masochism even when it is in specific and consensual circumstances. Those with masochistic fantasies can have more than one favorite, because masochism becomes even more difficult to define as the variables on masochistic fantasies increase.

It's All in the Mind

Masochism is much more than the embracing of physical pain; masochism is first and foremost a psychological experience, conceived in the subconscious and conscious mind. Scenarios of ritual sacrifice to a higher purpose or being, objectification, and humiliation, among others, are favorite, often reinvented masochistic fantasies. Some masochistic fantasies can be enacted; others start, and stay, solely in the mind. As it is conceived in the dark garden, or in the shadow land of Jung, masochism will always remain a paradox and a mystery. As a psychic image, rooted in the shadow land of our imagination, masochism is one way the depths of our psychic life can be expressed. Masochism is the expression of the different ways our soul suffers and loves.

Unfortunately, sex manuals usually concentrate on positions and technique and fail to establish the vital relationship between sex and the soul. Sex, SM or vanilla, is a very spiritual experience. During vanilla sex, penetration is the first communal moment, then at orgasm the souls touch. In SM sex, the flower blooms in the mind first and just the barest lick of the lash, or brush of a hard cock, or softly spoken command will elicit a more intense and spiritual response. There can be rapturous delight in submission (sexual or otherwise), in worship or service performed in wild abandon, and in being freed from the bounds of guilt and "normalcy." Freud said the fantasy of masochism may begin in childhood when the wish for an incestuous relationship with a parent is repressed. He referenced it as the "Oedipus Complex," after the ancient Greek character, Oedipus, who, in fulfillment of a prophesy, unwittingly killed his father to wed his mother. This spiritual ground can be the meeting place of guilt and sexual love.

Some have related the masochistic experience to punishment and reward, but punishment and reward do not nearly or clearly express the masochistic experience. In masochism, the embracing of pain or suffering is already part of the reward, not a forerunner of it. What does this mean in terms of sexual gratification? Gratification is not limited to the moment of orgasm but is deeply dependent first on the excitement of the mind and then the arousal of the body. The masochist enjoys the anticipation of "pain" or punishment, as well as the pain in and of itself. Both gratification and punishment give pleasure—and pleasurable humiliation. It is a time when we do not turn away from our pain but seek to embrace it and turn it into an erotic event. Experiencing our masochism can feel like a psychic orgasm: a violent yet joyous lack or loss of control. In masochism, our soul can be elevated beyond the body and its sensations. It may be one of the psyche's efforts to keep the body in contact with its spirit.

Masochism can also be an attitude that embodies our feelings about our pain and suffering, and it is worthwhile exploring that attitude. Some love their pain and suffering and offer it to the higher power as a gift; others struggle and rage before finally feeling they have put up enough of a fight before submitting. In my variety of masochism, I have recognized the value and meaning in my pain and suffering, and it has led me to a deeper knowledge of myself. Recognizing my masochism as a fantasy of my soul has given me more compassion and humility, and has had a healing effect on my spirit. Accepting my masochism has allowed me to explore parts of my psyche and discover new facets of myself that I had overlooked or ignored.

If you strip masochism of its spirituality and its sense of worship and submission, masochism will lose its vital connection to the soul. If you ignore masochism's ideal, its ancient values, and its idea of chivalry, if you do not acknowledge the spirituality in it, masochism will become pain without passion, higher purpose, or learning value. When we use sadomasochistic techniques for a one-night stand or as a quick thrill, we are undermining the beauty and trust of the SM relationship. Alternatively, if you see masochism as a sin or pathological condition or as a condition that needs to be "cured," you have overlooked the healing values of exploring the dark garden. If you ignore your deeper motives and the needs of your soul, then you are left with nothing more than unromantic, unreflective, violent sex.

The Deconstruction of Ego

Among our basic psychological experiences are suffering and sacrifice, repentance and atonement. And although those feelings may be humiliating to our ego, they have profound meaning to our soul. They can give us wanted humility and have the power to heal us. In these fast-moving, "me"-oriented times, we can easily forget that passivity can be as important to our soul as assertiveness. But we cannot speak to our deeper sense of dissatisfaction unless we are willing to delve down to the basics, or baseness, of life as it affects our own concerns. This is what I call the deconstruction of ego.

Masochism is a downward spiral that challenges the values and goals of the ego. It is an exploration of the depths of suffering and pain that one

is willing to submit to for the betterment of the mind and enjoyment of
the body. It is a fantasy of being beaten not caressed, of being humiliated
not exalted, and of feeling pleasure in what others would call pain. It is relinquishing control, and sometimes the self, to a higher power. Masochism
is an acknowledgment of radically different perspectives and perceptions of
suffering. In romantic masochism, we can turn our perception of pain into
pleasure, even almost religious ecstasy, and not reduce ourselves in the
process. Masochists are frequently people of inner strength, with strong
egos able to "cope," and a great sense of individual responsibility.

Maybe these are the very qualities that render their masochism necessary and understandable. In combining pleasure with pain or humiliation, we can help prevent a one-sided attitude: too much belief in our
competence, too much faith in our abilities. Some people call this one-
sided arrogance, others, pride. Can we consider masochism, then, to be
a cure for one-sided egos, for people who are about to drown in their
own accomplishments? Could masochism then be looked at as a cathartic experience rather than an unnatural desire? Could we also say that
masochism is a natural product of the soul which will bring forward its
own vision and subsequent cure? If we recognize the soulfulness and
spirituality of masochism, we will embrace and control masochism's
downward movement and its passion and need.

Masochism is first a psychological position. When we have masochistic
fantasies, we first strip ourselves in our minds, then we expose ourselves
and humiliate ourselves as only we know how. We make ourselves defenseless. We expose our egos, and through these depths of pain and pleasure, we can effect radical changes in our egos. For some, this is a necessary
process for the sexual experience and for the health, well-being, and vital-
ity of the soul. On rare and special occasions, a masochistic experience has
given me almost a "divine" revelation about my inner, most secret, self.

Embracing Pain

In a religious context, masochism was once considered to be a cure for
souls: to seek penance was a move toward the soul's health. Penance was
both a relief and a joy. Part of masochism is confession and exposure, and
part is atonement and penance. Through the desire to be punished, as well

as actual punishment, one can find sexual or spiritual satisfaction or both. There is no denying there is pleasure in it. And if you need to use the whip to get on with it, then there you have it. But the fantasy of the whip, once applied, binds us, creating and re-creating itself, and cannot be stopped.

As we agreed before, the concept of punishment and reward does not adequately express the masochistic experience because what others perceive as the punishment is also the reward. Masochism begins in the mind; you have been fantasizing about this, eroticizing it long before you felt the first lick of the lash, real or imaginary, caress your flesh. In pain, a masochist can find moments of exquisite pleasure and burning passion. Pain can be an excuse to release emotions that are too strong or scary to let loose in any other context. Releasing these pent-up feelings through pain are part of the relief and joy found in masochism. The pain unites the imagined with the reality in a profound flesh-and-mind experience. The body is often relegated to an inferior position, but in masochism the body is of great significance because it is the vessel of enlightenment, the carrier of the pain-transformed-into-pleasure. In masochism, body and soul occur at the same time, and the experience is a revelation.

On some occasions, when I have asked my master to give me a severe caning, I have also asked him to bind my wrists behind my back and gag me. The binding of my wrists frees me from the desire to struggle, and the gag stifles my cries; both help me to increase my tolerance for pain and my pain level. Then he bends me over the arm of the sofa and the caning begins, slowly at first to make me feel sexual, then harder and harder as my endorphins work their magic. When I am ready, he gives me the last hard strokes. The pain is blindingly beautiful in its intensity. I reel in ecstasy when he reduces me to a wanton, shameless thing who begs and grovels at his feet for mercy. I am empowered by my lowly position of choice on the floor, enriched by the red stripes marking my flesh. I am cleansed by the pain I absorbed, and, in pain, I find pleasure.

Masochism and the Pleasure of Humiliation

It could be said that the final element of masochism is humiliation. Buried in the fertile soil of the dark garden, our humiliation fantasies are the last piece needed for a deconstruction of ego and expanded knowledge of the self. Though our humiliation fantasies may shame us, it is the shame it-self that is the source of our sexual excitement. Our humiliation fan-tasies may be the most exciting ones of all because only we know what buttons to press to make these fantasies sexually satisfying, emotionally empowering, and gratifying experiences. Our fantasies of humiliation could include being verbally humiliated, physically humiliated (like being slapped, spit on, stripped in public, or publicly disciplined), or ritualistically humiliated. Once faced, our humiliation fantasies cannot be denied or suppressed.

In masochistic humiliation, one can find pleasure in the loss of old tired self-images and attitudes. When playing SM games, one needs to communicate one's desires to one's partner so one can have those desires fulfilled. Giving voice to these fantasies breathes life into them; to speak them to another person, to confess them, makes them all the more real for us, and the confession is part of the humiliation. Some may say that humiliation felt in romantic masochism is not "real"; that the fact that it *is* a fantasy, not a reality, doesn't make the scenario humiliating. I don't agree with this. The fantasy scenario might make the humiliation safe, but the humiliation felt is quite real. If we keep our deliciously dirty lit-tle fantasies to ourselves, then how can we feel humiliated by the con-fession and where is the pleasure in it? But we are creatures who love to fantasize, my friend! We need, and enjoy, our fantasy productions, and our pleasure is constantly refining and reinventing itself. Our hu-miliation is real no matter how far-out the fantasy situation may be to another. The fantasy reflects the dreamer's humiliation and shame, their pleasure and excitement.

Humiliation as Ritual

Masochism is an artful fantasy and has its ritualistic aspects: In many masochistic fantasies, everything must be just right to achieve the desired effect. The more imaginative the fantasy, the more apparent the ritualistic features are. Some masochistic fantasies center around the lit-eral sacrifice of the self for a higher purpose, or to serve a god, or for the blood lust of the crowd. In this type of fantasy, the humiliation is always the same although the window dressing and scenarios can change to keep the fantasy fresh. The end result is always the same even though the explorer may have taken a different route.

Bride of the God

I am walking through a strangely beautiful and eerie forest in a place long forgotten to man. I know it is dangerous to be in the forest. Tales of big, hairy men besetting the unwary went around in my head; those lost, never found. A twig snaps; my heart hammers insanely. Nervously, I look around but see nothing except for the tall, silent trees. I realize I have wandered too deep into the wood and I am lost. I swallow my panic and try to retrace my steps. Suddenly, the way in front of me is blocked. I look up and catch a glimpse of a tall, well-built man with long dark hair, wearing roughly sewn leather clothes. Something crashes into my head from behind, and I hear him laugh as the world goes black.

I wake up in a crude hut surrounded by tall, long-haired men. I am naked and tied to a wooden table, the object of much curiosity and attention. Upon seeing that I am conscious, the men untie me but hold me firmly as they help me to a standing position. They place me on a wooden seat with a hole in it which is positioned over a barrel, and they hold me in place. An animal bladder, filled with water and equipped with a wooden nozzle carved into the shape of a penis, is brought. Several of the men spit upon the thing, and one of them inserts it quickly deep in my anus. He squeezes the bladder and I feel the water begin to fill my belly. I struggle but too many arms hold me down; one grabs the nozzle and holds it firmly into me. Soon the bladder is empty and the nozzle removed; a leather-covered butt plug is forced into my passage. The men are standing around, watching me closely. One cups my breast and squeezes it, nodding his appreciation to the others. Another twiddles with my nether lips; finding them wet, he laughs to the others and shows them my slimy shame.

One of the long-haired men, obviously the leader, signals to the slimy-fingered one and the plug is roughly pulled from my anus. To my humiliation, the men gather around me while the water explodes from my bottom. When I am empty of the water, another bladder with a penis-shaped nozzle is brought and inserted in my quim. Once the leader deems me clean there, too, the men bathe me and shave my underarms, my legs, and my nether parts clean of hair. I am shocked into silence, into nonresistance. The events of the afternoon seem unreal to me, as if these things are happening to someone else and I am simply watching them unfold. After the rough ministrations of the men, the leader hands me a cup of steaming tea, sweet and fragrant, and I drink it down thirstily. Upon meeting the eye of the leader, I know from his smile that the tea was drugged. He nods to me as if to say, "it will be easier for you this way." I tilt the cup back and drink the last drops. The men leave me alone in the hut to curl up on the table with my fears.

Eternity passes before the men return, this time with strap restraints made of roughly worked leather which they attach to my wrists and ankles. I allow them to do this to me in a dreamlike state, and I realize the drug the leader had slipped into my tea is working. They lead me out of the hut, and although I am unbound, they completely encircle me with their bodies so there is no chance of escape. As we walk, I am able to glimpse through them, and to my amazement, I see that the clearing is filled with people. The men urge me forward into the circle where their god awaits his sacrifice.

He is terrifyingly beautiful to behold; his long hair, shot with silver gray streaks, flows down over his shoulders and obscures part of his face. He is taller than the other men, with strong, hairy arms and legs and a strangely hairless chest. In front of him, his engorged manhood bobs in the air as if seeking me. The god's spear is enormous and seems to pulsate and grow as I near him. The men close in to herd me toward him. He steps up to me and begins to sniff me loudly. The bestial sound of it excites me, but I stand very still, afraid to move, afraid to breathe. Then, throwing his head back, he roars his acceptance of the sacrifice.

The men surge towards me and manipulate me to the ground at the god's feet. My arms and legs are pulled open, the crude cuffs secured by rope to pegs in the forest floor. The forest people, led by the men, chant and sing, throw flowers and herbs, and scream in god-induced ecstasy when their fearsome god mounts me. His priapus is huge and red-hot, my agonized cry as he pierces me splits the air as the half-man, half-beast god of the forest pounds into me. The forest folk begin to copulate around us as the god leads me in the oldest dance known to man. As he pummels into me, each thrust makes the stars in the sky explode in my head. As he pumps me more furiously, I scream and writhe under him in pain and ecstasy; his long, hot pole in me has become the center of my universe. I open myself to him and he feels my submission. He *roars to the heavens as he pounds into me and shoots his white-hot semen deep inside of my belly. As he spurts into me, the fire comes down from heaven and consumes me, burning me up, making me an offering to the god.*

Although our humiliation fantasies may cause us some embarrassment, or even distress, there is great beauty to be found in the ritualization inherent in a good masochistic fantasy. Humiliation, and the abasement of the self, is a prime theme in SM. Often the two combine and provide a meeting ground for intense pleasure. As in this fantasy, the combining of humiliation and pleasure only happens at a certain time and under very specific circumstances. I present myself as a human sacrifice to create an exciting sexual drama of submission to a god-like force.

⌁ 10 ⌁

Mind and Matter:
Lost in Emotion

The fantasies in the shadows of the dark garden are an important dimension of our life and an integral part of our erotic mind. We push
these erotic aspects and impulses that we deny into a part of our minds
that I call the shadow land and that Carl Jung aptly named "the
shadow." Each and every one of us has a shadow land in our erotic
mind, which is where our repressed erotic images and impulses (our
prime erotic themes and sexy scripts) collect and coalesce until we are
ready to explore them. The shadows are the darkest when we refuse to
look at them; exiling them from our conscious thoughts can make these
fantasies fester and take on distorted proportions. To be more fully developed sexual beings, we need to learn to accept our dark fantasies as
an integral part of our psychological makeup, give them a healthy outlet, and try to understand the compelling motives behind them.

Shadow Land Dreams

Our darker fantasies will sometimes burst into our consciousness,
making us feel perverted or weird, because of our fantasy's utter dis-
regard for societal mores and personal values, like those in cultural
scripts and intrapsychic scripts. Often our shadow land fantasies involve masochism, bondage, coercion, humiliation, exploitation, objec-

114

tification, pain, dehumanization, manipulation, rape, and a whole list of other violations, vile and villainous, large and small. Fantasies involving erotic violations are a powerful force in the SM exchange, and many submissive fantasies are based on one or more of these violations. In the shadow land, the usual order of things can be reversed, and the onslaught of the unexpected can be controlled when we write our own script.

We can explore our sexual selves by playing out these erotic and emotionally charged fantasies, complete with props and wardrobe, in the safety of a consensual, trustful, and communicative relationship. Because these are fantasies and can be explored safely in the dark garden, these sexy scripts are very titillating. They can make us feel very naughty or wicked but they are usually harmless. Many of them are bathtub fantasies that we really don't want to act out but giving thought to them brings them into the light and helps us expand our self-knowledge. In our sexual enlightenment, we now know that although they are not rational, these fantasies are normal expressions of our erotic imaginations.

The denial of our shadow fantasies begins in childhood when we start to absorb the societal mores that may cause us to repudiate or suppress certain sexual aspects of our erotic personalities. As children, we fear that exhibiting these erotic aspects may lead to disapproval, punishment, or worse, from those on whom we depend for survival. But in adulthood, the fantasies in the shadows unlock the secrets of our inner self and should be explored, not denied. If we can recognize and integrate these erotic aspects slowly and comfortably into our consciousness, we will be able to experience an expanded self-awareness. Starting to explore and learning to accept your shadow land fantasies will contribute to your emotional wholeness and well-being. It is by making the darkness conscious of itself that we become enlightened; it is by giving these fantasies voice and shape that we are able to keep them within safe boundaries.

Humiliation Games and Mind-Bending

Who among us is not aware of the power our lover's words have over us? Who is not aware of the million messages his glance can convey? Who has not quivered with passion at his touch or has not been ignited by something in his look? Who has not felt the cruelty of a lover's rejection, yet been drawn to it like the moth to the flame? Who can say they have loved, truly loved another, and have not been aware of The Other's power over us? This power, a facet of love, is an exotic mixture of mind-before-body and the thrill of the chase, and a passionate blend of sexual anxiety and anticipation cushioned by the safety net of protection the expectation of returned love extends. In SM, the safety net of protection is enhanced by the heightened trust, respect, and communication necessary between the two players to explore the dark garden of their sexual fantasies.

Playing humiliation games is like exploring your mind's outer limits because these games are intensely emotional and psychological. With the right partner, they can be as satisfying as sex and as mind-expanding as an out-of-body experience. Humiliation games in SM, if done with caring and love, can actually build up a person's confidence and set them free. The question is: What do *you* find humiliating? What humiliates one doesn't ruffle a feather of another. Enthusiasts of hard canings would be humiliated to be beaten with rubber kitchen gloves; someone not into pain might find it hilarious. Some find dropping to their knees to kiss the master's boot to be humiliating; others do it without a second thought, and yet others may find groveling to be an uplifting and thrilling experience. Any scene can be a humiliating one—if *you* find that particular thing to be humiliating. Only you know what is humiliating to you, and to make your scene really powerful, you need to communicate this to your master.

In my humiliation scenes, acknowledging my demon out loud by saying, "Yes, master, I *am* your slut," frees me from guilt about feeling highly sexual around him, being a slut for him, exhibiting extremely wanton behavior, and enjoying it. My fantasy was to play "the little whore," but my generation (and many others) was taught that sexuality was not for nice girls. So, once my master commanded me to play the whore, he gave me permission to safely explore this persona. I am being a good girl by "obeying" him and doing as he commands. I have promised obedience, and he, knowing my wants and limits, has given me his permission to be the slut. My master has freed me from guilt by taking the decision out of my hands. This sounds like a paradox, that is, humiliation, or consensual degradation, for the purpose of uplifting, but with the right partner under the right circumstances, it can be a very spiritual experience.

From mild embarrassment to real degradation, a humiliation game, or mind-bend, can exist on many emotional levels. Mind-bending can start with playful teasing and stop there, or it can expand into playful ridicule. Playful ridicule could then escalate to the use of selective but extremely derisive (NOT degrading or disempowering) language. As the submissive accepts and agrees to each new humiliation, the subsequent ones become progressively more severe. With this type of game, I would strongly suggest that you prenegotiate very carefully and clearly your emotional limits in this area. The playground is in your head, and your master will not be able to read your body signs until, perhaps, it is too late. I say this because our set of emotional limits is deeply embedded in us and is less susceptible to change and expansion. Emotional limits are also harder to identify when breached because sometimes even we don't know our own bête noire. Our emotional limits are harder to predict and, once breached, take longer to heal. As the signs of our physical limits, like welts and bruises, are easily visible and heal quickly, our physical limits can constantly be tested and pushed and expanded because we have the knowledge to condition ourselves to "more." Since what takes place in the mind needs to be communicated verbally, the enhanced trust and communication skills you have developed in exploring SM with your partner will support you now. After any humiliation scene, your master should be especially kind and supportive of you because of the emotionally charged nature of the game. At the end of a humiliation scene, all parties involved return to equal stature.

Coercion and Consent

For my humiliation fantasies, and those of millions of others, to be really good, there has to be some sort of *coercion and consent* at play. Coercion and consent are a powerful aphrodisiac in a submissive's fantasy mix. At first the submissive is resistant to the will of the dominant or to the humiliation to be imposed upon her, but then her own imagination begins to work. It is the ultimate degradation that not only does she ultimately consent to the humiliation or punishment, but she begins to like it and want it. A fantasy of this sort can be constructed to remove guilt and therefore give the submissive permission to enjoy her sexual slavery. Psychologists believe that sexual submission is a means of relieving sexual guilt. For those who view sexual desire as a moral flaw, this may hold true. For those who don't, erotic coercion and subsequent consent can allow the submissive to abandon herself to sexual pleasure.

Coercion and consent fantasies often have ritualistic elements, such as being chosen for a religious ritual. The fantasy could be that, as the town virgin, she alone has been chosen to work for seven years as temple prostitute or serve the goddess in her temple. Of course, she has been chosen for this, and her protests would not be understood. She doesn't want to go, but what can she do? It would bring disgrace upon the family and herself if she were to refuse or run away, so she goes. She is exhibited nude in the temple, and is utterly humiliated. But through her haze of misery, she hears the local people admiring her as the bride of the god or human embodiment of the goddess, their savior. They look at her and exclaim that she is surely worthy tribute. Each day as she is led out of her room to take her place on display, she quakes in humiliation at what is to come. But slowly she has come to like it too. She has been set above the other humans by her very dehumanization, and she grows to want it.

For me, part of a good humiliation game is knowing ahead of time what will happen to me, because it is usually a thing I both fear the most and want very much. The time I have to dwell on it is deliciously excruciating. Will I let him? Will I say my safe-word, give my signal? Will I be able to see it through? This would be when I coerce myself into consenting. Often when we played, my lord kept his plans to himself. He knew me, and my fantasies, as I knew his, and he knew that I trusted him implicitly. But sometimes he told me his plans for me that evening. I loved it when he related to me in his melted butterscotch voice what he had in mind for me that evening. I would kneel between his thighs as he sat in his favorite spot on the sofa. He would lean forward, I would kneel up and drape my small arms around his strong neck. His lips to my ear, he would describe to me in filthy words how he was going to "use" me that night. He would pause dramatically to ask me if I had heard him or to ask in a gentle tone if that was all right with me. I knew his questions were rhetorical, yet they weren't. If he did say something I didn't like, I could beg in my soft slave's voice to be let off from that one, and he would acquiesce.

It drives me wild to know what is going to happen to me, to fear it and to love it at the same time, to anticipate it with the most delicious dread and thrill, and to wait for it to happen to me. As I wait, a struggle takes place inside of me between the part of me that wants it and the part that doesn't. The ultimate humiliation is that I not only consent to it but that I like it and want it, and when he withholds it from me, I beg for it. Under this premise, millions into SM are lovingly, playfully "forced" to do exactly what they fear most. Often what they fear most and what they want most are exactly the same. I just love it when that happens to me!

Verbal Humiliation

I would be very happy if the word "abuse" was totally disassociated with romantic, consensual SM lovemaking and techniques. We know SM is not abuse, so I prefer to call this particular flower in the dark garden "verbal humiliation" rather than "verbal abuse." Not only do I think "verbal humiliation" is a nicer term for what we do, I also see it as a more accurate one. Let me give you an example of what would be verbally humiliating to me versus what would be abusive.

During a very hot, sexy scene my master dips his fingers between my thighs and finds me to be very wet. In his hot fudge voice, he whispers "Whose fat (referring to my swollen nether lips), slimy little thing are you, then?" This makes me more swollen, as in fatter lips, and even slimier because this is exactly my kind of humiliation. Alternatively, if he said that same phrase to me over dinner, and the people at the table next to us overheard, I would be somewhat embarrassed, maybe even annoyed, because he would have allowed outsiders to hear of our personal life without my permission. I am *not* into public humiliation of that sort at all, though I would get over it. However, if during an argument, he called me a fat, slimy thing, I would be very angry. I would consider it to be a form of verbal abuse, like being called "stupid" instead of saying I am thinking with my quim.

Abuse, like harassment, whether sexual, verbal, or physical, is what the recipient considers to be abusive. Romantic, consensual SM humiliation games should make you feel a pleasant and erotic sense of shame and be quite enjoyable when done right. Understanding the rewards of verbal humiliation requires you to open your mind to the infinite possibilities of the sexual universe inside you, and not be afraid to explore there. You will not walk in this garden alone: Your master will be, as ever, your partner and protector. Because of the intimate nature of verbal humiliation, it works best between two people who know each other well. Each of us have different turn-on buttons in this area, if we like verbal humiliation at all. What turns one person on, grosses another out, or leaves them cold, so your new heightened communication skills will be necessary to make verbal humiliation satisfying and rewarding for both players.

It's How You Say It . . .

Dirty talk is a form of verbal humiliation that is a popular SM technique with sexual explorers, though most don't realize it is part of SM. If your mate likes to call you his "little bitch-slut," and this turns both of you on, it seems you have been indulging in some mild SM all along, without even knowing it!

But now let's assume that he has hit upon a name, or nickname, for you that you do not like. I had a lover once call me "skinny," and when I objected, swore to me he meant it nicely. I just didn't see it that way. I think of myself as slender or slim, even svelte. Furthermore, I couldn't make him understand that skinny was insulting. Perhaps it was all just too new for him, and he hadn't accumulated the necessary erotic vocabulary yet. In any case, the Pillow-Talk Thesaurus (see Appendix A) would be of enormous, and amusing, help. It lists alternate words for every body part, yours and his, as well as action words and verbs for those of us who don't get turned-on by the f-word and such. The thesaurus is followed by a list of Feeling and Emotion Words for the Slave and Master (Appendix B), which will help describe all those new feelings and sensations you are experiencing on your walk through the dark garden.

Just as names can be empowering or disempowering, words can make your spirit soar or they can anchor you firmly to the earth; they can elate or depress, exalt or deny, free you or fetter you. And sometimes they have two meanings, depending on societal and personal definitions. Let me give you an example. When I was growing up, there were certain girls who "earned" the title "slut," whether or not they were sluts. It might have been hung on a particular girl by a jealous classmate, or because she wore a certain style of dress, or simply because she was the new kid in town and was *different*. Even as a teen, it was okay in my mind to be the slut of The One but not to the many. Call me a one-man slut, if you like. The other teens I knew did not understand the difference: To them, a slut was a slut was a slut. Since then, I have felt that the word "slut" was much maligned and could have as many good connotations as it did bad.

Having said that, now consider this: What's in a pronoun? Such a small word, a pronoun. Now consider the pronoun "my." And now, imagine my master saying to me, "Claudia, you are *my* slut." Since I like this sort of play, my heart trip-hammered in my chest when he said this. However, if my master had said to me, "Claudia, you are a slut," I would definitely be put off some, maybe even a little insulted. If he insisted upon calling me "a slut" instead of "his slut," I would become very upset and even angry. Such small words, like *my* and *a*, can make a big difference in evoking the right feelings about your submission.

Rape Fantasies

Having a rape fantasy is a source of great embarrassment and confusion for some; yet for millions of others, men and women, a rape fantasy, imagined or enacted, grows in a carefully tended plot in the dark garden of SM. A rape fantasy could be a bathtub fantasy: a scene that is thrilling to enact in our heads but one we really don't want to happen to us. There are safety nets in a bathtub rape fantasy in that you can control how, where, and when you are violated, and who your violator will be. Also, you can redirect, or stop, the action at any time during the fantasy. You alone write, direct, and enact your script. These scripts are deliciously dangerous and thrilling to fantasize about and are a frequent theme of the SM dreamer.

Sometimes, when a rape fantasy is often repeated in the erotic mind, it begins to take on a ritualistic aspect. Although the location, time of day, manner in which you are raped, and even your assailant may change; but if you are always raped for a higher reason or by a higher being, then there is some ritual to your fantasy. If you dream of being raped by a god, or higher being, or king, or even an alien from outer space with powers greater than ours, and your rape by him elevates you to a position akin to a sacrifice, your rape fantasy has taken on ritualistic aspects. As we have said, ritual plays an important role in some SM games. Since our fantasies constantly seek to reinvent themselves but our Pet remains the same, we change the scenario and the window dressing to keep the fantasies fresh and exciting.

Explorers with a taste for more exotic blooms may choose to act out their rape fantasies safely, with the consent and help of their dom. These are not real rapes but carefully scripted scenes where the submissive has almost all of the say in what action is to occur. It is her right to decide the particulars of the scene and tell her dom, or coconspirator in this case, exactly what she wants done, how, where, and when. And, of course, it is her right to call off the scene any time she wants. The dom must be equally willing to play his part and his input not only is helpful, but desirable, especially if he feels his limits are being pushed. But essentially the submissive always tops from the bottom in this scene.

Some submissives have and enact rape fantasies just because they are such hot fantasies. For them, the fantasy could be enacted purely for the adrenaline rush of being chased or knocked to the ground by your lover, or in the thrill of fear as he covers your mouth with his hand, or even a sort of spiritual surrender by violation of the physical body. Your surrender may be accomplished by a real struggle with your "rapist" where he ultimate overpowers you, mounts you roughly, and uses you again and again. My master climbed in through a bedroom window which was conveniently left open while he was out at the pub. A short struggle ensued and he "won." Another's fantasy may be that she doesn't fight at all, only begs and pleads, cowers and trembles with fear as her violator rips, or cuts, her clothes off. One night, when I "ran to the corner shop," my master lurked in waiting for me, hiding out in the house. I came in, pretending that I was alone. In this scene, there was no struggle; he just fell upon me after I entered the apartment, made me his captive, and "raped" me while I whimpered, mewled, cried crocodile tears, and begged for him to stop. It was absolutely brilliant.

Other submissives enact a rape because they enjoy humiliation and violent sex; a rape fantasy can easily combine both. In a rape fantasy where humiliation and fear are the main aphrodisiacs, the actual "violence" of rape may take a back seat to verbal threats and taunting with tortures to come, bondage, face slapping, and physical intimidation. Other submissives may use a consensual rape fantasy to reenact a real-life rape with her loving dom. If this is true for you, your dom *must* be told this beforehand to ensure the emotional safety of both of you. You must give him enough information, details, and particulars to ensure that it *is* a fantasy reenactment and *not* abuse to be suffered anew. Is your motivation for the fantasy rape an attempt to cleanse yourself of the experience? Do you want to retape it in your head as a loving experience? Do you want to fight back and lose, or fight back and win? Do you want to give in without a struggle? The answers to these questions are important, and you must communicate them to your dom before proceeding. Also, after a scene like this, your dom must be ready to give you all the love and support you need and then some.

Rape fantasies can get very hot and very believable, but in the heat of the moment, let's not forget that it *is* a fantasy. No matter how hot it gets, your prenegotiated limits should always be respected, and if you elect to use your safe-word or signal, as always, all action should stop immediately. Rape fantasies with a loving partner can be an opportunity to rewrite a scenario that was once abusive and turn it into a loving or cathartic experience, or it can be an opportunity to live out a hot fantasy envisioned by millions. Proceed carefully at first, then enjoy, enjoy, enjoy!

Resistance Scenes

There are many types of resistance scenes and many roles to play, but interrogation scenes seem to be a clear favorite. In an interrogation scene, the dom plays a role that is an embodiment of power. This could be a police officer, a general from an enemy army, a ninja, torturer, or even a prosecuting attorney. Many women, myself included, enjoy scenes where the physical embodiment of power (our master) wears some sort of uniform. (I love a man in a well-fitted, darkly menacing uniform.) When I play interrogation-resistance scenes with my master, I find it deliciously humiliating to be ordered to strip. Ordering me to disrobe, instead of stripping me himself, makes me feel more powerless, more at his mercy, as I take off one item at a time. To strip slowly, hesitantly, under his hard, scrutinizing eyes is incredibly exciting to me and impresses upon me that there is no escape from him, my torturer, my captor, my master, my lover.

The submissive could take on roles like "murder suspect," "spy," or any sort of prisoner. You could portray a web-surfer who got a hold of government secrets and got caught selling them, or captured by bad guys who want the secrets for free. The object of the game is this: You have information, or you know something he wants to know and he tortures you to obtain this information. The desired information could be anything: nuclear secrets, buried treasure, or your middle name. Upon receiving the desired information, your torturer may decide that "you're lying," or that the information was inaccurate or insufficient, which guarantees you more delicious torture.

Part of the fun of a resistance scene is that in the verdant garden of SM, you are once again relieved of your sense of responsibility. As the submissive in a resistance scene, you can give yourself permission to struggle, go limp, shout, mewl, run away, cower in fear, whimper, scream, threaten, or plead, whatever you wish, and let it become a cleansing experience for you. Doing any or all of the above can be remarkably cathartic, and you could feel relaxed and sexy for days afterward. The dom who enjoys this game is one who would like to push his own limits and will press on, even if it means getting a little nasty. (Oh, I love nasty.)

Although these scenes can be incredibly hot, playing this close to the edge can be emotionally risky. Sometimes during the scene the submissive will experience real-world panic, fear, or anger. We have already agreed that because this is fantasy land, these emotions have no place here. They are real-world emotions and should be expressed and resolved in the real world. If these emotions arise in you while you are playing resistance scenes, you have two options: stop the scene, or play it through. If you choose to use your safe-word and stop the scene, communicate your problem, feelings, reservations, or fears as best you can to your master. (Sometimes these things are difficult to verbalize and take a little time to get out.) This will help you to work out the problem together.

Playing the scene through to see what happens is somewhat riskier emotionally. There can be emotional fall-out from a played-through scene that both you and your master must be sure you are ready for and can cope with. A flood of tears, crying, sobbing, even a temper tantrum during the scene may become cathartic for you later on, but is he prepared for it now? If you think your resistance play may be venturing into the deep waters of psychological limits (which usually arise abruptly), please be sure to let him know prior to the fantasy enactment that these reactions are a possibility.

When playing at rape or resistance scenes, you may want to consider a new set of rules designed especially for this type of play: If you are fighting, struggling, mouthing off, protesting in the proper phrases, consider these actions to be signs that all is well and proceed at will!

~ 11 ~

Objects of Beauty and Usefulness

Among our submissive personas, there may be one whose desire is to be treated as some*thing* rather than some*one* else. Objectification is an SM fantasy in which the submissive becomes less than a person, or sub-human, for a temporary period. It is a powerful and compelling fantasy; objectification, under its many guises, is a force in human imagination. To see it in its darkest form, consider those otherwise normal people who inexplicably develop a romantic obsession with murderers or gangsters or those who thirst for the gory details of lurid crimes. Many of our jokes revolve around laughing at the pain or misfortune of others. To enjoy the sight of another person being inhumanely treated or violated, to be able to laugh at the pain and misfortune of another, requires us to see that person as *less human than ourselves*. The widely known, but rarely admitted to, sexual kick some people get from these spectacles comes from the darkest side of our nature.

Although SM has found a place for objectification in its dark garden of pleasures and fantasies, my form of SM objectification rarely explores the darkest facets of the human personality discussed above. Many of us may be uncomfortable with the thought that we are mentally able to reduce another person to less-than-human status and by their reduction to subhuman, enjoy their pain and suffering. Some tops have therefore reported having trouble playing at objectification or depersonalization games, stating that this type of play approaches or breaches their limits. But that is not what we are going to explore here.

For our purposes, what I refer to as "objectification" will comprise the more playful submissive acts of being treated like an animal or pet, or, alternatively, like an inanimate object. These playful types of alternate personae are easier to understand because a lot of them are pleasure- or service-oriented personae or personae who wish to cease being an independent entity for a time and serve a higher purpose. The "higher purpose" for a submissive with a nurturing spirit could be to give a gift of selflessness to the dom, which says that you acknowledge and appreciate all of the time and effort it takes to top you and enact your fantasies, that you realize that topping can be hard work, and that the master could use a breather once in a while.

The Object of the Game

Fantasies of objectification rarely involve sexual, or even noticeably erotic, activities. Because the main turn-on is psychological, objectification can be used by the master to humble the submissive for arrogance, to punish her for an infraction, or simply to give himself a rest. Those who find the thought of being the master's footstool, or dog, or pony-girl intensely erotic have a desire to explore the ultimate powerlessness of being less than human. Sex is usually not an issue unless the object the slave has become is the master's sex toy. In objectification surrender, the submissive becomes something *other,* something of the dom's creation, and revels in the state of helplessness and passivity she has attained as an object.

Objectification play will be fun for the sub who enjoys it when the master exerts tight control over her every move. When the lord ignores your personality and treats you like a thing, like an object, incapable of thoughts or feelings, you are free to experience the total and voluntary subjugation of your will to the master's, and enjoy your powerlessness guiltlessly. When I have been an object, I have felt extremely peaceful and calm, and at one with myself and my master. My universe centers on the object I am to become for him. By centering on the object, I try to become the object I am imitating. I think back to having read of a Native American tribe whose belief system held that all objects, living and inanimate, had *animus*. Animus was neither good nor evil, it was just the life force, or spirit, of the object. By thinking of the life force of the thing, and of what makes a good footstool a good footstool, I endeavor to imitate the life force of the footstool. I ask myself what are the qualities of a footstool? To be still and motionless, to be properly positioned under the master's feet, to provide stable comfort for them and to elevate them, and to keep his feet warm and give them a soft place to rest.

Breathe With Me . . .

As I recite and repeat these qualities like a mantra, I begin my deep breathing exercises (see chapter 14, Sex Acts, for a relaxation mantra). Don't underestimate the power of controlled breathing during SM play. Some think breathing is the single most important skill for those who wish to experience pain or attain the state of objectification. It is almost impossible to get into a panic, or out of control, when you are breathing deeply and regularly. With practice, you can stay very still and relaxed and achieve an almost trancelike state. Teach your top to be aware of your breathing, like a labor coach would, because your breathing can help him read your body language. If you are breathing irregularly, or holding your breath, your top should verbally instruct you to breathe, place a hand on your chest or back to remind you to breathe, or take deep, audible breaths himself to encourage you to match your breathing to his.

To be a truly good object, I find that I must be able to enter a very special place, which some call "sub-space." For me sub-space is when the master becomes the center of my universe, and the real world turns into a scrim curtain background for our passion play. The breathing exercises and object-mantra I make up help me to focus and then attain an incredible lightness of being. What I am referring to, in either case, is the state of mind that the submissive enters when the master has touched a cord in her, and a deep connection has been made between them. When I was there, all that existed for me was my master: the sound of his voice, the rhythm of his breathing, the fall of his footsteps, his touch, his scent, and his needs. The strength of his presence and the force of his personality were all that I needed, or wanted, to keep me connected to the earth. An invisible umbilical cord anchored me to him, my Rock of Gibraltar, so that I could soar the heights of my passion, and explore my sexuality and sensuality. My trust in his protection of me was implicit while I explored the shadows in the dark garden we had cultivated together.

Objects of Usefulness

Although fantasies of being a footstool or other piece of furniture, objet d'art, or human sculpture are not among the most common, they are, nonetheless, a very powerful force in the erotic mind. Besides, human furniture is very low maintenance. In this SM scenario, the allure is in the helpful yet helpless nature of the object, the willing passivity that the submissive assumes. Objectification fantasies are very different from animal fantasies: When a submissive becomes a footstool, she is becoming an inanimate object. When she becomes a dog, although a dog is obviously not human, it is still a living thing. To become a dog one has to think like a dog; to become the master's footstool, one can assume the position, suspend thought entirely, and recede into the inner sanctum of the mind. These fantasies have some similarities to bondage and humiliation in that the submissive has to remain still in the commanded position until given leave to rise. Additionally, some type of sensation, or tiny torture, may be inflicted upon the submissive (like tickling) to excite or humiliate her. She, as an object, must remain the passive recipient.

Some dominants disapprove of objectification games, stating that the games are too passive, and they prefer to have a submissive who is more lively. Having been both the objectifier and the object, I do not see what their problem is. If the sub was likely to turn into an actual footstool, like something out of *The Twilight Zone*, I would understand their objections. But this is a temporary state—the sub does not remain the object forever. And for the sub with a giving nature, becoming an object of beauty or usefulness to serve the master in this way is a gift of selflessness to the dom.

The Footstool

The gift of objectification tells the master that you appreciate all the hard work (and it does take some effort!) he has put into fulfilling your fantasies. Knowing this, I don't wait until my master orders me to be his footstool; instead, I offer myself to him for this service. There are certain times when I sense he would like to be alone with himself and just *be* himself. He needs to let his defenses down in a way that only happens when one is totally alone: when no warm hazelnut eyes are looking at him, no little face is seeking his smile, no homey noises are coming from the kitchen. At these times, I know he will truly appreciate the thoughts and emotions behind this particular service, as well as the service itself.

To offer him this service, I would crouch on the floor right in front of his feet in the footstool position he favored most. Then I would curl an arm around his ankles and begin to kiss his feet. (I didn't care whether they were bare, socked, or booted.) When I performed this offering of service, even before the master accepted my offer, the butterflies in my stomach would begin to flutter. As I reassumed the position under his feet, feelings of deep submission had started to build in me. By the time he had placed his feet just so on my back, I was dripping with excitement at serving him in such as impersonal way.

As I crouched on the floor, unable to see him, or the TV, or anything else in the room other than the square foot of carpet under my nose, I would close my eyes and let the sounds of the world become white noise around me. I would concentrate on his feet as they rested on my back. I focused my entire being on his feet, picturing them in my mind, seeing that the second toe was slightly, sexily, longer than the first, and seeing as if for the first time that his feet were quite sexy. I focused on the warmth emanating from them and the alternately hard and soft spots on them as he rubbed them on my ribs and vertebrae. Then I would picture in my mind's eye what we looked like as man and furniture; I imagined what his feet looked like resting upon my naked body. The image was powerful and sent me into a more deeply submissive state. I no longer existed for myself, I existed to serve milord in any way he saw fit. I felt I was truly his slave in those moments in the chivalrous sense of the word because I had put his needs before mine. The rest of the time, he was very busy satisfying me!

The Ashtray

If you have an ashtray fantasy, I have some pointers for you to make your ashtray experience a safe and happy one. I have used my cupped palm and my extended tongue to catch his ashes and the trick to becoming this object safely is *distance*. The cigar or cigarette should be at least four inches (but not more than eight inches) from your palm or tongue when he flicks it. The flick should be "deliberate," not tentative: a good, firm tap to release the ash in one piece, well aimed over the proffered palm or tongue. When catching the ash in the palm, the palm can be cupped. As soon as the ash lands, I close my hand over it and shake it like dice, in case there is still some live ember there. This actions "puts it out," and although I've gotten a little warm, I've never been burned.

The tongue is a little trickier because obviously you can't throw the ashes in the trash can later, and ashes are very hard, if not impossible, to spit out. Ashes caught on the tongue have to be swallowed or else don't offer this service. Here's the best tip I can give you: Do not swallow your saliva before sticking your tongue out. This will put out any last bit of life in the ash and prove helpful later on when you need to swallow. So, collect your saliva on your tongue and make a little pool of it, *then* stick your tongue out. Your master should flick his ash so they fall directly into your little reservoir—the saliva will cause the ashes to keep their cylindrical shape as well as put out any lingering embers. Then, curl your tongue back into your mouth and swallow quickly. You'll never even taste it!

Objets D'art

An objet d'art can give the master as much joy as a footstool or any other piece of furniture without it being of any useful purpose. The purpose of art, the *job* of art if you will, is to decorate one's surroundings and to give pleasure to the eye. Or, to put it another way, the usefulness of art is its decorative value. Although this is not a common fantasy, popular objects among practitioners are candelabra, tables and table bases, sculpture, pillows, and hat stands.

Becoming a standing sculpture and a candelabra are my two favorite inanimates when my master and I play this game. I have also been a table—balancing my master's dinner tray, complete with beverage glass, on my back! When at a friend's house or private party, I have offered my services as his ashtray when that article was not in sight. If the objet d'art also happens to serve some useful purpose or another, like the candelabra, then you are of double value to your master!

Being his candelabra can be done in any number of interesting and deliciously sexy and humiliating positions, and I don't think you need me to explain them all to you! Tapers, or tapered candles, burn very hot, as do beeswax candles, plastic-coated candles, and candles with scents and dyes in them. The safest (and I think sexiest) way to be a candelabra is to set candles in glass jars on your outstretched arms if you are standing, or in a row down your vertebrae if you are crouched or bent over, or strategically placed on your torso as you lie face up. Yoga enthusiasts and the very limber will be able to assume many unusual and difficult positions where the candles can be set on the legs. For those who really do like it hot, a woman's nether openings, front and back, make good holders for those long, white, dripless tapered candles! (CAUTION: This is a very sexy fantasy, but hot wax *anywhere* on the body can cause serious burns!)

Interesting things can be done with a human being as sculpture. Anne Rice explored many styles of objectification in her Beauty Trilogy (see Recommended Fiction Works) and Beauty as sculpture was one of them. I like to think I am beautiful too, beautiful enough to be sculpture for my master, and because he plays this game with me, he must agree. I love to be a sculpture when I am nude or only wearing high heels and other ornaments. Other times when I am his sculpture, he drapes my head and the upper half of my body in a large square of black flocked material, then artistically arranges my limbs until I am pleasing to his eye. Other times, he poses me on a chair, or over one, so that I am exposed to his gaze. Often he poses me in positions that are a little difficult to hold, especially over a period of time. That is when I call up my breathing mantra and object-mantra, and sink deeper and deeper into sub-space. On those occasions, I have gotten so deeply into my role as sculpture or footstool that my master had to call my name several times to bring me back!

Being an Animal

Have you spent a pleasant half hour amusing yourself by watching your cat frolic in a sunbeam, batting frantically at some unseen mote, then suddenly lie down for a nice nap? Have you laughed at the goofy abandon with which your dog fetches and retrieves the ball? Have you ever wondered how it would feel to live such a care-free yet totally human-dominated life? Have you ever wanted to play the cat or dog? Or perhaps your fantasies of an animal persona take the shape of a pony-girl trained to elegantly pull the master's cart while dressed in fancy equipage?

You, my friend, are not alone. Animal play is a golden opportunity to shut down the brain and be delightfully and joyfully uninhibited. Some equate playing the pet with being lovable: Puppies and dogs are cute and cuddly and offer unconditional love. Others view animal play as freedom from the rules and restrictions that control human behavior. An animal can be *tamed* by a good trainer, but it cannot be civilized so it is exempt from civilized behavior. Additionally, if the animal fantasy is one of being a dog or cat, part of the fantasy's appeal could lie in that the animal has no privacy, or expectation of it, in its relationship with its master.

Its entire life is controlled by and lived out in full view of the master. The no-modesty-or-privacy aspect of humiliation in the master-animal relationship makes canine-feline games a popular fantasy. By becoming an animal, or a pet, the submissive is able to experience an emancipation from her humanity while totally subjugating her will to that of her human master's.

A beautiful bottom, a joyous submissive, can find delight and gratification in being treated like a pet—perhaps she likes to curl up in the master's lap, and be cuddled and stroked like a Lhasa Apso, a sweet tempered lapdog. Maybe this makes her feel cherished and cared for in a hard, cold world. Maybe the release of power and tension through the fantasy of being a pet helps her discover a hidden strength or value in her character. Perhaps it teaches her patience or tolerance, or gives her space to be at one with herself. Or maybe animal fantasies give her a place to free herself of herself, and center herself on another without re-criminations or guilt. Then again, maybe she uses it as an excuse to do nothing but be close to the master, her tongue lolling as she exposes her belly to him. For a beautiful, powerful bottom, her submission can be a walk on her dark side with the full brilliant light of the sun shining on her face.

Among submissive women, the most prevalent animal personae fan-tasies are of being a dog, cat, or pony-girl. Lately, bird-girl fantasies have come to my attention. If you have the time, try to make up a mantra about the particular pet you are about to become. Think of the animal-mantra as you "dress," or the master dresses you, for the role. As each pet has a set of very appealing qualities uniquely its own, and this will help you with your mantra, I would like to spend a little time with each.

The Doggie in the Window

For the submissive who dreams of the slavish relationship of master and dog, the canine fantasy scenarios are endless. Dogs and puppies get, and need, a lot of attention. They get their backs scratched, and their bellies rubbed. Long-haired dogs get a bath from the master and then a nice brushing. All dogs can be taught obedience commands like sit, stay, come, and heel. A dog can be taught to stay off the furniture, or can be brought to dog obedience school. In the home, they also can be taught tricks like rolling over, begging, speaking and singing (howling), and how to fetch the master's slippers. The master can play games with his dog. He can take his dog for a walk on her pretty new leash; she can sleep curled up on her new cushion at the master's feet. She can lap her water and eat her food—leftovers from the master's plate—from special dog bowls on the floor.

Other doglike actions for you to imitate: A dog will pant when she is hot—panting cools her off. Practice a sexy pant in the mirror when you are home alone. Learn how to wag your "tail"! Observe the differ-ent ways dogs sit and lie down, and pick those that look best when you do them. Practice in front of a mirror to get that real doggy feel. Put your hair up in pigtails to make big, floppy dog ears. Watch your own dog, or a friend's, and see what dogs do at home. Watch the dog shows on cable TV and see the paces they are put through. Some of the paces will work for human dogs too. Other amusing dog things: Why did Fifi circle that same spot fifty times before lying down in it? Why do many dogs walk in a circle when they want to be taken out for a walk? Dogs are loud sniffers. Dogs are also very good at licking things. Need I say more?

Pussycat, Pussycat, Where Have You Been . . .

If you feel the canine persona is too subservient or goofy for you, perhaps the feline persona is more your style, and that of your master's. If your master enjoys an independent pet, you will greatly enjoy becoming his cat. Because of the less-dependent personality of the cat, you are in a fantasy situation where the master has little control over your actions (cats rarely listen and are notoriously hard to train), but you are free to express what could become one of the sexier personae of your submissive side. If you have a cat, I know you have spent many hours watching your beloved feline amuse itself by lolling around, twisting its body this way and that with impossible ease and effortlessness, leaping to catch a fly, and doing hundreds of other cat things. I personally liked to lie stretched out atop the back of the sofa (my master's sofa was up against the wall) and take a catnap while he reclines on the cushions. I actually felt feline when I was in this position!

If you don't have the genuine article—a cat—to study, rent the video *Batman Returns* with Michelle Pfeiffer as Catwoman. She had very feline moves, very slinky and cat sexy, with cat class and cat style, much to be admired and emulated. Some readers may remember Julie Newmar as Catwoman in the *Batman* television series. She's the six-foot beauty with the legs that go from here to there and back again and a sultry voice to drive men wild. Either one is eminently qualified as a role model for a cat persona. Go see *Cats* to pick up some excellent pointers on the cat world. Practice a new sexy meow! Whether you are a big cat or house cat, cats are sexy.

Pony-Girls

Until recently, pony-girls were more of a British phenomenon than an American one, then suddenly, ponies began to spring up across the United States. I first became interested in human ponies when I read Anne Rice's Beauty Trilogy. Although Rice's ponies were all men, the methods and treatments used to subjugate their human personalities in favor of the equine fascinated me. Naked except for leather harnesses and pony-boots with hooves, with butt-plugs of streaming tails made of real horsehair protruding from between their cheeks, Rice's pony-boys were often rented out by their masters to transport young and old, rich and poor, through the streets of the village. Eating and sleeping in the stables, and taking their leisure in herds in enclosed fields, the life of a pony-boy was one of body, brawn, and mindset with no *mind*—physical exertion, even prowess, but no mental powers. I like to think that everyone, just once, wishes that it could be true, if only for an hour.

But when Rice wrote her Beauty Trilogy, a woman's fantasy of becoming a real working pony-girl was exactly that: a *fantasy*. Unable to support the weight of a man on their backs, the pony-girl's training was limited to prancing, practicing their gaits, and looking good in the pony outfit. Then, it dawned on someone that whereas one pony-girl could not support the weight of a man on her back, a pony-girl hitched to a cart could pull one along very easily. Two or three pony-girls could pull the master longer and faster. The pony-girl's dream of being a working animal became a reality.

The pony-girl rig reached perfection in my eyes with the 1995 debut of Master Keith and ponies hilary, suzi, and melanie at the Skin Two Rubber Ball. Built by the Master himself, the cart is actually an elegant chariot with room enough for the Master and a guest. The oversized wheels make the chariot easier for his three corsetted ponies to pull in tandem. The pony-girls are similarly dressed in corsets, lace-top stockings, thongs, and low-heeled pumps. Feathered headdresses complete the panoply. Their reins, bits, and harnesses, including behind-the-back arm restraints, were designed by Master Keith, as was the device that hitched the ponies to the chariot. The ponies trained several times a month, being put through their paces by the Master. They were drilled in pulling the chariot, halting on command, backing up, and turning corners. When the Master and his ponies hit the stage at the Rubber Ball, the four thousand attendees went wild, and the dreams of many became a reality.

Feathered Friends

When given her choice of masks in *The Story of O,* the submissive O chose the elaborately feathered headdress of a predatory owl to conceal her features. How does the dichotomy of submissive and predator in O echo our own feelings? How do we blend the submissive and predatory sides of our natures?

In O's case, her choice of the predator owl as her alternate visage expressed her understanding of her duality. Let me use the gyrfalcon as an example. Although the owl lives in the wild and the gyrfalcon lives in captivity to her master, their predatory natures are inherent and very similar, until human domination enters the scene. Whereas the owl hunts for itself, in falconry the gyrfalcon is carefully trained to hunt on command, then retrieve the prey and bring it back to its master. The falcon's natural instinct to hunt has been harnessed by the master, and trained to suit the master's purposes. In return, the master cares for the bird, feeds it, and sees that it is never suffers the deprivations to which animals in the wild are subject. A hood keeps the bird sitting quietly on the master's leather gauntlet, and delicate straps of leather keep her taloned feet attached to his wrist until her hunting skills are required by him. The falcon was a cherished and highly valued pet. Additionally, the female of each species used in falconry was more highly valued for hunting than the male because the female was larger and more powerful.

In the kingdom of tamed animals, all live in totally human-dominated existence, but none more so than the bird. Cats and dogs usually have the roam of the house, if not the furniture. Ponies are exercised regularly and shown at events and competitions. But birds? Birds are usually kept in their cage. Although many of the large exotic birds seem highly trainable, few people bother to do so. Hence, out of all of man's pets, the mind of the bird is among the least known to man. But I found my time as a bird to be very interesting, and very different than time spent as any other animal.

When I first fantasized about being his bird, I considered wearing wings and a feathered mask. But upon looking at myself wearing only high, thin heeled shoes with ankle straps, I decided I looked more bird-like in the nude. (I have long, thin arms and legs and often compare myself to a flamingo!) Some friends have remarked that I have birdlike movements when I dance and move so I dwelt on what I had done to make them pass those particular comments. Then I focused on the birds I had seen and made up my bird-mantra. What else did I need? I needed my master to enact the fantasy and a perch, and the perch should be in a cage. My master, the fanciful lord, secured two cages: a tall, upright bird cage and one with a perch.

We had agreed that my role was to be very passive: He would move me from one cage to the other and play with me as he wished while I was in captivity. I was allowed to coo and make bird sounds but was only allowed to speak the words he taught me. A safe-signal replaced the spoken word. In the tall standing cage, I posed, and preened my feathers, and observed my lord as he sat on the sofa in much the same way a real pet bird would. (I hoped.) I snaked my head from left to right and back in that weird and wild swinging-swaying motion I have seen birds do, what I call "the weird neck thing," or WNT. I extended my arms and pretended to fluff out my feathers. I inclined my head at him, gave him my profile, and fixed him with a bright, beady eye.

He rose from his seat and approached my cage. I burst into a fluster of happy bird activity. He stroked my head feathers (my idea) and fed me little bits of fresh fruit (his idea) through the bars of the cage. Then, using the fruit to reward me when I said it correctly, he taught me to say, "Hello, Master, how can I serve you today?" and "Yes, Master, whatever you wish," and, finally, "Thank you, Master." So pleased was he with my performance that he moved me to the cage with the perch. Previously, he had strategically attached leather wrist restraints to the top of the cage and leather ankle restraints to the bottom of the cage. Opening the door, he helped me in and sat me over the perch.

The perch came about midthigh when I was seated, leaving my exposed bottom hanging over the bar. When I reached up and grabbed the top of the cage to steady myself on the seat, my master quickly buckled the leather restraints around my wrists. My arms were effectively held over my head, and the clip hooks attaching the restraints to the cage gave me something to hold on to. Then my master spread my legs wide and buckled a restraint onto each ankle. Now I was balanced and held in place by the leather restraints clipped to my cage. He turned my cage to face the mirror and I was delighted by what I saw. My lord stood next to me, completely dressed, powerful and sexy in his black jeans, pullover, and leather boots. Through the bars of the cage, my nude body, embellished by the leather restraints, glowed with the submissive fire ignited in me by my lord.

As I looked at our combined reflections in the glass, I couldn't help but notice how exotic we looked—he, completely dressed and free; me, naked and bound to the cage. He looked handsome and human and I looked small and delicate, and, yes, like a bird. As I gazed at our reflection, I felt the pull of sub-space. Slowly, I turned into a bird, a caged, captured, and frightened animal. I pulled on the restraints as if beating my wings, struggled against them as an animal would. And all the while I struggled, I knew as a human that my fight was futile. I fought against the restraints, knowing my fight, and ultimate "defeat," would make my submission more intense emotionally. I fought for the sake of the fight itself, and I fought to enjoy the physical pleasure of struggling. And in losing, I sought the ultimate joy of surrendering to him and my inner self and becoming his helpless captive, a bird.

To calm me, milord reached his hand between the bars and began to fondle and stroke me. I "struggled" against the restraints, but it was more like moving into and onto his hand. It was my favorite kind of torture: to be bound and exposed, my body totally accessible to him and his whims. His long, slender fingers worked their magic on me, over and over, through the bars. My movement was limited and I could speak only those phrases my master had taught me. Isolated from the civilized world, I was his willing prisoner in luxurious captivity. In a gilded cage, I sat impaled upon his hand and said, as he had taught me, "Thank you, Master, thank you, Master" each time he gave me an orgasm. He gave me several before withdrawing his hand and returning to the sofa. From there, he watched me avidly as I hung draped over the perch.

At this point, I was a bird—a green conure the master had hand-fed from birth. I knew the sound of his footfall and his whistle. I knew the different timbres of his voice: happiness, sadness, tension, anger, love, sternness. I was his bird and he was my whole world. I made cooing noises, happy bird sounds, happy to have a handsome, caring master to take care of me. I arched my back and tightened my muscles (I knew this would make my body look incredible) and gazed at him. Then, still holding his gaze, I put my head on my arm and visibly settled down to await his attentions. His next endeavor was to teach me how to say, "Please fuck me, Master." I hurried to get the pronunciation right, but not too quickly. I didn't want to make it too obvious that I was out of my mind for him!

When I said the phrase to his satisfaction, he released me from my restraints and helped me out of the cage. I was still his bird, caged or not. He hand-fed me a piece of fruit and told me to say it again. "Please fuck me, Mas . . . ter," I trailed off. His tongue was in my mouth and he was pushing me to the floor, spreading my legs with his legs. Breathless and speechless, I was delighted when I realized he was going to honor my request!

Props for Pets

Thousands have spent millions indulging their animal-persona fantasies, yet you need not spend much at all to have just as much fun. Fantasies of being the cat or dog abound, and just a small investment in props or wardrobe fleshes out the scene. Do your shopping at the local pet shop for a touch of reality: actual animal wear! For a cat, get the appropriate collar: a thin dainty one, decorated with a tinkling little bell, or sparkling rhinestones; a heavier, thicker one, made of leather, for a dog, each with a leash hook, would be an ensemble in itself. (My cat collar is a thin band of red leather with rhinestones, a bell, and a leash hook.) A leash is always a nice touch for a dog and, of course, bowls for food and water for either can be placed on a mat on the floor. A small ball you can pick up in your teeth is a good toy for a dog, as is a rawhide chew toy. Cats like to play with string and fluffy things, and have been known to bat a ball around with a determined paw. Many costume shops regularly stock a selection of cat ears and tails, and having ears and a tail always made me feel more feline!

For feathered friend fantasies, a real cage is the single most important prop you can have. You can wear a feathered mask, or your master can have a small falcon hood made for you and leather tethers, too, but the mind-set of the bird was much easier for me to capture once he put me inside the cage. Unfortunately, bird cages that are strong enough to hold humans are very expensive, because they have to be custom-made. Furthermore, our two cages were made of welded cast iron, and their weight was considerable. The feeling of submission, the wave of helplessness, that opening the door to the bird cage invokes is hard to duplicate without the cage itself.

Pony-girls, both working ponies and show ponies, will need a padded bit or padded bar-gag, head gear, and reins. For the show pony, head plumes give an elegant look to the panoply, and can be effected with millinery feathers. Either pony may like wearing stockings and low pumps or boots, a corset, G-string, and bra. Of course, any and all pieces of wardrobe are optional! Additionally, a team of working ponies may need regular drilling in proper pacing to pull the cart, back it up, and turn corners. Back at the stable, a lunge tether can be used to restrain the pony during grooming. A lunge tether, well under twenty dollars from the local riding shop, is a length of rope with a tear-drop shaped ring braided into one end of it for easy attachment to a stationary hook and an easy-open hook on the other end of the rope for attachment to the bit. I find this particular item to add a very realistic touch to a pony scene—my lunge tether is red with gold rings!

~ 12 ~

Erotic Discomfort

Fantasies of helplessness abound in the dark garden of SM. Who hasn't, at least once, dreamed of being overpowered, held down, or cuffed to the bed while "The One" forces himself on you over and over again? Ultimately, he overcomes all resistance and pleasure is wrung from your happily helpless body. From the romance of the ropes to sensory deprivation, dreams of being helpless are a powerful force in the erotic mind of men and women. How provocative it is to know that even though I am helpless, I am still desired and desirable; how reassuring to know that helpless as I am, he still wants to be with me, care for me, look after me. There can be a great uplifting of the spirit, a victory of the mind combined with the exaltation of the flesh, in voluntary helplessness and sensual surrender. Many people still carry feelings of guilt about enjoying sex; enacting scenes where the submissive "has no choice" but to obey by being made helpless can relieve those feelings and allow her to enjoy a more enriching sexual experience.

Bondage . . . Helpless and Hopeful

Bondage occupies an interesting plot of soil in the dark garden. Many people who have no interest in any other aspect of SM, or use no other SM techniques, are fascinated by the beauty of bondage. For those in that category, perhaps the fascination started in childhood. Stories abound of children tying up themselves or their friends, so strong was the pull of the ropes. As children we were too young to realize, or understand, the significance of tying someone up. We were too young to grasp or analyze the change it had on their, or our, emotional state; we only felt it.

In romantic bondage, a good dominant will be aware of the emotional effect of restraint, and he will use it to enhance the experience and tighten his control. In bondage, the submissive can focus on the sensations she is being given—living in the moment—and release anxiety and stress caused by the outside world.

Experimenting With Helplessness

As adults exploring the dark garden of our sexuality, there are a few types of bondage we may want to experiment with. I want to discuss some of them here with you; later on, you will invent others of your own.

In *love bondage*, a scene is created to heighten the submissive's awareness of her body and her vulnerability. Love bondage, or sensual bondage, is usually done with soft, silky ropes and involves teasing the submissive. Once she is bound, the dom teases her into arousal and then prolongs it without giving her any orgasms. The skillful dom can tease and retie her for hours, heightening her senses and intensifying her need and desire for release. If properly done, she will be afloat on a sea of blissful, craven lust, hungry for any attention from the master. His slightest touch will send a frisson through her spine to explode in her brain and between her legs.

Another type of bondage scene that grows rampant in the fertile soil of the dark garden is one combining *bondage and submission*. This scene is created to bring the submissive to a state of surrender and make her yield to the power of her lord. Bondage devices are often used as window dressing in this scene to signify the submissive's status. Collar and leash replace a necklace; wrist and ankle cuffs replace bracelets and anklets. Usually each token is assigned a meaning: When the collar is on, you are his to command, or the token may have some ritual of acceptance the submissive must perform such as kissing the collar as a symbol of your acceptance of his dominance over you.

My master used to find it very entertaining to tie my legs together just above my knees then send me off on some little task. If, bound this way, I executed the task to his satisfaction, he would then tie my ankles together as well and send me off on a more difficult task, like serving tea. Remember to walk on tippy-toe!

A less sensuous form of bondage is what I call *rough bondage*. Rough bondage would be used for rough play or to give punishment. Although one can easily see and find the sensuality in being tied down for punishment, the bondage in this scene is to make one hold still for the other activity. In the complex way SM fantasies are conceived, the bondage aspect of the scene frees the submissive to experience the other sensations given to her (the punishment and pain) without fear of guilt or reprisal. Her chains, or ropes, set her free as she thanks her master for each stroke of the cane that he gives her. Unable to struggle or free herself, she accepts her position, loves it, and subjugates her will to that of her master's.

Safety Tips

Before embarking on your journey into bonded bliss, you must be aware of the safety factors involved in engaging in romantic bondage. Bondage, by definition, is restriction, but in real life we don't want to restrict anything important!

In general, applying to all forms of restraints used in bondage, your dom should be able to insert two fingers snugly between the limb and whatever he has put around it. The wrists, when bound together, should have at least a few inches of rope or chain (if cuffed, a couple of double-sided clip hooks) separating them. The restraint that is fastened too tightly presents the danger of loss of circulation, or possible nerve damage; the restraint fastened too loosely can slip when you, in a welter of passion, pain, and pleasure, pull on them. Additionally, the cuff or restraint should not press against your wrist or the nerve at the bottom of your thumb; the nerve can become pinched before the hand falls asleep. This is where your two finger fit is a sensible move. If you are using rope, make sure it does not pinch the skin. Never allow anyone to suspend you by the wrists as they are delicately boned, filled with nerves and veins, and were not designed to take a body's weight. If your master ties your hands over your head, make sure he leaves several inches of rope or chain between your restraint and whatever he has tied you to so that you can hold on to it. This piece of rope is not only comforting but gives you something to pull on during those moments of agonizing ecstasy.

The neck is also a very delicate part of your anatomy. Never put the neck at risk by putting ropes, especially with slip knots, around it, pulling or tugging on the back of a collar, or attaching the collar to a stationary object.

Standing bondage, an image that is undeniably erotic, is a demanding position, and some cannot "stand" it for more than half an hour. For those with low blood pressure or poor circulation, ten to twenty minutes might well be long enough. The safest standing position is with your arms out almost straight from your shoulders, with your elbows comfortably bent. By far, the most comfortable position for bondage is lying down, but you should not be left unattended if you are face down on a soft surface. If a gag is part of your fantasy, then you never want to be gagged when you have sinus problems, a stuffy nose, a cold, flu, or cough. The caring and responsible dom you are grooming him to be will need to be taught these things to ensure your safety and a fun, sexy SM encounter for both of you.

Where nerves run close to the surface skin, it is important to protect them from damage. Prolonged or extreme pressure should not be applied to the underside of the thumb, the inside of the wrists, the crook of the elbow, the joint of the knees, at the groin, and, of course, the neck.

Your restraints should be checked every ten to fifteen minutes or so until you or your master can discern if you can safely stay in bondage longer. He should "order" you to shake your hands and wiggle your toes, and to rotate your ankles and wrists, to ensure that they are not becoming numb. If they are, he should remove your bindings immediately, then stimulate the limb by rubbing it.

In bondage, many scenes begin as a collaboration because putting you into bondage safely requires cooperation from you while it is happening. After you are suitably trussed up, you may start playing another scene that includes sexy struggling and squirming, begging and pleading most eloquently, and other delights found in the dark garden. At its inception, bondage is, more so than some other SM games, a mutual effort. As a submissive in bondage, it is your responsibility to keep in communication with your master, telling him things he will not be able to perceive on his own, such as dizziness or lightheadedness, numbness, nausea, or anything else unusual.

Often when I am removed from bondage, I am giddy and a little unsteady on my feet, like walking on the earth again after just having walked on the moon. This is a common phenomenon. Some submissives actually fall down! Your master should know this and help you to stand, or support you, until you can reorient yourself and get your legs back underneath you.

Shoes: Tools of Control and Punishment

The power of high heels, stilettos, and fetish shoes work in a uniquely dual way: the high-heeled shoe imparts grace and beauty to the sub while providing the dom with a tool of control over her. Using shoes as a means of controlling the submissive is considered part of bondage and a form of punishment. In referring to shoes as part of bondage, I am speaking of the height of the heel, or stiletto, as being uncomfortable and limiting to the slave. Inhibiting her movements will intensify her feelings of helplessness and increase her dom's control over her. Walking in stilettos takes practice, and the slave may have some difficulty in the execution of her duties. Common household tasks became enormous challenges when you are balancing on five-inch heels! Wearing stilettos may make some chores painful to perform, or take longer to complete. High heels can make a slave clumsy or likely to give inept service. Pain emanating from the bound foot and the subsequent distraction of the slave's attention can cause the slave to make all sorts of mistakes, thereby putting herself in a position to be punished!

High heels and stilettos can also be used by the dom to punish his slave. Using shoes as the instrument of discipline leaves open the possibility of displeasing her lord once again and being punished further. I loved to be made to wear the black stilettos and ordered to execute the same task over and over again, being "corrected" as he saw fit until I did the task perfectly. Then, a new task or a higher heel would be introduced and the training continued. Additionally, starting with shoes as punishment is relatively gentle and leaves plenty of room for taking things to a higher level. To me, the ultimate in slave-training shoes, the shoes perfect for bondage and discipline, are the fetish toe-shoes with the six- to seven-inch heel. To wear these shoes standing, I must be holding on to a rope or a chain overhead; basically, all I am doing is standing on my toes, with little or no assistance from the shoes. This position is a mix of real and mental bondage. When wearing the fetish toe-shoe while serving the master, I must remain on the floor because the heel prevents me rising or standing; indeed, it prevents me from assuming any position other than on all fours on the floor. I must serve him on my knees at all times because the shoes will not allow me to serve him any other way. Having only floor and crawling rights helps me to forget myself and serve him—which is surely the desire of any sensual submissive!

Mental Bondage

To some the motivation of bondage is surrender; to others embarrassment or humiliation is the most provocative aspects of bondage. *Humiliating* bondage would be any bondage that "forces" the submissive to expose her genitals to her master. A verbal dom would tease his slave about her vulnerable position, her exposure to him for his pleasure and amusement. This type of bondage doesn't need any equipment, like leather cuffs or rope, to enact. I find humiliating bondage to be just as satisfying when no physical restraints are used. Physical restraints free one from responsibility by rendering struggle futile; "invisible ropes" or *mental bondage* requires that the submissive use her mind, her willpower, to keep herself in position, making her a coconspirator in what is to come.

One evening my master and I played this very game. The rules were simple: He taught me two positions to assume. Position one was bent over the arm of the sofa with my hands behind my back for penetration, or gripping the sofa arms for caning. Position two was crouched at his feet. I was to stay in position one and submit to him: his use of the flogger, the canes, his hands, his cock, dildos, whatever, until I couldn't bear it any more. At that time, I was to assume position two and he would stop. Then things got really interesting. He told me that "when I had had enough of a rest, I was to reassume position one to show him I was ready for more punishment and penetration." And, he would know when I was taking "too long," he added, smiling wickedly.

How lovely to be able to decide when I was ready for more hard strokes of the cane, more deep penetration! How deliciously humiliating to rise and splay myself over the sofa arm—to deliberately spread myself for his gaze, knowing what would happen next. I willed myself to the sofa, motivated by lust and the desire to submit to the pain and to him. The strength and desire in my mind gave power to my limbs, the courage and beauty of my actions exploded in my brain as I bent over the sofa arm and clasped my hands behind the small of my back. One thought repeated itself in my head: No ties bind you except the bounds of your own free will. I anticipated with giddy delight the next three strokes of the cane alternated with three deep stabs of his spear.

The cane worked its cruel magic; when he stepped up behind me to take me, I was wet and ready for him and begging for the pleasure of penetration, of his cock inside of me. The promise of penetration made me hotter for the pain: more pain, more penetration. In this way, we were also able to extend the duration of our scenario because the rest periods allowed my endorphins to do their work, constantly enabling me to take and want more and more and to bring our play to a higher level.

Sensory Deprivation

Combining bondage with sensory deprivation is another well-cultivated flower in the dark garden. Sensory deprivation is when the dom exerts his power over the submissive by restricting or controlling one or more of her five senses. If he has cuffed you, then one of your senses has already been taken from you. It is thrilling to want to touch him, to yearn and ache to touch him, and yet not be able to because of the luxurious bonds he has placed you in.

Blindfolds and hoods, gags and earplugs are also used, most effectively, by the dom to deprive you of your sight, speech, and hearing. Application of any one of these devices greatly increases the feelings of helplessness experienced by the submissive. The use of one or more of these items, each applied at a different time, creates an even greater sense of helplessness and submission. A loving dom will increase his submissive's pleasure while in bondage and sensory deprivation by surprising her with a variety of sensations, both pleasurable and painful. When bound, gagged, and blindfolded, it is impossible to know when, how, or with what one will be touched. The anticipation can make you on fire with desire for him.

A Good Word for Gags

The classic red ball gag seen so often in SM pornography is an object of horror and fascination to many a submissive. A gag invades a part of our body that we normally have use of and unrestricted control over: our mouth. The intruding gag changes your perceptions, even your demeanor, as well as deprives you of your speech. For some, the emotional impact of being gagged is enormous; the ability to communicate has been taken away, and this reduces them more than the loss of any or all of their other senses put together. In some cases, even the expression in the submissive's eyes changes when the gag is applied.

Personally, I find the look of a gagged woman to be highly erotic: I like to look at myself when gagged and observe the changes in my physical appearance. Once the gag is firmly yet comfortably in my mouth, another part of me is freed from societal mores; the gag removes my need to cry out, to protest against what will be or is being done to me, and to beg and plead with my master not to do exactly what I want done.

On a physical level, gags not only alter your senses by depriving you of your speech, but they force you to breathe more slowly and concentrate on each breath you take. This slow breathing, in turn, forces you to relax more. It is hard to panic when one's breathing is regular. Any submissive in love with and experienced in bondage will tell you, "relax into the ropes, you'll enjoy it more," and I can't agree with that enough.

Sensory deprivation is sexy and fun and can send the submissive into an altered state of perception and consciousness where the heat of his breath on your neck flows over your flesh like lava from an erupting volcano; his lightest touch alters the orbit of the planets in your own private universe. Sensory deprivation can send the submissive on a silent and blind journey to the center of her soul. Who knows what knowledge she may find there?

Bondage and sensory deprivation are synonyms for trust, and trust should not be given or taken lightly or without knowledge of its inherent responsibilities. Bondage and sensory deprivation scenes can be very powerful and forge a deep bond between the dom and submissive that is stronger than the ropes and restraints they so love. Through the smoke and mirrors of SM, one will see upon closer observation that the one who appears to be helpless, defenseless, and exposed is showing her strength and courage by the trust she places in her master. Her master is enthralled by the trust she places in him. In bondage, the techniques of SM are applied to attain a strange and wonderful state that transcends sexuality.

~ 13 ~

Sensual Sensations

When he's been and gone, and then I hear his name, will I still feel the same sensation? Who is to know? But the butterflies that flutter in my stomach at his approach are sensations. The unfolding of my consciousness when I see him, or the blossoming of my mind like night-blooming jasmine in my erotic garden, is a sensation. In the more physical sense, sensation is also a perception associated with the stimulus of a sense organ or a specific body part. In and of itself, sensation is neither good nor bad. It just exists. It is the individual receiving the sensation who has the ability (or not) to eroticize it. Take tickling, for example. Some people love to be tickled; others hate it. Some were ticklish as children but outgrew it as adults, others were ticklish as children and stayed that way, and still others were never ticklish to begin with. Tickling is a sensation that demonstrates each person's potential and perceptions vary.

A slave to sensation, sometimes called a sensation slut (whichever you prefer), enjoys the thorns as much as she does the roses, but her fun may also lie in the fact that in a sensation scene, she gets to do absolutely nothing other than experience and enjoy all the different and lovely sensations her master is giving her. Sensation scenes are often coupled with bondage scenes, the classic being "tie her up, tease her silly, and make her come." Bunny mitts, feathers, chamois cloths, leather and wool gloves, wartenberg wheels (like a pie crimper with needle-sharp edges), a square of velvet or suede, long fingernails, gentle fingertips, tongues,

151

breath, his hair or yours, floggers, clothes pins, nipple clamps, ice cubes, hot wax, cold feet, and warm hands all provide hours of sensational pleasure in the right hands. Amass your toy chest, ladies, and try them out on yourself wherever possible. You can select an order you would prefer for your toys to be used or let him surprise you. Discuss this in full with your master before proceeding, and have a simply sensational evening!

Pain: Part Two

Pain is a facet of sensation, and like sensation, in and of itself, it is neither good nor bad. In the dark garden of SM, it is the sub's ability to eroticize pain, combined with the ability of the dom to give "good pain" that turns it into a good experience. How does he give you good pain? Well, that would depend on two things: his expertise with his implement of choice—he must practice! practice! practice! (and not on you!)—and on how you are feeling at the time. Pain is a funny thing. Sometimes it hurts and sometimes it doesn't. And sometimes, it doesn't seem to hurt enough! And if given with the right buildup, pain doesn't even hurt. This is because those endorphins our brain keeps releasing when we are aroused enable us to take more—harder and faster—when properly built up.

If you aren't feeling all that aroused, then a warm-up beating is necessary. That feels more like a nice massage, if done with a flogger, or a cheek warmer if he has given you a hand spanking. If you are feeling aroused when he starts to beat you or to give you pain such as nipple pinching, then he can start at a higher level. And he can bring it to an even higher level.

Pleasurable Pain

The first level of pain could be called a warm-up for the real beating, or a sensuous massage, which is done with a variety of instruments. None of these "instruments of torture" will actually hurt you; some are the equivalent of getting hit with a wet noodle, pain-wise. This level of pain, the sensuous massage, is for those who only want the sensation of being whipped, or the feeling of being disciplined or humiliated.

Doms usually begin the warm-up by trailing any number of things from the home over the area—let's say in this case, your bum—to sensitize it. Favorites are a soft, furry or fuzzy cloth, feather, his fingernails or fingertips, his hair (if it's long enough), a feather duster, plus all the other things you found in your house. This can also include a lot of teasing and fondling. When your bum and your mind are both tingling and ready for more, you will know he has done his job well. Perhaps now you will ask him to hit you "just a little harder, please, Master." If you are one of those, now is the time for the deerskin flogger or a nice hand spanking. If you are not, the "pain" stops here and the other things you have planned begin to happen.

What the warm-up should have done is made you feel sexy when perhaps before the "beating," you weren't that aroused. Your brain responded to the stimulation and sent out our little mind-friends, the endorphins to help you along, and they did. Now you want more, and you want it given to you with different things.

Midlevel pain is for those who wish to explore pain and see how far they can go. Sometimes called the love-hate pain, this pain level uses a mixture of pleasure and pain that also allows a gradual buildup, but this pain starts at a slightly higher level than sensuous pain. Inventive doms will occasionally throw in one harder stroke among the others that will produce a hurts-so-good-response. This pain, or beating, can be tricky, however, because if you are not entirely warmed up and feeling sexual, you may not be ready for this much pain.

The final level of nonpunitive pain is what I call trance-pain which, for a masochistic or very aroused submissive, is the highest level of arousal attainable through pain. At this stage, each blow or new sensation is like a whole new universe exploding inside and outside of us waiting for our exploration. We can spiral into the depths of our masochism through this pain and gain new knowledge and understanding of ourselves. It is pain to bring you to your knees, groveling at his boot because you have discovered a new level of self and have been elevated by it.

Pain as Punishment

Punitive pain is the most extreme level of pain, not necessarily because this pain is any greater than that of another beating per se, but because punitive pain is not erotic. Nor is it meant to be. It is punishment by pain, no warm-up, no little caresses or rubs with a hard cock, no large hand on your breast, just punishment. But interestingly, sometimes an hour or more after this punishment, I do begin to feel sexual and want him inside me.

There is always some little bone of contention over punitive pain being nibbled at in the SM community; those against it say that it erodes the hard-earned thrust of the SM relationship. Well, you did negotiate this beforehand, didn't you? Did you specify whether punitive pain was allowable? Did you also say what you preferred your punishment to be? So, if pain as punishment is part of the fantasy mix for both partners and both have agreed upon it, where is the erosion of trust? Next, they say, punitive pain is abuse. And again I refer them to my above response: If both parties have agreed to it, what is abusive about it? Some people get turned on simply by the word "abuse" in a romantic, consensual SM setting. "Abuse me, Master, please . . . " that doesn't sound bad to me. I think this bone of contention over punitive pain is just another attempt by the "my kink's okay—yours is not" crowd to impose their will upon everyone.

Knowing Your Body

Before he can give you a beating that you will enjoy, he will need to know which areas of you are safe to hit. Look at your body, front and back, and observe where you carry your padding. Is it around your thighs? Your bum? Those areas, the well-padded ones, are safe for a nice disciplining but not much else at first. You can get hurt if you are hit in the wrong place! We're not trying to achieve real pain; this is *pleasure* through pain. He needs to learn your body, and if he's not using his hand, he needs to be proficient with his equipment before he can use it on you. A hand tends to go exactly where you send it, whereas a flogger requires that one practice aim and technique first.

Generally, you should never be hit where there are bones protruding; this would include your shoulder blades, vertebra (and possibly your back), your ribs, arms, calves, hands, wrists, neck, jaw or cheekbone, your upper bum (right below your waist), your hip bones, knees, tops of your feet, or in the face. Face slapping is an art in itself and must be done correctly to prevent possible neck injury. The head should be held steady by his free hand and not left to snap around upon the blow's impact. Avoid hitting any tendons, ligaments, or joints. You should never be hit in the area between the bottom of your rib cage and above the crack of your bum. There are not only bones there, but lots of soft organs. You should never be hit in the midsection.

Breasts and nipples, however, are a different matter. Many women like a little (or a lot!) of breast slapping, and they *are* soft and cushiony with no bones, tendons or ligaments that can be injured. He can hold your breast in his hand, and slap it downward, or slap it up from underneath. He can tie them up and slap them. Nipples can be pinched or pulled. Interesting things can be attached to them which can be used for torture and adornment. Whether you want to add this to your list is an entirely personal choice. Some women love this, but other women's breasts and nipples are much too sensitive.

The inner thigh was made popular as a new erogenous zone for beatings by *The Story of O,* but unless you are very well padded there, this may not be a good idea. I don't have any padding there at all, so I find it to be excruciatingly painful and unerotic to be hit there; it's actually a scene breaker for me. Also, there are lots of major tendons between the thighs and pelvic area that are close to the surface of the skin, and these should never be hit.

Temperature Play

Who among us has not sunk down gratefully into the embracing warmth of a hot bubble bath or Jacuzzi/hot tub when we are chilled to the bone? And who doesn't appreciate the comforting whir of the air conditioner when it's ninety degrees in the shade, with humidity to match? We use different things to regulate our body temperatures in the everyday world; in SM, we use other items of hot and cold to heighten our anticipation and increase our arousal. These products and items, when used on sensitive parts of the body, can command your full attention whenever they are applied to the skin, but everyone's skin is different and each person responds differently to stimuli.

Hot Stuff

If you are interested in experimenting with mentholatums such as Tiger Balm, Vicks Vapo-Rub, Mineral Ice, or Ben-Gay, please be aware that each of these products differ in intensity. Some people break out in rashes from them, and others have allergic reactions to the product itself or to the menthol in it. And for some people, nothing happens at all except for the desired sensation! If you are unsure about how your skin will react to such an application, test it on the inside of your elbow. After an hour has passed with no adverse reaction to the substance, proceed but still use caution. Keep observing the test skin because mentholatums are hard to remove once they have been applied, and an adverse reaction is under no obligation to appear in a hurry (and I can vouch for that!). Make sure that all residue from the mentholatum is washed off his hands if he is going to stroke your face, especially near the eyes. The strong scent alone is enough to make your eyes water.

You might be tempted into trying one of these items on your quim or rosebud opening (as I was), but some authorities think this practice to be ill-advised. They state that mentholatums upset the "natural balance" of the mucous membranes and mucosal tissues, which I find to be credible. However, players who have used mentholatums for years report no adverse affects, and I don't have any to report either. I have found the hot sensation of Tiger Balm on my nipples to be divine, but the product does feel hotter on these spots than when used on other areas of the outer skin. I'll leave those especially hot areas to your imagination. If you do get too hot, wash the product off with lots of cold running water and tons of soap, dish washing liquid, or shampoo. Witch hazel can be used to wash off mentholatums, and plain yogurt will help to cool down the hot spots, too.

Ice Dreams

Of course, cold is the opposite of hot, and cold can provide intense sensations all by itself or after another skin sensitizing treatment. An ice cube trailed gently over buttocks that are red hot from a spanking is a delicious treat for the squirming submissive. Use of the droplets falling from the ice cube to cool the hot spot which makes the submissive wiggle with anticipation and wonder where the next drop will fall are popular techniques, too. Wondering where and when the next icy drop will fall drives her wild and heightens her arousal. The two major problems with using ice are the fact that it melts (and you can slip and fall on an unseen puddle) and that it can cause frostbite. One "problem" is easy to deal with and the other is easy to prevent.

Keeping a towel handy to mop up any errant drips and drops caused by the melting ice will prevent anyone from slipping and falling on an unseen puddle. Simple as that, problem one is solved. Now for problem two: frostbite. Preventing frostbite under the extremely limited time you will be playing in is relatively easy.

If the ice cube sticks to your fingers, then run it under water until it doesn't. This will also melt away any sharp edges or protrusions on the ice cube which may cause unerotic pain when it is inserted into the opening of choice. And last, never leave the ice cube in one place long enough for the skin to become numb. If numbness occurs, immerse the area in warm, not hot, water. Numb skin cannot transmit signals that it is being burned.

With the proper safety measures, there is no reason not to enjoy all the erotic discomfort and sensual sensations that you can handle!

～ 14 ～

Sex Acts

Have you ever been loved so completely that the sound of his voice in your ear caused your body to shudder and explode with such intensity that only weeping could bring you full release? Have you ever been tasted until you believed you could only be satisfied by consuming the tongue that devoured you? This is the miracle of physical love, and it can be so powerful that it can convince lovers that there is no other life under the stars but theirs.

Sex is a merging of the soul and body of one person with another, and penetration can be a remarkably spiritual experience. But sex, of any sort, is not required in an SM scene unless you and your partner want it to be. Additionally, if sex is to be included, it can happen during a scene or after it, even before it, if that suits your fantasy. (One night, when we were already dressed for an SM party, my master bent me over the bed, pulled my dress up, and had a "quickie" on me before we went out—to keep me in the right frame of mind for later. I loved it!) Intercourse as part of SM sex comes with its own set of misconceptions, usually about "rules." There are no rules here except mutual consent; the only limits are your own needs and desires and those of your partner. And if anyone tries to tell you differently, say, "Rave on, sister!"

Many couples who play regularly at SM have kept a place in their love lives for vanilla sex. Even the most perverted of the Perverati like a little vanilla sex from time to time and fit it in to suit their tastes. Many couples also make a distinct separation between SM scenes and straight sex. Furthermore, as your tastes change and expand, and as you enact different sexual personae, the right time can change from one scene to another. As I pointed out above, the right time is whatever time you and your partner say it is.

Since information and instruction books on cock-to-quim sex abound, and many of them, like *The Joy of Sex,* are very good, I'm not going to go into the more common garden variety of bedroom games. If you are reading this, you are already playing in the dark garden and don't need me to explain the missionary position. What I do want to discuss before moving on to some wonderful sexual variations is an interesting phenomenon we ladies should learn more about.

Female Ejaculation

Since female ejaculation is not the norm for most women, it is often misunderstood by those who do experience it. Some women quite naturally expel large quantities of fluid from the vagina when they have an orgasm. Among these women, some will have an ejaculation every time they orgasm; in others, it happens occasionally or even frequently but not each time. To some it may happen only once or twice. But unless the woman has found and read what little there is on this topic, this poor soul may think she is pissing herself, or wetting the bed, and end up being embarrassed about her bodily functions. This is female ejaculation and I wanted to include it here because, obviously, there is some misunderstanding about it.

There is much we do not know about this phenomenon, but we do know that this fluid is not the same vaginal lubrication we secrete when we are aroused, nor is it urine. We also know that female ejaculation is more likely to occur because of, and during, vaginal penetration, although a few women ejaculate every time they come. Furthermore, ejaculation has no bearing whatsoever on the quality or quantity of the orgasm—some women ejaculate and others don't.

The first time I ejaculated, I didn't understand what had happened and neither did my partner. (I ejaculate infrequently.) He thought I had lost control of my bladder and wet the bed; I didn't know exactly what had happened, but I knew that this wasn't urine. But his reaction embarrassed me—he freaked out because of the way my body behaved during sex. Would he have liked it better if I had been dry as a bone? Wouldn't it have been better if he had just gotten a towel?

If you or your master can touch your G-spot, exerting pressure on it may cause you to ejaculate. This spot is on the roof of your quim, on the side closest to your stomach. In some women, this spot, which is like a tiny little sponge, can actually be felt with gentle fingertips as it lies buried in the vaginal wall. Even if you don't ejaculate, touching this spot with a rhythmic pressure is highly enjoyable, so teach your master where it is!

Oral Sex

What man doesn't go nuts for a good blow job? And what does it take to give one? There is no such thing as a "generic" blow job; the right amount of pressure varies greatly from man to man, as does the degree of sensitivity. Then, as each man has his preference or style, what turns him on may turn another off. Additionally, it is not easy to get used to a hard rod down your throat; it makes you feel like you are suffocating or are about to throw up. It makes your eyes tear and smears your makeup. If cock sucking is not currently one of your favorite things but rather an issue you compromise on (doing it occasionally to please him), all of this could make giving him a BJ (blow job) less than appealing. Why go through so much trouble for something that you can take or leave?

The profound intimacy I experienced during SM sex with my master cannot be compared with any other sexual experience I have had. When I became submissive to him, I found that my boundaries (not my standards) began to drop; that I looked with new, accepting eyes at things I had shunned or not thought of before, and found myself opening up to them in the deepest, most erotic ways. Some of you will sympathize when I say I hated giving oral sex, even in a vanilla setting. The man's hands on my head knotted my hair and messed it up; his cock down my throat made my sinuses back up and my eyes tear. To add insult to injury, my eye makeup ran into my eyes and stung them, then the mascara made black tracks down my face. This turned me off quickly: burning eyes, runny nose, and general dishevelment are not any of my erotic buttons. I didn't want to behold myself in this messy state, let alone allow him to see me; I was uncaring that I had gotten this way in giving him pleasure.

My master, however, had different ideas about oral sex, and how I looked before, during, and after it. When I first started to go down on him, I did it gently, getting used to him before doing the things that I liked best. As I nuzzled and lipped him, I began to notice that the skin on his cock was soft and slippery silky under my lips, like crushed velvet. It was quite delightful, really, the nicest cock skin I had ever been near. So I adjusted my neck, opened wide, and took in some more of him. Then, a little more, and yet a little more. It was then, with my nose so close to his groin and hair, that I noticed he smelled absolutely wonderful! I don't mean clean and soap-good *only*; yes, he smelled clean but it was more, and different, than that. He smelled like he was anointed with a delicious, intoxicating essence of himself. One of his loves is the forest, and the fruits of it, and somehow, this love was captured in his scent. It wasn't musky or musty; it was more like pines and winter berries, combined with his own essence and the delicious smell of sex.

Enjoying myself for the first time in, oh, maybe my whole life, I lifted up my head to take a better look at this organ-from-heaven that I was sucking. I was so glad I looked—it was beautiful! Truly beautiful. It was perfectly formed, long and thick, with a very nice generous nob-head with a large cum-slit; the nerve pulsed and throbbed up the front of his shaft as I handled him. His medium-size balls were high and tight, close to his body, and fitted perfectly into one of my large hands. "Oh, Master, your genitals are so handsome, you smell so good . . ." I trailed off, eager to occupy my mouth with better things than talking.

He allowed me to continue caressing him for several minutes before I felt his hands in my hair. "Oh, no," I thought, "here it comes." "It" was the part I hated: even a gentle thrusting caused a clogged nose, runny eyes, and smeared makeup. His grip tightened on my head and pushed me further down on his cock. When I tensed, he stopped. When I relaxed, his hands began their relentless pressure, "forcing" my head down on his shaft, making me take in more and more of his cock. He knew he wasn't really forcing me; he felt me relax my throat, then I began making these certain little noises that he knew meant "yes, I like this, keep going, more, more." (I *said* I was greedy.) Then he asked me if I was ready to take him "his way." I didn't really know, or care, which way his way was—I have my "word" (which in this case was actually a signal since my mouth was full!)—all I wanted was more of his delicious cock!

"Oh, yes, your way, Master, your way," I lifted my mouth from him long enough to gasp out the words. Both of his hands grasped my head and positioned it over his cock. "Just open your mouth," he said, his voice like hot butterscotch, as I started to tongue him. "I don't want you to suck or tongue me. This is for my pleasure, not yours. Now open your mouth, I want to pump your face." I shivered with fear and passion and anticipation as I obeyed him. I dropped my jaw and cushioned my lower teeth with my tongue. He began with rhythmic strokes, using them to open my mouth wider. When I relaxed under his "assault," he started to deep throat me. His engorged cock blocked my breathing, and in my struggle for air, snot exploded from my nose. I began to gag but he held my head in place, far down on his dick. I gagged again before he let me up.

I was gasping for air, snot was streaming over my lip, and tears were rolling from my eyes. I knew my mascara was in long black streaks down my face and my hair was a bird's nest. I felt wet and smeared and ugly and confused and asked to go to the bathroom to straighten up. Instead, he gathered me to his chest and held me in his arms. My eyes widened and my mouth fell open when he said, no, I didn't need the bathroom, I was beautiful like this, and the makeup streaks and tears and snot were like badges of love and devotion. Taking a tissue, he wiped the snot from my nose like I was a child too small to manage this task for herself. Smoothing down my up-ended hair, he said it was a crown of glory, and he would have me no other way. Tears of joy rolled down my cheeks as he bent to kiss my mouth, the mouth that had so recently held his delicious member in its warm, wet folds. His tongue parted my lips and he kissed me deeply, savoring the taste of himself in my mouth. Before that, my motto about oral sex was "Neither a giver nor receiver be." Now I look at oral sex in a different light, dark and sexy, and fantasize about the next time!

Head Tips

Beginners to the art of the BJ should have the use of their hands so they can wrap their fingers around the base of the shaft and stroke the part of his cock that doesn't fit in their mouth. A man's common complaint is that the woman doesn't apply anywhere near enough pressure when she grips his member, so grab a firm handful! When taking him into your mouth, it helps greatly to inhale as you take him. This will help you control your gag reflex. If he starts to pump, and you start to gag and heave, tell him to back off some and let you take him in at a slower pace, your own pace. Deep, rapid thrusts will make even an expert choke and heave, and should only be done to the submissive if, and when, she likes it.

If you want to acquire a little expertise in BJs, maybe you would like to practice on a dildo first. Find one that is very soft and flexible, and about the same size as him. And remember, a cock is much easier to suck than a dildo! Practice on the dildo when you are alone until you develop a "technique" based on his preferences, combined with what you are comfortable doing and what you do well. To extend your throat, let your head fall over the edge of the bed or arm of the sofa. Remember to inhale as you take him in. Cushioning your lower teeth with your tongue or lips is something he will appreciate. Try licking, and gently nibbling; use your lips and tongue on the big vein that runs along the underside of his shaft. Wrap your lips around the head and flick your tongue back and forth over it. Gently suck, or lick, the nerve nexus just below the nob. In addition to going straight up and down, try a corkscrew effect, or rhythmic strokes (shallow, shallow, deep, deep). If you weren't too good at this before, even the slightest improvement on your part will send his libido spinning!

Anal-Oral Sex

Before you blurt out "you want me to put my tongue where?" and turn up your nose at the mere thought of this practice, please read on. In the vanilla world, the act of anal-oral sex is called "rimming" or a "rim job"; in SM, we refer to it in general as part of "body worship," in the specific as "ass-worship." It can also be called "eating him out." As unglamorous and unromantic as these words sound, the act itself when done in love can play a very special and dual role in the SM relationship. As you can imagine and appreciate, ass-worship is not something you would be likely to do on a one-night stand. When an act like this is done between two caring partners, it can be an affirmation of their relationship, a tribute to the special trust between them, an act of devotion, or a physical manifestation of their love. Additionally, the submissive who enjoys a touch of humiliation will be thrilled when commanded to perform this service for her master.

Consider it this way: He has been playing with you, mastering you for three or four hours, touching you, hurting you, caressing you, depriving you, teasing you, and pleasing you. Over and over he has brought you to the brink of orgasm, many times he has let you come. He has been a master of control, over himself and over you. But he has not yet penetrated you—with anything! By now you are out of your mind with desire and your openings are aching to be filled, or perhaps you are flying, attached to the earth by your connection to him. You beg him in your slave's voice to enter you, please, go inside you, penetrate you; you are long past caring which of your openings he takes. You know what you must do before he grants your wish, you discussed it beforehand. But, he asks the question anyway, it is part of the plan, and your humiliation and exaltation. Your voice is small and soft and loaded with emotion as you say, "Yes, Master." He positions himself to receive you and you extend your tongue. When done in love and consent, an act that the world-at-large perceives as degradation becomes an elevation of the spirit and a communion of the body and soul.

Let me say that I think ass worship is more prevalent than research and studies show: Who tells everyone *all* their secrets? I don't—do you? But if you would like to experiment with ass worship, allow me to make a few suggestions. In many instances, a person's distaste for the anus stems from feelings that the area is unclean. Asking the master to wash, or washing him yourself, will help in that regard, but some would argue that to wash before would defeat the purpose. Others argue that it would be missing the point to wash. To wash or not to wash—this is something for the two of you to decide together; no one else's opinions counts.

Of course, if the receiver has an upset stomach or any other stomach problem, sitting on your face is a big and definite NO-NO. Another plus for the proponents of washing is that hepatitis A or B can be transmitted by anal-oral sex, and hepatitis is not a nice illness. It puts you off your food, saps your energy and strength, makes you turn funny colors, and totally obliterates your sex drive. It does not go away in a week, or even in two—it lasts a long time and takes a chunk out of your life. Washing is a good idea for this reason, and if a nice bath together appeals to you, in the next subhead there is a section called "Getting Closer." In it you will find a description of how to load one of the secret weapons in a woman's private emotional arsenal: a bubble bath. Adapt freely to accommodate two!

Anal Play

Hidden between the folds of the buttocks is what the Marquis de Sade lovingly described as the "rosebud opening," the orifice of preference among the devotees of the lonely prisoner of the Bastille. If taken literally rather than as a political statement, the works of the Marquis wax poetic about the joys of sodomy. But unlike the Sadians (followers of the Marquis de Sade), who idolize the pleasures of the rosebud opening and rear view of the naked body, many adults are alienated from their anus and the erotic pleasures to be had there. This could be caused by societal taboos, guilt or fear caused by religious beliefs, pervasive attitudes about the lack of cleanliness of the area, or general embarrassment about anyone fiddling around "back there." Additionally, many women are turned off to the pleasures of anal sex because of a previous painful experience. Perhaps they would like to experiment again, especially because anal play can be a very erotic and submissive act, but they feel they have no one they can trust to reeducate them to have a physically and emotionally positive and pleasurable anal experience.

Some of you may be feeling guilty or embarrassed by your desire to explore your potential for anal eroticism. For you, perhaps anal relaxation and pleasure cannot be attained without a fantasy of being sexually overpowered: taken by force or swept away, tied up, and then sodomized. These fantasies are not unusual in the SM setting; in fact, in SM these fantasies become even more powerful, more compelling. When speaking about sodomy, I often refer to it as one of my ultimate acts of submission and one that I enjoy greatly on both an emotional and physical level. Sex should only and always be pleasure oriented, and there is no reason why anal sex should be traumatic or painful. It should be a uniquely satisfying sexual experience and an intense form of intimacy—if you take the time necessary to educate yourself to these pleasures, that is.

Because of my own love of the joys of anal sex, I would like to help you become more at ease with this part of your erotic anatomy by sharing with you some of my secrets to a pleasurable anal experience. Since you are conducting your own erotic exploration, and what I am recommending is a whole routine, try to perform it when you have plenty of spare time and know you won't be disturbed.

Let's first discuss the way you think of your anus and what you call it. Calling your anus your ass hole is fine if that is a sexy, powerful, button-word for you. But if you refer to that orifice as your ass hole with all of the old and "dirty" connotations the word implies, stop calling it that and try thinking of it as your "rosebud opening," just as the Marquis did. Pink and shy, and delicate like a rose, this name should help you disassociate your anus from any previous unpleasant experience. (See The Pillow-Talk Thesaurus in the Appendix for other synonyms for "anus" that might appeal to you.)

Getting Closer

Now let's break out one of the secret weapons in a woman's arsenal and use it as part of our erotic exploration: a hot, foamy, fragrant bubble bath. Try turning off the bathroom lights and using some candles to illuminate the room with a soft, warm glow. Candlelight makes everyone look and feel sexier. Step into the tub, then relax your body and mind. When your limbs are loose and relaxed, concentrate on relaxing your rosebud. Focus on it, think of it relaxing and getting sweetly pink, and send it nice thoughts (I'm not kidding). Since the rosebud opening is very sensitive, it often reflects what is happening to the rest of your body: It is subject to stress, tension, anxiety, sadness, and poor diet. As you concentrate on relaxing it, promise your rosebud that you will *never* allow anyone to hurt it (and I'm not kidding on that one, either).

Pushing down as if you are having a bowel movement will aid you in relaxing. Then take ten deep breaths, focusing on your rosebud, and with each breath, concentrate on relaxing the opening further. Think of the times when you felt really, really good, in body and soul. Your rosebud opening played its part in that good feeling, too. When you are happy and relaxed, so is your rosebud. If you are having trouble focusing, try the relaxation mantra below or use it as a template for your own.

Relaxation Mantra

Make yourself comfortable . . . relax . . . sink into yourself, feet open, hands relaxed at your side. Close your eyes . . . and from this point on, do not speak. Block out unwanted noises and interruptions, make them white noise in your inner space. Don't resist the tide in your mind, don't resist the random thoughts that come up, but ride the waves of your thoughts in total relaxation.

Now, breathe deeply to aid relaxation . . . in through your nose and out through your mouth, ten breaths made audible in and out . . . one . . . two . . . three . . . four . . . five. . . . Take your time, fill your lungs then empty them completely . . . six . . . seven . . . eight . . . nine . . . ten. Now I want you to focus on your body, become aware of it, and repeat "relax, relax" as you focus on it. Feel the stress and tension drain away from you. Now, imagine your toes, feel their tension and concentrate on relaxing them. On to your feet, relax, relax, then move up to your legs and feel each muscle in your calves, and your thighs. Focus on dissolving your tension and sadness, free yourself of it, and let your legs open in relaxation.

Feel your spine, feel it relaxing, feel stress and tension melting away as you move up your body to your torso. Don't resist your body . . . let the thoughts flow in and flow out. Let go of your corporal body and breathe deeply, in and out, in and out Think of your lungs, filling and deflating as you breathe, think of your heart, hear it beating strongly in your chest, feel the blood rushing through your veins.

Now think of your genitals, think of them as a beautiful flower unfolding with the sun's caress. Locate a spot deep in your vagina, and relax around it,

let go of your pelvis and sink down in deep, warm relaxation. Now think of
a spot deep in your rosebud opening. So much stress and tension there, release
that stress now, remember to breathe deeply and regularly as you relax. Send
the stress from your rosebud, release that tension from your openings and keep
a relaxed awareness there.

Think of a time when you felt love, think of a time when you felt secure
and happy; think of the brush of a kiss, a warm, strong hug, the salt of a tear,
the sting of a lash. Recall the sounds and smells of love and sex, recall laughter
and smiles from your loved ones; recall of a moment of passion, the spasm of
orgasm, recall the heat of his body against yours and recall a time of great joy.

When you feel you are totally relaxed, begin to wash yourself slowly and
sensuously, luxuriating in the feel of the soap, bubbles, and cloth on
your skin. Lastly, wash your genitals, paying special attention to your
rosebud. Make each stroke as you wash a slow and caressing one; try a
long, paintbrush stroke then a soft, teasing, short one. Take as long
as you like, and don't rush but don't overdo it either. Then dry yourself as
slowly and sensuously as you washed yourself.

Next, I would like you to look, I mean really and open-mindedly
look, at your rosebud. If you do a "bikini trim" or shave completely, you
may already be familiar with the look of your opening. If not, let this
be the first time. You are exploring your sexuality, enhancing and expanding it with every page you read. As a submissive woman, you may
find anal play to be an extremely erotic act of submission, but before
you can release the pleasure and enjoy the passion of anal sex, you must
become familiar and comfortable with your anus, your ass hole, your
rosebud opening.

If this is the first time you are looking at how beautiful you are there,
you can assume one of several positions. You can try kneeling up with
your knees apart, and looking at yourself with a handheld mirror. Or,
you can lie on your back, knees up and open, and use the handheld mirror for visual exploration. Another comfortable and sexy position for
viewing is to lie on your side and reach your arm back with the mirror.
Bending at the waist and looking in the mirror works also, but this position is awkward and doesn't make me feel very sexy. Furthermore, some

women are turned off by the hair in this area. Everyone, and I do mean everyone, has hair there and if you really don't like it, at some time in the future you can carefully shave it off. Perhaps at the request of the master! (See chapter 16, The Body Made Beautiful.)

A Gentle Caress

Hopefully, you are still comfortable with your exploration and would like to continue. Perhaps now would be a good time to touch, to caress, your rosebud opening, either while you look in the mirror or just lie back on the bed. Feel the differences in the textures of the skin; feel the delicacy of the pleated folds that can expand and be stretched to transparency to accommodate a lover. Pay attention to what you are feeling and what the tip of your lightly questing finger is feeling. And be honest. If you are comfortable with the feelings, inside and out, very gently try inserting a finger with a smooth, short nail into your opening. Using lubrication will make entry more comfortable, physically and emotionally. But if you are not comfortable at any point, stop for now and try the routine another time.

If you are comfortable touching your rosebud and have gently inserted the chosen finger, focus on what the finger inside of you is feeling. Feel the latent tightness of your dual anal sphincters; try clenching and unclenching your muscles around your finger. (Those of you who have had children already know how to do "Kegels"; see Explanation of Terms.) Take a moment to appreciate the hot, silken feel of the skin in your rectum, so unlike the bumpy folds of your quim. Gently withdraw your finger and reinsert it with a little more confidence. You know now that this needn't hurt; indeed, you may have already experienced erotic pleasure from your initial exploration.

For many of you, looking at and touching your rosebud opening will be a completely new experience. For some, the initial experience will be liberating, and they may feel more intimate with their body, or on better terms with it. Some of you may have found the initial exploration to be intensely erotic; others may have disliked it immediately; and still others may experience a combination of the above. Any and all of these reactions are fine.

Out front and visible, the genitalia of a man requires a concerted effort on the part of the bearer to ignore. Ours are all tucked away, like a secret garden concealing blooms of unseen beauty, and ours require a concerted effort to *explore*. Many of you have already dealt with prohibitions concerning exploring your body and have overcome them. If you are one of these lucky women, then with your deeper awareness and self-knowledge, and a little acquired knowledge, you will be able to explore your rosebud opening with more ease.

Acquired Knowledge

Bottom or top, consenting to the nonconsensual or outright begging for the pleasure, your rosebud opening is a very delicate area, and certain precautions should be taken when playing there. If you still feel that a distaste for the anus can stem from feelings of uncleanliness, then make sure the area is clean. The bath in your relaxation routine will be more than adequate to make you feel clean and fresh, if you have the time. Refer to chapter 5, Cultivating Your New Sensuality, to refresh yourself on personal preparations. Perhaps you would like to begin, and end, your anal exploration with a nice bath or washing for both of you. If you would like to give yourself an enema, or instruct your lord how to give you one properly, please see chapter 15, Liquid Persuasions.

Because of the delicate nature of the tissue, certain procedures should always be used when engaging in anal play. The first and foremost of these is the generous use of the proper lubricant. Adult shops sell a large variety of lubricants, and most manufacturers will specify if their product is suitable for anal use. If they don't, the sales help in the better shops, like Condomania, can be a valuable resource in assisting you. If there are no adult shops nearby that you would feel comfortable visiting, any local drugstore will sell "Old Reliable," KY Jelly. It is important to remember that all water-based lubricants, exactly those suitable for use with condoms and latex, dry out quickly and need *frequent* replenishing. Everything that is to come in contact with or is to be put inside of the opening should be very well lubricated, and often. Avoid any anal lubricant that contains a numbing agent as it will mask pain. Anal play should not be an overly painful experience but an exploration of sensation. (Besides, that stuff tastes terrible if it gets anywhere else.)

A little anatomy knowledge will also help guide you through a pleasurable and safe rosebud encounter. When you explored your opening earlier, you would have felt the resistance of the external and internal sphincter muscles. These are the muscles you need to learn how to loosen and relax for pleasurable anal play. Another important detail of the anatomy of the rectum is that the rectum is a tube but not a straight one, making the angle of entry of prime consideration. Additionally, because all people are different, the angle of entry varies from person to person. Although the anus, or anal opening, is rich in nerve endings, there are not many nerve endings *inside* the rectum. The tissue there is thin and delicate and tears easily. Inside, the lower rectum tilts forward toward the navel, then back again toward the tailbone. Driving anything into the rectum on a forward angle rather than a straight one is bound to be painful, and could tear or damage sensitive tissue.

I am assuming that you are playing with your regular partner, so transmission of sexual transmitted diseases (STDs) is not an issue. Even so, since much bacteria lives in the anus, nothing should ever be taken from the anus and inserted into the vagina or mouth. If any burning sensation occurs in the rectal tissues or real bleeding (not a little pink froth) becomes evident, then all anal play must stop. And, until the two of you are totally comfortable playing here, both of you might be more mentally comfortable using gloves. Surgical gloves, or fetish gloves made of latex or of leather, are suitable for this play. Be sure to use a water-based lubricant if you are using surgical or latex fetish gloves to preserve the integrity of the rubber. Petroleum jelly and oils are not good for use with latex whether it be a condom or a glove. If cuts or abrasions are on the hand, the use of gloves is a must even with your regular partner. The donning of the gloves, either variety, can be worked into the scenario as a protective, humiliating, or other emotional factor.

Inviting Him In

Having made friends with your rosebud opening, having given it a name more evocative of the pleasures that lie there, after having had a long, loving look at the hidden beauty of your anus, and after having acquired some techniques and knowledge that have given you confidence, perhaps you are ready to have your lover join you in your exploration and experience. If he has approached you before about anal sex and earlier attempts have failed, it may be his technique, or lack thereof, or an inability to relax on your part. Practice the techniques we spoke of earlier if you feel the shortcoming is yours. In chapter 11, Objects of Beauty and Usefulness, there is a breathing exercise that should help you to relax and stay relaxed. Remember, deep and regular breathing is a secret ingredient of SM. If you feel his technique needs improving, you can help him by teaching him how you like to be touched. (For specific details and exercises to assist you in further exploration on your own for the mutual benefit of both, I would recommend *Anal Pleasure and Health,* by Jack Morin, Ph.D.)

The first thing you want to do is get into a position that is comfortable for both of you. Ask your master to lubricate his gloves and then to swipe some of the lubrication on your opening in a wide, paintbrush stroke, just the barest whisper of a caress. "Beg" him to touch you gently because your opening will tense in fear of anticipated pain. Remember your promise to your rosebud to never let it be hurt again, and concentrate on relaxing. Since the opening to the anus is rich in nerve endings, the slowest and lightest of caresses can create an enormous amount of pleasure.

Suggest to your master that he stroke your rosebud gently for a couple of minutes to give you time to adjust to "something" being there. The master should caress you until he feels you relax, or until you give a signal that you are ready for him, then he should try inserting his finger into you. The opening is the most sensitive part of your anal anatomy and entry should be done slowly and gently. Two things happen when something is inserted into the anus: the feeling of needing to move one's bowels and the tensing of the pubo-rectal sling. The pubo-rectal sling is the muscle that is about 75 percent responsible for continence and gas control, and when it tenses, insertion becomes more difficult. After you feel your anal sphincters relax, concentrate on relaxing the pubo-rectal sling. If your muscles are still too tight, he can keep his finger there until you relax, or with a little precoaching from you, he can coach you into compliance.

He can remind you to bear down, as if you were having a bowel movement. This will slacken the muscles some. If you are very focused, the master could talk you through ten deep breaths, directing you to push out and down each time you exhale. As you exhale, your anal muscles will relax, and your lord's finger will move into you. He should allow you to moan, even scream, if you feel the need because either one will keep your breathing regular and release some of the energy building up in you. Screaming will depend upon how soundproof your walls are and the tolerance of your neighbors. A gag will muffle the screams but still allow the release of some sound, as well as pent-up energy.

Until you, even in your role as submissive, are entirely comfortable with his technique, *take my advice,* leave the master-slave play out of it! Play the scenario in your head, talk about it out loud like we discussed above to egg him on, but do not allow him to "force" the issue. Anal sex and the subsequent thrill of breaking taboos, being ultimately submissive, or whatever, is extremely exciting but a slow, gentle entry is important, especially in the beginning. The best way to guarantee a gentle entry is to control it yourself. You can do this by taking him into you rather that letting him enter.

After he has loosened you to your satisfaction with his fingers, both of you should lie on your left sides like spoons, with you, obviously, in front of him. Remember we said that the angle of entry into the rectum is different for everyone? Keeping this is mind, position yourself at an angle to his body that lines up with your particular angle of entry, and take his cock in your hand to guide him in and stop him from pushing. (If seen from above, your joined bodies should look like the letter, K.) Lubricate him and your rosebud well, position yourself over him, spread your cheeks, and slowly, gently, at your own pace, work yourself down onto his cock. Push down as you take him in, do it slowly, and take a little more of him inside of you with each gentle downward stroke. Remember to breathe, to push down, and take as many pauses as you need. Withdrawing his cock slightly and reinserting it may help you to get accustomed to that full feeling. Don't worry about him; if you have gotten this far, he will be out of his mind with lust and rock hard, hoping it takes you all night!

If you feel resistance, it may be because you are unused to having a large, throbbing cock, or even a finger, in your ass, or it may be because the skin of your anus has become pulled taut. This could be from lack of lubrication, or because the tube of the rectum needs to be "pulled down." To pull the tube down, all you need do is to reach back, and simultaneously spread your cheeks with your hands and push your muscles down and out, as if you are trying to expel him. Do this a few times until his cock rests comfortably inside you. As your muscles loosen, and his head clears the internal sphincter, the two of you will roll over onto your combined bellies with him still inside of you and controlling the roll. This sounds harder than it is, and you have probably done this very action quite naturally during vanilla or quim sex. He should hug you to him, and on your signal, the two of you should roll as one to be face down on the bed. As he gently rolls you over, he should (just as gently) be pushing his cock into you. By the time both of you are face down, he should have another inch or two in you. If you did it correctly, the pain factor should have been very low (and quite enjoyable).

Although I have used this style of entry countless times, I am unsure about how it works. I think that as the two of you roll over, the action of him rolling you requires little or no effort on your part so you relax, knowing what he is going to do next. As you roll, the puborectal sling automatically relaxes, and that muscle is the next obstacle in the way of anal pleasure. Or perhaps rolling uses a different set of muscles and doesn't allow one to be tense anally. In any case, this method has worked for me most times and given me many highly pleasurable experiences.

Perfecting Positions

Among the many positions that the submissive may assume for anal play, some are more comfortable than others and provide easy entry; others can be unpleasantly painful unless you have been adequately stretched and lubricated. If anal entry is the pleasure you seek, let me suggest some other positions that I have found comfortable and exciting.

On your belly is a comfortable position, and because no muscles are being used to support your weight, performing your relaxation-breathing exercises will be easier. Try to relax every part of your body, even your fingers and toes. Let all tension flow out of you into space and leave you feeling free, floating. When you feel him brush your opening, relax, push down, and exhale as he enters you. When I am on my belly, I find it more comfortable to have a pillow or his arms elevating my hips. Also, when my hips are elevated, I have found that keeping my legs more closed than open makes entry less painful. Please remember that no matter how slowly and gently the anus is entered, a certain amount of pain will always be associated with anal sex. You can learn, as I have, to metamorphose this pain into one of the most exquisitely pleasurable sensations you have ever experienced.

Another comfortable entry position after you have been loosened is "doggie style," and the shoulder-to-floor variations thereof. You hardly need me to explain this position or its variants as I am sure you have been doing them for years now in the forward opening.

For those who wish to experience anal sex in a truly submissive position with a deliciously high but bearable amount of pain, *after* you have been comfortably stretched and loosened, try this position with your master. Pile several pillows up to make a wedge under your hips, so many pillows that when you kneel forward over them, your knees no longer touch the floor or the bed. Your legs should hardly be supporting your weight at all; your upper body, tilting forward comfortably over all those pillows will be supporting you. Spread your legs as wide as you can and relax *forward*. Then begin taking your ten deep breaths, relaxing your entire body as you melt into the pillows. Your master should position himself between your spread thighs with his cock pressed up against your rosebud opening. Now put your hands behind your back. Your master should grasp one of your wrists in each of his hands, and slowly, very slowly, pull your shoulders and upper body off the bed (or floor) by the wrists. As he pulls you up, you will involuntarily bear down, and your cheeks will spread. He should push into you very gently, in time with your exhales, as he pulls you back onto his cock. As your sphincter muscle relaxes and expands, he will be able to increase the pace and depth of his thrust. Make sure you (or your master) keeps your opening and passage well lubricated for maximum comfort and pleasure.

Many men think that placing the woman on her back is exciting— and it is!—but I find this position to be very uncomfortable unless he has taken me in one or more of the other positions first. The rosebud opening is stretched taut in this position and that makes entry unnecessarily painful. Later on, though, it is very exciting to look into his eyes and see his handsome face above you. Then, when you let your eyes rove to the spot where his body merges with yours, you can watch him enter you. The visual manifestation of the gift of submission, when added to the physical and emotional sensation, is very powerful and can be quite spiritual. Sometimes, when we do this, I think he is looking into my secret soul.

∽ 15 ∽

Liquid Persuasions

There is a long history of human interest in water sports, and, of course, these practices find fertile soil in the dark garden of SM. Some SMers find water sports to be advanced play, but water sports can be played on different levels, from light to heavy, just like other SM games. Many are quite casual about water sports on its lightest level, the golden shower. After all, anyone can pee, so lots of practice with the equipment is hardly necessary! But there are a few health issues I would like you to be aware of before you partake of the waters.

I am assuming you are playing with your regular partner, so some of the health concerns brought up here may not apply to you, but they are good to know anyway. HIV is not transmitted by drinking urine because the virus becomes too fragmented by the urine's acidity. However, it is possible to transmit hepatitis, and various other infections, through the golden nectar, but I hope you would know if your regular partner has hepatitis and any other problem. Don't brush or floss your teeth for several hours before you drink because it will open up little cuts in your gums. Don't eat broccoli, asparagus, brussels sprouts, or cabbage and try to stay away from coffee because these things will make the urine especially "pungent," as will tablet doses of vitamin-B and some replacement female hormones. If you plan on taking more than a little sip, drink plenty of water afterward to flush any excess urea out of your system, and any lingering taste out of your mouth.

The Golden Stream

Few of us think about how often we casually use the word "piss": I think I'll have a piss, this beer is as warm as piss or tastes like piss, I'm pissed off, I'm pissed. Now try to imagine what your reaction would be if your master wanted to piss on you, and I mean that literally. Would you still be so cavalier? But remember this is SM—Sex Magick—which also can mean "Smoke and Mirrors"—and things are not as they seem.

Before you flatly turn down this request, consider this: When you water a flowering plant, do you water the roots or drench the flower? You water the roots, of course. Compare yourself to this flower, turn yourself into the flower, a flower from your very own dark garden. Think of a dry, hot day—one of many dry, hot days unrelieved by rain. The sun beats mercilessly on your petals. Think of how delightful it would feel to experience the warmth of a summer shower flowing down your parched stem, dripping and sparkling on your leaves, and soaking into the dry soil at your feet. You are starting to wither when a shadow falls across your face. It is the gardener, come with his watering hose, to save you from the baking sun.

Carefully, he waters you from the waist (or neck or breasts) down. The water from his hose is warm and fragrant, and cascades down your skin, leaving in its wake waterfalls and rivulets of its own design. You needn't worry about him "missing." His hose is designed to be aimed at something, not spray the area willy-nilly. As for what some might perceive as the mess this practice involves, all you need do is use the bath tub.

Let It Flow

Many times a mainly vanilla lover and I have playfully piddled on each other when we showered together. This is the most common, and least threatening, way playful perverts experiment with golden showers. With all of the other water action happening in there, the odor of the urine becomes less strong, and the golden stream becomes diluted, then indistinguishable, in the relentless flow from the showerhead. And of course, the shower washes you clean when you are through. I never knew how erotic the act itself could be even without the security and guaranteed cleanliness of the shower; I thought of a golden shower as

fun and cute and harmless, although not particularly sexy. Until my first
SM golden shower scene.

One night, during a play scene that lasted until the next day, my
master brought me into the bathroom with him. This itself was not unusual: he often gathered up my hair and used it as a leash to "walk" me
into the bathroom on all fours, and keep him company while he emptied his bladder. His usual routine was to have me lift the cover and seat
for him, then with his free hand, he used my hair-leash to keep my head
close to his knee (and the bowl) while he peed. In other words, I was
plastered to his right leg, my face no more than six inches from his
stream and the bowl. But this night was different.

He brought me in there using my hair as the leash, but then he ordered me to sit on the far side of the tub with my back leaning up
against the wall. He had me place my feet on the opposite rim of the
tub and open my legs wide. When I was positioned to his satisfaction,
he stood between my feet, unzipped, and whipped out his lovely manhood. I was leery but I trusted him—he would stop if I wanted him to.
But when he let his stream flow, the most incredible thing happened! As
soon as the first rush hit my breasts and streamed down my belly, I got
so turned on I began touching myself and playing with myself as he
peed on me! It was so hot, so fragrant, so fresh from the fountain—it
felt divine. I never expected his ambrosia to be so sexy, to make me feel
like this; as his stream ran down between my spread legs and soaked
my fingers and quim, I came! He peed some more, and I came again
and again and again. Not one drop splashed my face, or wet my hair—
it was strictly from the breasts down. The sensation of his warm, fragrant urine washing down over me was unexpectedly and absolutely
delightful and I loved it.

Later that night, I told him that no pleasure, no joy, no figment of
my imagination could ever compare or compete with the happiness I
felt when I was able to give myself to him with such freedom. I was
thrilled to think that I could do almost anything with him, that the sky
was my limit, and there was no restriction in the manner in which I
could search for pleasure with him. He was my lord and master, the
very first I ever abandoned myself to, and as such he will always hold
a special place in my heart.

The Golden Nectar

The origins of any fetish or SM technique are greatly interesting to me, but, as you can imagine, much of what any SM author writes about is largely gathered from her own experiences, anecdotal evidence collected from colleagues, and relatively few scientific studies. Not much money is spent on researching the origins of fetish so imaginative types (like you and me) are free to spend a little time thinking up how a particular thing or action came to be a fetish. Drinking the golden nectar had me puzzled. How did this practice start and who started it?

Then one night, when I was watching *Rob Roy* for the tenth or eleventh time, a vignette from the movie presented a theory. In the vignette, after a night of heavy drinking, the Englishman, Archibald Cunningham, and a castle serving wench had just been rudely awakened by the Scottish factor, Killarn. As Killarn proposes his shady deal to Archie, Archie relieves himself into a chamberpot. When Archie finishes up, Killarn volunteers to remove the full, steaming pot from the room. As such a menial service is well below a man employed by the lord as the modern day equivalent of an "agent-accountant," Archie is obviously surprised by the offer. Then Killarn remarks something like, "This is almost pure spirits. There's many a Scotsman that would be grateful for it on a cold morning like this!"

Did people back then drink morning-after-a-big-one urine to jump start their engines like we use espresso and cappuccino today? It seems to me that no matter how much distilled liquor that urine contained, it still would have tasted more like piss than anything else. Did they eventually grow to like the taste of urine, from pleasant old associations, even if there was little or no recycled booze in it? Is that how the drinkers of the nectar came to be?

Whether you include drinking the master's nectar is up to you. I personally feel that it is unsanitary to drink anyone's urine excepting your own *but* I think taking a small sip once in a while is probably all right. One night my master and I each filled a little cup with our stream, then wrapping arms like a new bride and groom drinking a toast to each other, we sipped of each other's nectar. Just a small sip to taste the essence of each other, to commune with each other in a new and exciting way, to further cement and establish our relationship and commitment to each other.

Enemas

Who, you may ask, in their right mind would, *could,* find the thought of an enema erotic? It may surprise you to find out that there are tens of thousands who love enemas but are uncomfortable with coming clean about it. And it is not hard to understand their reticence on the subject. The idea of someone invading your anus with a nozzle that is attached to a hose that is hooked up to a bag of water about to be emptied into your body by way of your rosebud opening is not, for the vast majority, an erotic thought.

For thousands of years, people have used enemas as a means of purging, or a way to commune with their gods, or just for erotic pleasure. There is archeological proof that the ancient Egyptians purged using nozzles carved to liken the beaks of the sacred ibis. In Central and South America, ancient burial sites revealed enema bags made of animal bladders which archeologists believed were used by the priests to introduce trance-inducing drugs into their bodies through the anal canal. The ancient Greeks purged; Chaucer, who wrote *The Canterbury Tales,* knew of purges; so did the court of Louis XIV. Daily, many people administer or receive enemas without the eroticism of it entering their minds. Yet an enema can play a special role in the SM relationship.

To the submissive, an enema is a humbling affair, leaving no doubt as to who is in control. The SM enema scene exemplifies the dom's power in no uncertain terms. For some into enema play, role-playing of doctor-patient or older relative–child is involved; others simply prefer to remain the master and slave. In the master-slave scene, the submissive could be "forced" to accept the enema as punishment, discipline, humiliation, or as preparation for anal play. In all these scenarios, the dom's power is explicit.

Consider the scene: The slave is nude while the master remains dressed; the bathroom has become the play-space, and the master might opt to keep the bathroom brightly lit to add a little more humiliation to the scene. The naked sub can be made to lie in the bathtub, sit over the end of the tub, or made to assume one or two humiliating positions on the floor. She can be made to bend at the waist and grip the side of the tub, or lie on her left side with her knees slightly drawn toward her chest. If she is made to kneel with her shoulders on the floor and her hips in the air, her quim and rosebud are fully exposed to the master and are available for his pleasure and amusement. The slave presents her bottom to her master. He fills her with warm tap water or an enema solution, and then often inserts a butt plug so that she may not relieve herself without his permission. Forced retention is a turn-on and the plug adds to that full feeling. Then, either the master will order the slave to unplug herself, or the master may do it for her.

In an SM scenario, this is an emotionally charged situation. Not even your bowels are yours to control! The lord may choose not to leave the bathroom while you expel the water; this can be deeply humiliating and, for some, a source of sexual excitement. It also deeply impresses upon the submissive her helplessness and enforces the lord's power over her. The master controls what goes in and when it comes out. This invasion of privacy can be deliciously humiliating, and the calm, floating feeling one experiences after an enema often makes her more submissive.

Giving an enema isn't difficult, but there are some things you should know before you start. As with all things that will be inserted into the rectum, the nozzle should be well lubricated. A gentle stroking motion not only is exciting but accustoms you to the feeling of having "something" in there. It's best to use warm water, never hot or cold. If your tap water is unsuitable for drinking, it is also unsuitable for an enema. Warm distilled water can and should be used in this case. Some people experiment with wine or liquor enemas, but I don't believe this practice to be safe. Absorption through the anal passage is very quick: Some people are allergic to the sulfides in wine and alcohol, others have very low tolerances. If you must experiment with different fluids, try putting a little salt in the water. It aids in retention and using just a little (for effect) is virtually harmless unless you have a sodium problem.

The bag should be about two feet above your rosebud so that the flow in is gentle. Clear the hose of *all* air by making sure the water flows freely from the well-lubricated nozzle before it is inserted; excess air should never be forced into the bowels. The standard red enema bags sold in the United States hold two quarts; unless you are doing a course of high colonics, you don't need that much. Half a bag will do just fine. One of you will need to hold the nozzle or hose in place as muscle contractions will make it slip out. The master controls the flow of water into you—never full force—by pinching the hose with his fingers or using the clip to control it. You may need for him to pause now and then so you can absorb his gift to you. If you start to cramp or leak, he is giving it to you too fast. The master should be ready to stop the flow as soon as you say pause—there is no negotiating on this one, your word is law! When the bag is nearly empty, the hose should be clamped off immediately to stop air from being forced inside.

After a small enema, allow at least one half hour to elapse before you begin playing. This grace period will be sufficient for you to release any errant drops left behind.

～ 16 ～

The Body Made Beautiful

Long before recorded history and our own discoveries in the dark garden, body modification was practiced by ancient peoples around the world. Archeological records and findings demonstrate many varieties of body modification; piercing (of which ear piercing was the most common), tattooing, altering the shape of the head, foot binding, ritual scarification, and waist constriction were the most prevalent. Today, rhinoplasty (a nose job), breast augmentation, liposuction, and body building have replaced the flattened heads and bound feet of years gone by. Piercing, tattooing, and waist constriction are still with us and are three forms of body modification that have been embraced by SM. Before we get to my personal favorite of the three, corsetting or waist constriction, I would like to talk some about the body-spirit aspects of piercing and tattooing.

Erotic Piercings

Piercing of an erogenous zone has become very popular lately with SMers, tops and bottoms. In SM, a ring through the flesh denotes erotic servitude and is a unique way to combine the aesthetic with the sensual. For the top, being allowed to pierce the submissive is a powerful and heady experience, an enforcement of the top's control over the bottom. For the submissive, it is a more emotionally charged experience. The act of being pierced involves some degree of pain and hence may represent a challenge to the bottom. During the piercing, the sub may experience an adrenaline high in which the mind focuses completely on the body. Piercing has been compared with a rite of passage, a return to ritual in a society decidedly lacking in ceremony. The process may be a symbol of spiritual transformation and the experience, emotionally intoxicating. The moment of being pierced is a deeply personal and spiritual time for the sub, and some piercers also have reported being deeply moved by the piercing.

Piercings below the waist usually are done to enhance the sexual pleasure of the pierced one and her partner. This radically erotic alteration to the sub's body may only be visible to the sub's intimate partners, but the physical and emotional are everlasting. A piercing may just be for fun for some, but for many, the meaning is much deeper. The erotic piercing could signify the end of one way of life and the advent of another. It could be an act of devotion or a spiritual act. To her, her piercing is a visible sign of her ownership by a dominant. Romantic doms into ritual have designed ceremonies to celebrate the piercing of the sub, enhancing her feelings of value to the master and heightening her arousal. Physically, clitoral piercings may stimulate the woman when she walks or moves; emotionally, this is constantly reminding her of her sensual submission and her master. During a scene, the ring through the clitoral hood may be used with a leash or chain to control or restrain her actions. Nipple piercings are popular, too, and increase sensitivity during breast play. Some have reported that their pierced nipples have remained permanently erect!

In general, body parts that protrude, like the nipples, the labia, and the clitoral hood, are more easily pierced and heal faster than, for example, a clitoral piercing does. Also, I would imagine the clitoral piercing to be the most painful because of the large number of nerve endings there. The clitoral piercing can result in extremely heightened sensitivity for those who enjoy very intense stimulation and the deliciously delightful embarrassment of being intimately "handled" by the piercer.

Tattooing

Tattoos have been with us for at least five thousand years and have been alternately embraced and outlawed by peoples of the world. The fully preserved body of a man, who was frozen in ice in the high Alps three

thousand years ago, was found to have what appeared to be ritual tattoos. Egyptian tomb paintings depict the Brides of the Dead as having
ritualistic tattoos on their arms, legs, and bodies. The Romans, however,
frowned upon tattoos, deeming them to be a desecration of the purity
of the human form. The Roman legions must have been stunned when
confronted by the fearless Britons, their faces covered in blue tattoos!
When the seventeenth-century Japanese outlawed fancy or decorated
garments for all but the upper class, the middle and lower classes re-
belled by decorating their bodies with tattoos.

Reasons for tattooing are as varied as the individuals who sport them.
In *Modern Primitives,* no less than twelve reasons are listed, ranging from
the obvious to the arcane. Although I don't expect any of us to get tattooed to provide better camouflage when we are hunting naked, to acquire fertility, to frighten our enemies on the battlefield, or to make money
as a circus sideshow, these have numbered among the reasons others before us have indulged in tattooing. Other reasons cultures have used tattoos are to secure a place in heaven, ensure an easy passage through
difficult phases of life, ancestor worship, or to prevent disease and injury.
The prevalent reasons to tattoo in our time is to express visually the individual's inner self, represent an event in one's life, symbolize a person's
philosophy, or identify with a group. A tattoo is both art and a personal
statement, and can impart to the wearer an almost mystical power. The
images conveyed by the tattoo are a part of your definition of self.

Some elements of tattooing are highly erotic for those with SM interests. Doms find watching the submissive being tattooed to be erotic:
the use of needles, the discomfort (like an intense scratching), and the
energy level involved. A tattoo can be taken as a sign of willingness to
raise ourselves to the next level of passion. It can help to reinforce the
submissive's vision and spirit, and bespeak of an intensity and lack of
fear. Erotic tattooing is usually done on a part of the body not visible to
the casual observer. The submissive is often nude, or partially nude,
while beautiful or meaningful images are being drawn on her body. For
the submissive, a tattoo, like a piercing, is a significant symbol of ownership. Enduring the mild pain caused by tattooing can be an integral
part of her statement of devotion to the dom. And, as with a piercing,
the nudity required may invoke feelings of erotic humiliation.

Piercing and tattooing are the most radical of the three forms of body modification discussed here and should be done by a professional. Additionally, proper after care of a piercing or tattooing is absolutely necessary to prevent infection. Once the piercing, which is a wound, has healed, manipulation of the jewelry becomes an important aspect of erotic SM play.

Corsetting

I was in high school the first time I saw *Gone With the Wind*. My girlfriend and I went through a whole box of tissues and disturbed the entire theater with our noisy sniffling. Two things fascinated me about the movie: the wickedly dashing Rhett Butler and Scarlett's tiny corseted waist. Then, as now, I am a hopeful romantic and my schoolgirl fascination with Rhett Butler was easy to understand. Although my girlfriends and I were into sexy lingerie (chipping in to buy the birthday girl a new baby doll nightie), to them, my fascination with the corseted waist was less understandable. What I didn't know then was that corsetting for beauty, eroticism, or punishment had a long history for women and men.

The short version of it goes something like this. It seems that those ancient wonders (and terrors) of the sea, the Minoans of Crete (of the Labyrinth and Bull Dance fame) favored the wasp-waisted look. Both men and women wore corsets. The women's version enhanced the bust, which was often left bare in polite society. Corsets were popular in the sixteenth and seventeenth centuries, and again in the early nineteenth century. Corset training was popular at that time, as was corset punishment. Although tight lacing was warned against in Victorian times as causing damage to the internal organs and miscarriages, it was practiced anyway. Tight lacing was a means of controlling the wearer; unable to breathe deeply, move quickly, run, or eat a great deal, the woman was subject to the "vapors" from her tight-laced corset. Well, what do you expect when the ideal measurement for your waist was exactly the same as that of your neck?

In the dark garden, SMers indulge in corsetting for two main reasons: bondage and body modification. The corseted submissive, in

her high-heeled shoes and sheer black hose, is undeniably sexy. The
newly submissive woman is probably more interested in corsetting as
a form of love bondage first and then perhaps light body modification later on.

Luxurious Captivity

Many women who collect lingerie may have something called a
corselet among their lacy things. I still have the first one I purchased,
right next to my corsets. I think of a corselet as corset-in-training. I remember how sexy I felt the first time I wore it. Then I got the real thing
and I was hooked. A real corset can be ordered from a corset maker, a
fetish store, or catalog. There are many custom makers of corsets here
and in England. Now that I understand the fascination of the corset
more fully, I have three in graduated sizes.

Corsetting has been a part of SM erotica for years as a garment of
power for the top, and as a garment of voluntary surrender for the bottom. Corsetting that is used as a bondage technique is an infliction of
control on the submissive's body, shape, and mental outlook. Wearing a
corset creates a feeling of luxurious captivity while the constant restriction and pressure never lets the wearer forget her sexuality. This restraint
has been imposed upon her with her permission and her cooperation;
the corset wearer must actively assist in her own restraint. As a method
of control, corsetting lends itself very easily to SM.

Many dominants and submissives wear corsets; for me, my corsets
are the most sexy submissive garments I have. Although I do wear a
corset when I am alone, I prefer to wear one when I am with my master. Many other couples indulge in corset training because it can become
a shared erotic experience. Why do they do it? Because couples find it
sexy. It is something you can do together even if you are not going for
corset training. Corsetting can be a facet of love bondage for the submissive because she is not immobilized by the corset. Her movements
are restricted, so she must learn a new gracefulness. She has to adjust
the way she breathes because deep breathing is no longer possible; the
way she walks must change too because the waist is constricted; running is impossible and food must be taken in sparingly. These things

add to the overall sexy helplessness that the corsetted figure conjures up for the male. In the case of a corset dress, the wearer must literally be carried up and down the stairs because she is unable to move her knees enough to negotiate the steps on her own!

When I am alone and decide to get laced in, I do it because corsetting feels like I am giving myself a great big hug. I have a long corset that covers me from the top of my breasts to the top of my mons Venus. It is red satin with black lace over it and black satin trim with six spidery garters. I have especially long black silk stockings that I wear with it, one pair with seams and one pair without. Although I usually feel feminine, wearing a corset with the silk stockings and my stiletto pumps makes me feel unusually feminine. I love the way I look in my Victorian regalia. My nipped waist thrills me, my flattened belly delights me, my butt plumping so perkily out the bottom makes me giggle, and my cleavage sends me to the moon. And my name isn't even Alice!

As I settled into "breaking in" my first corset, I had to adjust my actions and positions to accommodate the corset. If I sat up for too long, my face and upper body became very pale. I assumed this was because blood flowed easily down past the restriction but getting back up above it was another matter. As a result, every hour or so I would have to recline with my feet above my head for a few minutes to get things flowing again. Even when asleep in the corset, I rolled around considerably more than usual, or so I was told by a reliable eyewitness or innocent bystander if you prefer, since his sleep seemed to have suffered while mine (in spite of the rolling) was affected very little.

Then I began to see lovely little changes in my body. My posture improved and my back hurt less. It was easier to sit and stand up straight than it was to slouch. Not a bad thing for a person who always wanted to be taller! I began to develop "lats"—the abdominal muscles running from under your breasts to your hips. That was as good as being, or at least feeling, taller! That was what happened with my first corset, a longline, size 24 waist. Then I bought two shorter corsets, both starting at midnipple and ending midhip. I altered one, the plain one, to start under my breasts and hold them up either with or without a bra. I left the lace one as it was. Both of these corsets are twenty-two inches in the waist, and I am looking forward to my days in a twenty incher!

Laced by the Lord

Knowing my lord had an interest in corsets, I took the small black satin corset with me on one of my trips to England. His eyes lit up when I took it out of the suitcase along with the hose and stilettos. Later on that night, he ordered me to put on the corset. He watched me intently as I undressed to the skin. His hot green eyes on my slender body drove me wild. Naked and kneeling at his feet, I worked the laces open with trembling fingers. Hurriedly, I wrapped the corset around my waist and reached around back and began to pull the laces tight in as organized a manner as I could considering I couldn't see a damn thing. "Turn around, Claudia, I'll help you with that," my master said. I liked what I heard in his hot butterscotch voice, and the butterflies started in my stomach. I knelt between his open knees and presented him with my back.

He fiddled with the lacings—it felt like he was straightening them out from my frenetic fumbling—and a moment after that, the most delicious sensation overwhelmed me. With his massive, strong hands, he laced the corset fully closed in one long coordinated pull! As he slowly pulled it closed, I worked my torso this way and that, settling my organs and rib cage as comfortably as I could underneath the steel stays and satin. And that wasn't all that happened! I had enjoyed wearing my corset alone but having him lace me into it sent me into sub-space immediately. It was as if he had, in one pull, put me in bondage (I love bondage), not with ropes or chains but beautiful satin and lace, exquisite, expensive, extreme. My breathing became shallower and not just because of the corset. I felt the familiar low ache in my belly and the subsequent wetness between my thighs. Taking one lace in each hand, he looped the excess string around my waist and pulled again, cinching me in another half inch before tying a pretty bow. Then he spun me around and ran his hands all over my corsetted figure.

That was when I wished for a smaller corset to bring to him. I imagined him tightening it for me over the course of the evening until what was twenty-two inches was now twenty. I dreamed of the attitudes of submission I would have to assume to assist in my own voluptuous bondage and began fantasizing of a new corset regiment in my head.

First, I would be laced down to my standard twenty-two inches. Then after an hour or so had passed, I would lie face down on the bed and he would straddle me. I fantasized about how his legs in their leather pants would feel against my silk stockings and bare skin as he sat on my bottom. "Inhale," would come his deep voice from over my shoulder, his handsome face unseen. I would obey and feel the laces being pulled inexorably tighter, making it harder to breathe, to move, cutting into me, squeezing my rib cage.

He climbs off me and helps me to stand. Unsteady on my stilettos and breathless, I cling to him as he reties the laces around my waist. His large hands almost encircle my waist as he guides me back into the living room. He stands me in front of the mirror and smoothes my hair, strokes my face. "Very pretty," he says, his lips close to my ear. I look at my reflection in the mirror and mentally agree, yes, I am pretty. (All submissives are beautiful when they are being submissive.) A frisson runs up my spine and explodes in my brain; there's the low ache and throb and I'm wet again. Then he sends me to make tea. I am getting quite graceful at managing the full tray in stilettos and wearing a tight corset. I wonder when my next tightening will be?

I return to the living room and my pillow on the floor at his feet. I lower myself to it slowly; unable to bend at the waist, I sink down like one genuflecting. And wait.

Another hour passes before he asks me to stand up. He extends his big warm hand and I grasp it and rise. He steps away from me and goes to the door. Throwing a handy piece of rope over it, he ties one end to the doorknob, and closes the door. One long sinuous length slithers back and forth on our side of the door, hypnotizing me like a gold watch of old. He takes me by the arm and leads me to it. I walk as if I'm wading through water, balanced precariously on my six-inch heels. "Arms over your head, darling," he breathes in my ear. Without thinking I comply, wrists together. He grabs both wrists in one of his huge hands and uses them to pull my arms high over my head. Suddenly the corset feels loose; I take several deep breaths and rearrange myself inside it while he ties my wrists to the snaky piece of rope.

Standing on tiptoe, face to the closed door, I waited for him to lace me in that last inch. He untied my little bow of excess laces and unwound them from my waist. I inhaled without being told and heard his voice from behind me say "good girl" in his special tone. Then he began to pull. One big tug and the back was closed completely. He steps back a few feet; I hear his sharp intake of breath—he must like what he sees. He steps back to me and runs his hand, hot now, over my dangling, corsetted figure. I throw my head back, feeling his shoulder right behind me. I rub the back of my head on him and his hand travels up my torso to my exposed breasts and throat. My chest is heaving from corset restriction and desire, naked lust, and I moan his name. He manhandles me for another minute, rubbing my breasts, pinching my nipples, and touching me between my legs. When his finger grazes there, I gasp and open my legs. "Slimy little thing, aren't you?" he laughs at me. "For you, lord," I whisper. He smacks my bottom three times hard and unties me. His arm is there to support me as I fall free. I see myself in the mirror and love the way I look. My breasts are high and inviting, my waist nipped in and sleek, my belly flat, my ass protruding round and juicy from the back. I glow from my lord's attentions to me and my skin is hot all over. I am tingling with anticipation over his plans for the rest of the evening.

Has any of this convinced you to try one?

Corset Tips

The proper way to order a corset is to measure your waist, then order a corset four inches smaller. So a twenty-four-inch waist would order a twenty, and a twenty-six would order a twenty-two. Ready-made corsets work for some and some ready-made corsets can be altered slightly to fit your figure, if you are adept at such things. If you fall so in love with corsetting that a ready-to-wear one will no longer do, a custom-made corset can be made to fit your exact body measurements and in the exact length that is right for your body. If you are ordering in person, all custom makers of corsets will measure you in several places and give more than one fitting. Additionally, you can select the fabric or hide yourself and any trim or other decoration. If you are ordering by catalog, the company will provide you with the directions to measure yourself and usually provides a body chart to help you. Beautiful, well-made corsets can be gotten through catalogs so you needn't be hesitant to use a reputable supplier such as Vollers in England, Dark Garden in San Francisco, or Janette Heartwood in Laguna Beach, California.

Traditionally the corset is not meant to be completely closed when laced up. There can be a gap of up to four inches in back. I personally cannot stand the way this looks. It makes you look fat because pulling the laces bunches up the skin, creating rolls of flesh where none may have existed before. So my twenty-four-inch corset, when closed, is comfortable enough to sleep in. The twenty-two-inch corsets close all the way but are not as comfortable. After six hours or so, I am dying to get the thing off and move freely and breathe deeply. With corset training the idea is to slowly decrease the size of your waist by a combination of diet, exercise, and corset tightening. So someone into corset training may have a twenty-four-, twenty-two-, and twenty-inch corset, a regiment to slowly decrease food intake, and an exercise routine. Slender people can use it as a device to keep trim; couples like it because it is something that they can do together.

Corset Figures

According to an illustration in the March 30, 1929, edition of *London Life* magazine, there are four basic types of figures one can achieve with lots of determination. These are the hourglass superb, the wasp magnificent, the V perfectos, and the pipe-stem regal.

I think the corset figure most appealing to the American eye is the hourglass figure. Mae West sported one, as did Marilyn Monroe. My friend Betsy has an hourglass figure when corseted and so do I. This type of corset can make instant cleavage for almost everyone when properly fitted. The hourglass figure is a curvy, small waist with full lush hips below and bust above. This type of corset is what most ladies like you and I would be most comfortable in.

The other three styles are not prevalent these days because our corsetting "habits" are for pleasure and eroticism, not extreme body modification or punishment, or tight lacing. The day of the thirteen-inch waist as a standard has long passed. The second style, the wasp-waist, is much harder to achieve than the friendly hourglass superb. This type of training is usually started in youth and results in a long, narrow torso.

The third figure, the V perfectos, is one I have never seen in person. I am told it combines the hourglass and wasp shapes. I am assured this training is very severe; in time the lower ribs collapse completely, and the internal organs become severely compressed. The "ideal" after all this is full hips below a V-shaped torso.The fourth style, the "pipe stem" regal, is another I have never seen in person. This one is very peculiar looking indeed. The torso is long and narrow and looks like it has been fitted into a "pipe." The bust and hips are flared out above and below.

Most of us won't need to worry about collapsing ribs and crushed organs. Corsetting for couples is a great way to share an erotic experience, and needn't be carried to the extremes of fainting spells. Not unless you find the vapors sexy!

Ritual Shaving

One night, during one of those late night trans-Atlantic phone calls I loved so much, my master ordered me to undress and splay myself out on my living room sofa. I hurried to obey—I love phone games—and got naked as fast as I could. When my master asked me to describe myself to him, I put on my best phone voice and went to it. When I got to my quim, he asked me if I was shaven and I replied truthfully: I was sporting my standard bikini trim but, no, I wasn't a hairless slave. On his command, I shaved the offensive patch of hair off and admired the new, hairless me. My master felt very powerful at having his command obeyed even though I was five thousand miles away. And to prove my obedience, I did my hair and make-up, then took pictures of the new me to send him as proof of my devotion.

I don't know any woman unfamiliar with the use of a safety razor on her legs, under her arms, or maybe even around her nipples. If you do a bikini trim, you have already developed a shaving technique for a sensitive area that works for you. For the new shaver, here are some helpful hints before you get started.

First, trim the hair down as much as you can with sharp scissors. Then, climb into a nice hot tub for a soak, or cover the area you are going to shave with a warm wet towel. This will open your follicles and make your ritual easier. Make sure you shave in good light and use your fingertips to feel which way the follicles point. Do not shave against the grain: if your hair grows down, shave down, not up. I find this helps prevent in-grown hairs. Additionally, do not keep shaving the same spot over and over; those with sensitive skin will experience razor burn with repeated shaving. If you missed a few hairs, let me assure you they will still be there the next time you shave, and you can get them then. I do find that using a safety razor that has been "broken in" (used a couple of times) on my legs is of great benefit because a slightly used blade scrapes away less skin. Also, it is very important that you frequently rinse the razor under the faucet to free it of hair. A razor full of hair just drags and pulls and scrapes the skin, so dunk it often to clean it.

Some recommend wiping the area down with a high isopropyl alcohol solution before and after shaving. Take this under consideration before running out to the chemists. I would *never* do this because alcohol burns my skin, and I can't imagine a worse place for a hot tingling reaction that just won't go away. Others recommend using shaving cream or gel to cut down on razor drag, and although this usually works, often a shaving cream contains some kind of menthol product and I have had adverse reactions to those too (especially on the extremely sensitive skin on my quim). Additionally, some advise cleaning the newly shaved area three or four times a day for four or five days after shaving with an antiseptic, or antibacterial, soap. Sorry, I'm allergic to most soaps and wouldn't even consider rubbing one of my newly shaved quim. If you cut yourself, surely clean it with whatever antiseptics you have around, but remember most contain some alcohol and alcohol can burn sensitive skin. One recommendation I do agree with is that you shouldn't shave more than once every five to seven days to prevent painful and ugly in-grown hairs.

Now you are hairless and you love the way it looks and feels: so fresh, so clean, so youthful. But be warned. Since shaving removes not only unwanted hair but also a few layers of dead skin cells, the nerve endings in a recently shaved area are closer to the surface than usual and more susceptible to sensation than their haired counterparts. When the shaved area is an erogenous zone, the increase in sexual stimulation is remarkable. The feelings invoked by being shaven from the neck down are hard to describe. Like what happened between Samson and Delilah, a power dynamic is in play when one person removes the hair of another or does so on the command of the other person.

~ 17 ~

SM Players, Their Scene, and Their Etiquette

There are two general groups of people who engage, or indulge, in SM sex: the Spicers and the Kook-a-Maniacs. The first group, the Spicers, would be those who fantasize about SM and occasionally engage in it. I call these people "spicers" because they use SM techniques like cayenne pepper: only now and then to spice up their regular lovemaking. This could be anything from a once-a-year "birthday spanking" to a once-a-month encounter, or from simple name calling and nipple pinching to an elaborate anniversary treat. The majority of SM players fall into the casual, Spicer, category.

Kook-a-Mania

Then there is the other umbrella group: the Kook-a-Maniacs. As their name implies, SM sex is an integral part of the sexual repertoire. This group encompasses the Perverati, who are the movers and shakers of SM; the less-visible Fetterati; and the Fetishists. I coined the phrase "kook-a-maniacs" in loving description of those who do what we do, which is "kook-a-mania." The words Perverati and Fetterati were first introduced to me in London in 1996. The beauty and relevance of the two words struck me. By stripping away, or ignoring, prefixes and labels like "hetero," "homo," and "lesbian," the terms Perverati and Fetterati have leveled the playing field. Each title, or rank, denotes the player's level of involvement, not their sexual preference. This helps to promote a non-judgmental atmosphere among the Kook-a-Maniacs, and hopefully will one day make everyone an equal opportunity SMer. Let's talk about the Perverati, Fetterati, and Fetishists separately, as they each deserve a word of their own.

The Perverati

The Perverati are at the highest level of Kook-a-Mania, or SM involvement, and it could be said that they are totally driven by their sexuality. SM is a constant and enduring part of their sexual makeup, and they simply will not do without it. The Pervs join SM societies not only to make new contacts, learn new techniques, and seek out support from like-minded souls, but also to get on a good private party circuit, or the guest list at the best club parties. Some Pervs Emeritus have been in the scene for forty to fifty years! They were there at its inception in London, or New York, or San Francisco; they helped to shape its philosophies and guidelines and to form its language. Some of them have established SM societies and support groups. Other proponents have been quieter in their contributions to the demythification of SM, but all watch its development closely and take its victories and setbacks to heart. I am proud to say that I rank among the Perverati.

The Perverati are at the deepest level of involvement, and have become the showmen and women of SM. Many have found one aspect of SM they excel at and have turned their hobby into an avocation. These masters and mistresses can put the submissive in full-suspension bondage or full-body mummification; some are licensed body piercers, and others specialize in strict slave training. Some are whip angels with the single lash or flogger; some share their knowledge of handballing so that others can realize their dream. They have been known to travel around, often at their own expense, to teach others the proper use of the object of their passion.

The Perverati cater to their pleasure as their leisure time and finances allow. Some have converted the spare bedroom or the entire basement of the family home into a dungeon; others have closed off and soundproofed the garage and outfitted it as a dungeon. However, some

Pervs aver that a dungeon is unnecessary—all SM takes is the consent and creativity of both partners and the top's two hands. All agree that SM is an integral part of their sexual makeup, and they will *not* go vanilla. A Perv bottom once told me that she would "do anything her master desired of her." "What if he wanted you to turn vanilla?" I asked her. She thought for a minute, then said, "I'd leave him." Any Perv will tell you that SM sends their needles into red and keeps them there, making their playtime a transcendental experience.

The Fetterati

The next level of Kook-a-Maniacs are the Fetterati. Fetterati seems to be derived from the word fetish. The Fetterati are more private about their perversions, preferring to go to the club party, take in the Perverati demonstration, then go home and practice their favorite variety of SM behind closed doors. Occasionally, you will see a Fetterati master or mistress in public with a collared and leashed submissive in tow; you might also witness a flogging or a foot scene. But the Fetterati are quiet kooks and sometimes one only knows their association with the scene because of their fetish dress.

Most Fetterati are aspiring Perverati and watch avidly as their kookier fellow freaks demonstrate their superior talents. Although some amount of titillation *must* be expected as one watches these demonstrations, the Fetterati are also there to learn. Sometimes, when a Perv is seeking a "co-top" (a middle person to act as a dominant who is between him and his bottom), he will search the ranks of the Fetterati for a likely candidate.

The Fetishists

Neither a showy Perverati nor a quietly freaky Fetterati, the Fetishists occupy their own niche in SM. All Fetishists have a specialty. A Fetishist's love could be for latex or a high-heeled fetish shoe; the fetish could be for the master's armpit or the hidden erogenous spot behind his knees. A fetish that is developed very early in life is a sexual attachment to a nonsexual object or body part. If the fetish is developed later, the attachment could be for a traditionally sexual part of the body or for a newly acquired passion. But we don't discriminate here; all kooks are welcome.

The Fetishist does discriminate and is not satisfied with the sexual encounter unless the object of the fetish is there. I would think this to be both limiting and limited unless the Fetishist can incorporate other interests or related activities into the scene. I am curious as to how many women Fetishists there are because it seems to me that many more men are Fetishists. I have a "fetish" for shoes, but it is a girl thing, not an SM thing.

Spicer or Kook-a-Maniac, SMers come from all walks of life. Males and females, tops and bottoms, and those wonderful, special switches could be the people next door or up the block. They look just like everyone else, sound and act like everyone else, but then, maybe not. SMers have a great sense of humor and occasionally let their proclivities peek through. An answering machine message may announce, "We're all tied up now and can't come to the phone." Or you may overhear a conversation about a gym horse found at a yard sale, now recovered in leather and painted shiny black. The director's chair in the corner of the den could be doing double-duty as a "bondage chair." The folding massage table leaning discreetly against the wall is really a rack, or a torture table, or bondage device.

An inventive and creative bunch, many who indulge in sado-masochistic sex are college-educated, white-collar workers and postgraduate professionals. They have the leisure time and discretionary income to spend on SM or their fetish. I was deeply involved in SM while working full time as an assistant analyst in an audit and analysis unit.

Before You Leave the House

Basic social skills are necessary for anyone, and more so for those who wish to build respectful relationships. Because of the intimacy and eroticism of SM interactions, it is critical to acquire and hone these skills. For those who make friends easily, some of these suggestions might seem silly; however, if you are shy or don't make friends easily, some of these suggestions may help.

In earlier chapters, we discussed several steps that could be on your list of personal preparations before a romantic SM encounter-for-two at home: showering, shampooing, shaving, oral hygiene, manicure and pedicure, and your wardrobe (such as it is). These same outward preparations will improve your chances for meeting like-minded people and making friends with the same sexual tastes as yours.

If you are venturing out, while you are making your physical preparations, you will need to prepare your mind for what you are about to see. When I was a newcomer to the public scene, what surprised me most was the "my kink's okay; yours is not" crowd. The cross-dressers don't like the whips and chains crowd; the male doms don't like the professional female dominants; the bloodsporters think the foot worshipers are silly. Imagine the chagrin of someone who has just come out of the closet, who may have struggled for years to come to terms with and express her sexuality, only to have it put down by, ridiculed, poked fun at by someone who really should know better. This is breaking the prime directive of SM: Thou shalt not ridicule another's fetish or fantasy! Some people definitely think that no sexual fantasy is politically incorrect—as long as it meets their personal criteria! So be as tolerant of others as you would like them to be of you. Besides, in the strange and ever-expanding dark garden of SM, later on you might find you enjoy the very object or action of your earlier derision.

If you and your master are going to an event, you will naturally want to dress appropriately for the occasion. There are standards in dress codes, but the subtleties change depending on the venue or situation. If you are attending an SM meeting, lecture, or demonstration, your basic black cloth outfit (jeans and shirt, skirt and top) will be eminently suitable. Usually at this type of event, only those on the panel, serving the group, or giving the demonstration, will be in fetish dress. Whatever you wear, it should be clean, and look good on you. Remember about first impressions—your outfit is an expression of who you are so choose it carefully.

At a full-out, fancy-dress SM event, the dress code unfortunately can vary at the door. Some clubs, or doormen, admit those wearing head-to-toe black, others do not. Red latex is no problem but a red cloth shirt is. For the submissive woman, this is not so big a deal. Lingerie and a collar will qualify as "fetish" dress, so will a sexy dress (in the hope it will be removed later on); for a man, a pair of leather pants will fulfill the minimum requirement, as will a uniform or uniformlike look of some sort. Gauge your future wardrobe for these events by what you see others wearing.

My mother always extorted me to wear clean underwear "in case I got hit by a car and had to be taken to the hospital." (As if I ever wore dirty ones! I just love lingerie and have always had way too much of it.) I guess the shame of ragged underwear would have killed her faster than the car would have killed me, but there you have it. If you think there is even the slightest chance that you and your master might feel comfortable enough to do a little public playing, please wear sexy lingerie or at least clean underwear. Don't you want to look as beautiful as you feel?

Fetish Wear

Fetish wear plays an important role in the private and public life of the SM couple. A particular garment or style of dress can appeal to those into the ritual aspects of SM, or the fetish aspect. When going out to a club, or SM party, event or weekend, fetish dress establishes the group identity. And the pleasure of dressing for SM play is certainly not limited to those garments, or lack thereof, that we may wish to adorn ourselves with during our private playtime.

Dressing for fetish is a passion with both males and females, tops and bottoms. When dressing in fetish, the master, or lord, or whoever is titularly in charge, has the opportunity to indulge his fantasy as fully as any woman. A shirt with ruffled plackets and cuffs replaces a button-down shirt and tie. Smooth black leather knee-high boots disdainfully kick everyday lace-ups out of sight under the bed. Pleated trousers now occupy the hanger his custom-made leather pants just vacated. Their delicious aroma wafts through the room as he slides them up his legs, over his thighs, and settles them on his hips. He carefully tucks the shirttail into his trousers before buttoning them. The toothy whoosh of the zipper sends a matching frisson up your spine. He turns to face you; a smile splits his craggy, handsome visage; unexpected dimples, put there by some benevolent goddess to soften the ruggedness of his face, dot both cheeks. The dimples deepen with his smile, making you giggle in anticipation of the reverse action later on.

For a woman, dressing in fetish can be a chance to explore different sexual personas or for her imagination to take flights of fancy. Whereas a man must always have on some piece of leather or latex or PVC to meet a dress code, a woman can wear a tutu with fishnets and high heels and still pass inspection. Costumes are very much appreciated in fetishland, and a woman has so many more choices than a man. Ballerina, governess, nun, goddess, nymph, harem-girl, angel, devil, cyber-girl, all would be welcomed in. Another advantage for the submissive woman is that she can wear a regular dress to the club or party, and change or disrobe inside. One doorman told me with a wink that he *always* admits a woman wearing a pretty dress in the hope that she will take it off later on!

One thing I would like to see change is the definition of fetish wear. I believe dressing in fetish is more than wearing something made of leather, latex, or PVC. It is also uniforms and baby wear, chain mail and lace, nudity and mummification; it is Gothic dresses and vampire capes, Victorian corsets and ruffled petticoats, suede chaps and bolero jackets. In short, the definition of fetish wear should be broadened to encompass whatever outfit or costume the wearer feels expresses her (or his) alternate reality, alter ego, or SM persona. This style of neofetish dress could be called OTT, meaning "over the top."

Etiquette When You're Out and About

An SM play party can be held in a private home or in a public establishment rented out for the night to a group or society. Some large cities have clubs that host SM nights on a monthly basis; others are large enough to sustain an SM club that is open two or three nights a week. Some entrepreneurs throw roving parties: one venue this month, a different one the next. In cities where commercial dungeon space is for rent, the entrepreneur can host private parties in an elegant and fully equipped facility. Because this type of party is by invitation only, the players are quite serious and the scenes frequent and heavy.

Club parties in the United States differ greatly from those in the United Kingdom in that all the best U.K. parties have at least three "rooms" or distinct areas where different tones are set. There is usually a large dance area with a good beat deejay, a "juzshy" zone where one can lounge around and hear a more mellow sound meant to encourage conversation, and finally, an equipped dungeon with a third deejay playing ambient sounds for erotic events. In the United Kingdom, SMers mix with Goths who mix with TVs who mix with the leather boys and dykey girls. In the United States, especially on the East Coast, there is little or no crossover crowd except for special events, but good dungeon manners should be a constant worldwide. Although rules may vary from party to party, some rules are fairly standard for both top and bottom.

A public scene is an invitation to watch, not join in or volunteer. If anyone wants your help, you can be sure they will ask for it. Many SMers welcome an audience as long as no one interferes, stands too close, calls out rude remarks, or speaks in a loud, distracting tone. Don't have nonscene conversations near a scene; if you are overheard talking about what a rotten boss you have, it will surely distract the players and undermine the eroticism of the scene. If you see a scene you would like to watch, make sure you don't stray into the top's play area. A good top will have cleared a space for his scene, knowing how much room he will need to swing his whip or wield his cane in safety.

Private play-parties have multiple purposes: You get a chance to observe others in general, and, in particular, someone you may be considering bottoming to. Others attend for the rewards of being out in a group of like-minded individuals. Parties give you a great chance to be a responsible voyeur (that means looking, not touching, not talking, and not interfering!), and voyeurism gives you a great chance to learn new techniques. Playing at a party where the screams of delight and the moans of pleasure from the other bottoms surrounding you can be enormously arousing. Play parties are great fun, and everyone wants to stay on the guest list and be invited back. So how do you accomplish that? If you know what to expect, and what is expected of you, misunderstandings and faux pas can be avoided. First impressions are important, and a bad first impression can be difficult to change once established.

At a crowded house party, try not to sit, lounge, or store your personal props and toys on the bondage or dungeon equipment unless you are about to use it. The larger pieces, like the rack, spanking bench, cage, Katherine wheel (a wheel mounted perpendicular to the floor that spins 360°), and so on, are often very sought-after toys and should not be monopolized by your toy bag. If your scene is going to be unusually loud, unruly, messy, or intense, make sure it is okay with the party organizers, or in keeping with the club's policies, before beginning your Drill Sergeant routine. If your scene is a messy one—many clubs have prohibitions on hot wax scenes, shaving scenes, and blood scenes because of the mess— use a sheet, tarp, or even a garbage bag to protect the floor, then clean up all spills immediately. (At home, dried wax can be removed from the carpet by a using a *warm*, not hot, iron on a paper towel over the wax spot.)

House Rules

Most club parties and private parties held in commercial dungeons in the United States have a dungeon master, mistress, or monitor (DM), whose responsibility it is to make sure that scenes are consensual and house rules are obeyed. If the DM asks you to stop doing something, please stop right away whether you feel you are right or wrong. Stop the scene, and if you feel you must state your case, or press your point, take it away from the play area. In a club, house rules are rules for a reason: Maybe they need to comply with the local liquor code, or nudity laws that you know nothing about; maybe there is a church across the street that in some way limits their license. If you can't live with the house rules, by all means leave rather than sneak around trying to bend them. How would you feel if what *you* had done caused the club to be closed down for a violation of this or that law? Alternatively, at a private party, bending whichever rules you feel don't apply to you will violate your host's trust in you. You may be asked to leave or may be excluded from future events.

Sometimes what appears to be an unfair party or house rule may be a rule for no other reason than it prevents a two-tier system. I am speaking about house rules that require all couples who are being sexual to practice visible safer sex standards. The exclusive or monogamous couple is not exempt from this rule because that would create a double standard. Additionally, this rule will support safer sex standards among those who are playing together but are not monogamous or in a relationship. I support safer sex in all its forms, and when I encounter this rule, I save being sexual until I get home and can play my way without offending or upsetting anyone.

The Mindful Master

My understanding of the dominant role is that one person takes on the responsibility for someone else's physical and emotional good time and well-being for a prearranged period of time. This applies to the experienced top as well as the novice. It is part of the master's "job" to protect me, make sure no harm comes to me, and that I enjoy myself being his sub. The good master not only is in control of himself, and his sub, but of any other person present. His protection of you, before and after a scene, not only during one, should be evident to those around you. His aura should surround you like a shield and engulf you in its warm, protective glow while it warns onlookers that you are protected by a strong and capable master.

It is acceptable to approach a master and ask if there is any possibility of *joining* in the scene—I stress joining in because no responsible master would just hand his valued sub over to another. If your master feels this third person is acceptable *to him*, then it is your master's responsibility to make sure the third person is acceptable *to you*. Even if you are bound, gagged, blindfolded, and suspended by your ankles from the ceiling, it is your master's responsibility to make sure that you are fully aware of what is happening. And that you consent to it.

Your master should be mindful of your physical comfort and safety at all times, even when you are not involved in a scene. In extreme cases of self-centered, insecure, or overly demanding masters, the poor sub may have started out kneeling at his feet in what was a quiet corner but now has become a busy thoroughfare; her master, chatting away with his friend, is oblivious to her plight, but there she must remain until he notices her predicament and gives her permission to move out of the footpath.

At one party I attended, there was the Mindless Master and Senseless Sub doing a single lash scene in a hallway. Although there were enough rooms in the house that we didn't need to party in the hall, the hall was the Mindless Master's choice, and that was that. Of course, the Mindless Master could care less that his choice of venue for the flogging totally and effectively blocked the only route to the bathrooms and smoking section! We, on the far side of the bathroom, could not catch his eye to signal him to take a break yet we didn't want to be as rude as he was and walk through his scene and risk getting hurt by his lash. Being Pistress Niagara herself, I found a nice cup and filled it up. Others weren't so fortunate, or uninhibited, or maybe they just couldn't find an empty cup. Finally someone at the far end saw what was happening and got the Mindless Master's attention by pretending he didn't know the "Master was at work" and shouted for him with great urgency from the other end of the hallway!

The Shielded Slave

One would think it would be normal to show some respect no matter where one is, but, like we said before, some throw social conventions out along with the sexual ones. Listen up. It is *never* appropriate, permissible, or acceptable for anyone to walk up to you, or any sub, and begin to paw her. Her sexy outfit is for the benefit of herself and her master, real or imaginary, present or in absentia; it is *not* for the jollies of just anyone that happens along and has a free hand! Why would anyone think it would be acceptable to grab at the exposed parts of her body? Because she's there? A masterless sub deserves the same respect as a collared one until she gives her permission for another party to do deliciously wicked things to her. If she can't dress to express her sexuality at an SM party, where can she express herself? No one should ever touch you without the express permission of your master and your consent.

What if you don't want to give your consent? Then don't—but do it politely. You need no reason other than you don't want to. No other excuses or reasons are required and should not be demanded from you. (Then things could get impolite.) All you need to do is say, "No"; "No, thank you"; "Thank you for offering but no"; "No, thank you, our interests don't seem to be the same"; or "No, I don't feel any chemistry between us." All are polite answers, and all communicate effectively and clearly the word NO.

Additionally, the master doing a scene with his submissive is not an invitation for every slaveless master in the room to line up to ensure his turn cracking the whip. Lone males, strange masters, and the generally uninvited of either sex should never touch or assume they may touch the submissive in any way, shape, or form. Never assume that the submissive would welcome being touched unless he has heard the words from her own mouth or has heard her give her consent to her master. Fortunately, this "whip-line" seems to be a phenomenon in only one club in New York and has not caught on elsewhere. Let's hope it never does.

The Collar and the Casual Observer

Although at this time you and your master may choose to do no more than watch a scene, there are a few more rules you should be aware of before you go out. These rules will affect how you interact with those who are standing next to you at the bar or sitting near you at a table. Unfortunately, a lot of clubs are filled with the offensively curious, in spite of a strict dress code. The offensively curious often have no idea of proper manners, SM or otherwise.

The foremost of these regards the rules about the "collared" slave. In SM, a collar is often a gift; but whereas most gifts are forever, a collar is not. The collar given to the sub by her dom always remains the dom's property. Although we would like to think of our relationship as lasting "forever," forever can be a much shorter time than either anticipated. A collar bought by your dom is a symbolic reminder of your submission to him. Such a gift can evoke deep emotional responses in both the dom and sub, and the gift of a collar can almost be compared to that of an engagement ring.

What does this mean in an SM setting? Sometimes this means you are not allowed to speak to or interact with the collared one unless you have the permission of her top first. She is not allowed to respond to you unless she has her master's permission; she will not take orders or guff from you until or unless her master gives her the OK. As she is clearly someone else's slave, you are certainly not allowed to touch her in any way. The submissive is protected by her collar, as well as the master's aura of authority.

A word here on proper capitalization: when writing to an SM couple, or when referring to them in writing, it is nice to observe the formalities and address them properly. The rule is simple: the top's name always goes first and is given initial caps. The bottom's name is always second and in all small letters; for example, Mindful Master and sensual slave, or Master Val and slave claudia. Of course, one should *never* address the envelope in this style, only in the traditional one. Save the fun stuff for inside!

Slave Contracts

To the woman just discovering her submissive persona, the thought of signing a slave contract is a red-hot fantasy. Fantasies about SM contracts are common, and SM fiction abounds with just such scenarios; the classic is *Venus in Furs* by Leopold von Sacher-Masoch. Although in the *Story of O* by Pauline Reage, O did not sign a paper contact, but she was constantly required to verbalize her commitment. But imagine it: Here is this piece of paper that signs away your rights to your body and makes you chattel, the property of your lord and master, his to do with as he wishes, when he wishes, where he wishes, as often as he likes. It seems, at first blush, to be the ultimate form of being owned, looked after, and securing one's place in the master's life. And there's your signature, bold and clear, at the bottom. What more do you need to fuel a submissive's fantasy fire on a cold night?

Hot fantasy that it is, remember that no one, top or bottom, can stay in role twenty-four hours a day, seven days a week, 365 days a year.

In a serious or committed SM relationship, contracts between the dominant and submissive can serve many good purposes. Both of you may wish to set your goals, limits, obligations, and expectations down in writing because it is easy to forget who said and agreed to what during your negotiations. Writing it down puts an end to confused memories of who said YES or NO to what and when. The contract will make each person's role and responsibilities clear. If you would like to experiment with a contract, try a very short-term one for just a night, or a weekend. If you enjoy it, then you can renegotiate your contract and do another short-term experiment. After that, you can make the duration longer, or introduce new play. Occasionally, you both may want to reaffirm or repledge your loyalty, or you may want to renew your vows of submission. Of course, these contracts have no force in law but they do carry some responsibilities.

Before I signed my first and only slave contract, I stopped, thought about, and reread each word I had written. I knew that by committing those ideas and fantasies to paper and giving him full permission to act them out with me, he would. I also knew that if one of those things slipped my mind, he was entirely capable of showing me that paper and asking me if I had written it and signed it. And by the terms of my contract, he was fully within his rights to do this. So I gave each word, each phrase, careful consideration before writing it down. Was I ready to relinquish my safeword for something more abstract? Was I ready to submit without knowing exactly what was going to happen to me that evening? Was I ready to trust him fully and completely like I have trusted no other in my life? Do I think he is intelligent and sensitive enough to know when I need to work and not to play, need to cuddle and not to assume the position? The butterflies in my stomach danced and whirled. YES. YES. YES. Then I signed my name and sealed it with a fresh lipstick kiss!

Your first contract should not be so advanced, or far-reaching, as the one I wrote between myself and my master. Because my master and I are experienced players, and I lived five thousand miles away from him, our rules and parameters were very different from those of a couple who live together. My time with him was a two- or three-weeklong unbroken, romantic interlude. Because we saw each other so seldom, each moment, each day was precious and special of its own. These were truly fantasy conditions as we were largely untroubled by the stress and trials of an everyday relationship.

The contract for a live-in relationship, married or not, should be realistic in scope, and could specify important things such as times when the contract does and does not apply, reassignment of chores to facilitate playtime, a date the contract expires, a meeting time to renegotiate the contract, who covers expenses for toys and wardrobe, rules for appropriate conduct including manner of dress and off-limits activities, and what will be the punishment for infractions. The fact that you have a contract does not mean that you no longer need to communicate, negotiate, and consent; it does not eliminate the need for safety. And remember to include your safe-word in your contract!

Although I wrote my first contract myself at the request of my lord and master, ideally the contract should be created when you are together. Even though I took great care in writing my contract, I left out things that I felt should have been implicit, and these omissions caused trouble later on. I did not specify in the contract that I wanted the contract and the attached list of fantasy scenarios to be kept between us in the strictest confidence and never shown to another person. It just never crossed my mind that my contract, a very intimate and personal thing, as you can imagine, to say nothing of the list of dirty deeds, would be shown or "shared" with others without my permission. I thought this would intrinsically be implied and I was wrong. Make sure everything is clear to both of you.

Alternatively, a slave contract between two responsible players who are not in a relationship could be just a list of fantasy scenarios. This type of contract is nothing more than a written expression of the fantasies of one, or the other, or both. Carrying no more weight than saying "let's play dress-up," this type of contract can be a list of what the slave would like to experience with the master of the moment. Although hardly as romantic or serious as the committed contract, the benefit of this contract is that it gives the top a concrete idea of what the sub would find erotic.

Ideally, either a committed or a casual contract should help you define your relationship more clearly and enhance your communication skills. Either contract should be realistic in scope; it does not exist only to turn you on. The committed contract is an obligation, and should be taken seriously by both parties. But in the meantime, don't hesitate to use it as a hot fantasy!

The Basic Rights of a Relationship

Whether your setting is SM or vanilla, whether it is casual or committed, sexual or not, dispossessing yourself of sexual conventions does not mean you are free from social ones. I think that there are basic rights that each person is entitled to in a relationship. Each of us has the right to a courteous response, and the right to have your own emotions and point of view, even and especially if yours are different from others. Each of us has the right to live free from blame and accusation, and the right to feel stable and secure. You have the right to receive a sincere apology for any jokes, comments, or behavior that you find offensive or insulting. You have the right not to be called by any name that belittles, degrades, or devalues you. Other rights include living free from criticism, fear, belittlement, and judgment. We each have the right to live free from emotional and physical abuse and threat and to live free from outbursts of hostility and rage.

Each human being has the right to encouragement and respect. You have a right to the expectation of privacy and a right not to be lied to. You have the right to pursue and enjoy peace and harmony. It is your right to give your full, informed consent, and to withdraw that consent any time the situation no longer pleases you. You have the right to be free of another's emotional roller coaster and the right to protect yourself against those who would put you on one.

It may seem that some of the "rights" are self-evident; therefore, it may seem a waste of time to write them down. But all relationships, SM or not, physical or platonic, light or for keeps, require a foundation on which to build. All too often, the rights of one are trampled, muddied, or simply overlooked by the other. Some seem to think that their rights are more important than the rights of others; some simply have no concept of others having any rights at all. Respect for the rights of the individual is the foundation of any relationship, but too often no one knows what those rights are, or have very different concepts of the rights of the individual.

Knowing these rights, or something similar suited particularly to you, to be your rights and the rights of others, is one of the most important flowers in your dark garden. It is more important than all of what you have read before, or will read next, because respect for others is not donned like a coat, but something that comes instead from the mind and the heart.

Emotional Blackmail

A caring relationship, obviously, does not consist of any degree of emotional blackmail. Emotional blackmail is abuse, and it has no place in a healthy relationship, SM-flavored or not. What is emotional blackmail? "Do as I say or I'll leave you." "You have two choices: do it or end the relationship." "This is the way I want it to be; take it or leave." Any statement like this is an attempt at emotional blackmail. It leaves no room for negotiating or compromise. It makes no attempt to find middle ground for both to feel comfortable. Giving only the illusions of choice, it *forces* one partner into giving (unwilling) consent. This is basically a nonconsensual arrangement and, therefore, not romantic SM as we have defined it. Who is an emotional blackmailer? Any top who has taken away the submissive's freedom of choice by threatening to leave her if she doesn't consent is an emotional blackmailer. How can her agreement be considered consensual under such a threat, even if she says YES?

An emotional blackmailer can also be demeaning to his submissive. Demeaning differs from humiliating someone in two important ways: When you demean someone, you are causing them harm either emotionally or physically, and that is nonconsensual. Humiliation and headgames in the SM arena is consensual and negotiated by both partners. It does not tear down, it builds up. It is wanted, enjoyed, and planned by both partners. How can it be demeaning when someone cares for you so much that they want to try and fulfill your every fantasy?

SM is a wonderful sex aid but it is not a suitable substitute or cure-all for a failing or dysfunctional relationship. Please be aware that SM games or play will not help or enhance a relationship that is not already a healthy one. Marital problems warrant professional attention and should be addressed in a therapist's office—not in an SM scene or dungeon. SM sex is fantasy enactment in a healthy and consensual setting. It can be a safe place to heal, to grow, and to change, with the care and support of the right partner.

Recognizing Signs of Abuse

Although I would like to think that everyone playing at consensual SM today is a responsible adult, I must admit that violence, or abuse, does occur in the SM community, much as it does everywhere else. And, unfortunately, abuse does try to masquerade as SM. It is sometimes hard to know, even to the eye of the most experienced perv, what is a consensual scene and what is not. So look not at the scene itself, but at the players enacting it.

First let's define the purpose of violence, or abuse. The purpose of violence is to cause either psychological or physical harm or damage or both to someone (or something) without their consent. A violent person can be anyone, regardless of their race, creed, sex, age, social status, profession, whatever. Violence can be motivated by a desire for revenge: for insults and infractions, slights and snubs, whether they are real or imagined. It can be fueled by anger or fear; it can feed on itself. Violence is a way of forcing or intimidating one partner into accepting modes of behavior nonconsensually. It is a vicious cycle and often escalates in severity as the cycle goes around.

How can you recognize signs of abuse? SM abuse is not different from vanilla abuse. The first sign of abuse is that the scene is unpleasant for the receiving partner. Some examples of abuse would be one partner hurting or restraining the other against their will; repeatedly violating limits in and out of a scene, and coercion into acts, especially sexual ones, to which the sub has not agreed. Other examples of abuse would include the top undermining the sub's self-esteem, harming of the sub's property by the top, and the belittlement or degradation of the sub beyond her consent. Extreme examples would be the top exploiting an illness, such as anorexia or bulimia, to enhance or cement to the top's control.

What can you do about an abusive situation? If you feel you are in an abusive relationship and are afraid to leave, seek the help of an abuse survivor's network near you. If there is none, try any hospital, clinic, or women's center. You can call a crisis or suicide hot line. Often these services will refer you; follow their suggestions until you get the help you need. If you feel someone is being abused, unfortunately there is not much you can do on a practical level. "Advice" could be construed as meddling interference from the top or bottom, or both, or, heartbreakingly, as a reason for a new reign of terror perpetrated on the sub by the dom for the "betrayal." Alternatively, the sub may feel she deserves this treatment, or believe that she doesn't deserve better. All one can do in this situation is hope and pray that she seeks professional help and finds the strength to move on to a new healthy life and relationship.

Epilogue: The Spiritual Side of SM

Throughout this book, there have been references to a bit of earth in your dark garden that SMers call "the gift." You know now that there is an *exchange* of gifts: the rare and precious gifts of your erotic submission to him and the one of his romantic dominance of you. By sharing your souls' darkest sexual desires, you have attained a state of heightened awareness that will enhance more than your sexual relationship. Sharing a romantic, consensual SM experience can be transcendental; it can take you and your master to another place together and open up a new world for you. Exploring the sexual being inside of us with a loving partner can be a safe way to heal and grow.

Long before you read this book you probably realized that all sex, as in the merging of one body and mind with another, is spiritual. You are inviting someone inside of you in every sense of the word, and that is a spiritual experience. Every orgasm that you have, every one that he has, is a spiritual experience, and more so when you experience them together. When you add to that the exotic blooms of SM fantasies enacted together in love and trust, your minds and bodies collide to become one universe, brilliant in its awareness of the combined sexual self and the merging of spirits. The enhanced trust and communication necessary to experiment with SM and the deepened love I have felt for my master has made SM sex one of the most spiritually uplifting events I have experienced in my life.

When I love someone, I love the side of him that walks in the light and is visible to all, and I love the dark paths he chooses to walk when we are alone together—especially when I want to explore those paths myself. I was fortunate in that it was relatively easy for me to come to terms with my sexual submissiveness—I had my earliest memories of sadomasochistic fantasies when I was five years old. I consider myself a submissive in the chivalrous sense, but I am submissive only in private and only to one master. Each of you will come to terms with your sexuality in your own time. Do not rush the gift, your own or his, or give the gift away in haste. Do not give it to someone who does not have your understanding of it, and therefore is not ready to exchange these special gifts. In the wrong hands, the energy flow, the power exchange, is all one-way, and the outcome can hurt.

In the right hands, the SM exchange of gifts is a visible manifestation of the love and trust you have built up in your relationship. Your honesty in communicating and understanding each other's wants and needs have taken your relationship to a higher level. The mutual giving, loyalty, and devotion are open and ongoing, making your relationship a serene haven in a stormy world.

The Depth of the Gift

One of the things many submissives come to love about SexMagick is the depth of the gift they can offer to their master. The chivalrous submissive will endeavor to become an extension of her dom and to submit to his will. As her limits will allow, she will surrender her sense of self and her individuality as a human being to serve him. As she does this, her self-esteem is not reduced, and she is not degraded or abused; instead, she is uplifted by her voluntary submission and exploration into the depths of her soul. Her trust in her dom is complete and knowing he is a worthy and responsible recipient of that trust, she can and does serve him without reservation. Each one respects their promise not to bring real-world problems into the dungeon.

My heart swelled with joy when I realized how much my lord trusted me when he allowed me to experience his sadism. The extent of his sadism is wide and deep, and it needed to be given free rein at times. Through his intimate knowledge of my sexual desires and his adept handling of the fantasy enactment, I often was able to attain a state of altered awareness, a different dimension where the reality of our fantasy took place and enter a physical state that enabled me to far surpass my normal bodily limits. At these times, I allowed him to cane me freely, as hard as he could, the strokes one right after another until, although I was coming and coming, I could take no more. Then I would grovel at his feet and beg him to slap me instead. Wrenched to my knees by the hair, his large hand would cradle the left side of my head as his right hand smashed in my face. After the third or fourth slap, I would come again, and freshly lubricated, he would "rape" me. It gave me enormous pleasure to serve him and tend to his needs: sexual, emotional, and physical.

Spirituality and Ritual

We have discussed rituals as part of our SM fantasies, and the word "ritual" has sacred resonations. Our deepest sexual secrets are sacred to us, and the sharing and enacting of those secrets can be like our own private religion. SM sex is a spiritual experience and, like a religion, has mystery and symbolism, rites and ceremonies. The fantasy enactment can wring from us, and endow us with, enormous physical and emotional intensity. To open ourselves in this way, to give up or go past our usual boundaries, and to drop our complex system of defenses expands our self-awareness. The expanding of two consciousnesses through the SM sexual experience can make you realize that there is no time when you are separated from your sexuality and that sex is spiritual.

I sought to find spirituality through SM because at an earlier age, I ceased to subscribe to the credos of organized religions that the mind should deny the body. (I have a nice body, I like it, why should I ignore it because the people God has working for him said so? Maybe they got the message wrong.) I believe that the mind and body work in tandem after the mind gets things on the path. Trying to separate the mind from the body can create a void that alienates people from themselves and from society. In a loving relationship, SM can be a bridge across that void and a span built into the innermost self. For those for whom organized religion held no meaning, combining SM, spirituality, and ritual can provide an alternative path to inner spirituality and worship that has been crafted to the needs of the individual.

Prior to the ritual, one may feel caught in a rut, bored with one's daily routine. One senses that there is more to life than the ordinary and the mundane, and SM spirituality and ritual can evoke very strong emotions. In days long gone by, spirituality and eroticism were intertwined, inextricably part of each other, but as I said earlier, mind (spirituality) has become separated from body (eroticism and sexual pleasure) and enacting an SM ritual can reunite the two. Some are drawn to the spirituality of the SM experience because it can make, and keep, a promise of physical experience. The promise of physical experience can be more important, and more enticing, than all the dogma and creeds in the world. Some are drawn to seek spirituality through SM for the mental testing the experience can provide. Others explore SM and spirituality because they are attracted to the personalized rituals one can create in the SM experience. As you can imagine, one may want to explore SM and spirituality, or seek spirituality through the SM experience, for one or more or all of these reasons. Many times these reasons overlap.

Outside the SM arena, they are very few ways to attain a state of spirituality through physical or emotional rites of passage. By combining spirituality, ritual, and SM, one can define what is needed for your personal development.

The Healing Power of SM

Old wounds can plague us, but what if by some magic power we were able to heal those wounds by reopening them? What if there are parts of us that we can only get to by going through those painful openings? I'm not saying that SM is a magic wand to solve all of our problems, but one can change and grow by working out these problems in a safe, protected environment with a loving and understanding partner. SM comes with its own dark spiritual energy that when properly channeled can transform both dominant and submissive. To some it will be a revelation that their dark side is as lovable and as desirable as the side that walks in the light. To know with utter certainty that one's shadow is deserving of love and can be loved is a manifestation of the steps we have taken toward self-exploration and acceptance.

I have experienced three states of altered consciousness, or three levels of ecstasy, while enacting SM rituals. When not in an altered, accepting, exploring state, my mind connects first, which then gives notice to my heart. My heart, in turn, notifies my body. After I have entered an altered state of consciousness through SM ritual, I am able to unburden myself of an emotional state that encumbers me. It is a frame of mind heavy with thoughts of things past and things to come; in this heavy state I am constantly thinking about "being," instead of expressing the lightness of one who just is. By this I mean that the order of connection is reversed: During a transcendental, or unburdening, SM experience, my body (sensation) turns on first, then my heart (catharsis) beats faster, and only then does my head (insight and ego deconstruction) engage.

These ecstatic states can reward one with new insights, knowledge, and creativity, and one can refine and define the self. Catharsis from a spiritual SM experience can leave one feeling cleansed, purified, and released from old issues. One can come away from the experience with feelings of well-being and new vigor, new zest for life. Catharsis through the SM experience is a release into a new purity and attaining a joyful satisfaction.

The three states of ecstasy—sensation, catharsis, and finally, insight—can provide a forum for the positive loss of inhibitions. As boundaries are broadened and redefined, one can experience a loss of fear, sorrow, guilt, and personal limitations. In this ecstatic state, one may lose a sense of time and place or the ability to form thoughts into words or structured sentences. One senses that the ultimate surrender of control over the self can reap great rewards, such as feelings of eternity, unity, and heaven, increased self-knowledge and inspiration, and empowerment from increased self-esteem. At no time is the connection between master and submissive more intense than during the spiritual and cathartic SM experience.

If you are using the SM arena to work out a lingering problem, be sure to talk it over in full with your dom before proceeding. Any attempt at addressing a problem by using SM techniques to bring it to the fore should have his full knowledge and support to ensure the emotional well-being of each of you. In a romantic, consensual SM setting, you can confront and settle problems and dilemmas from your earliest life by exploring your sexuality—it just takes time, patience, love, and someone who has a sexual appetite that complements your own.

Combination and Transformation

When you explore the dark garden together, you are combining two separate entities into one greater consciousness. As his willing receptacle, you take his passion and energy into you and combine it with your own passion and energy. This combination of energy and passion forges its own path in the dark garden and transforms both of you into something more brilliant, more self-aware than one can be alone. This combination and transformation is a particularly beautiful flower in the dark garden. We need each other to be who we are, and we need to like each other for who we are. This gives us the validation we all crave as sensitive and sensual human beings. To express our darkest fantasies and have our desires met, or perhaps even exceeded, transforms us, elevates us, and gives us added courage to explore ourselves.

There are an infinite number of sexy scripts in our erotic minds, and with the consent of a loving partner, we can enact many of those scenarios in a protected environment. We know that we can give our power to another because it is ours to give. The surrender of our power does not diminish us or degrade us, rather it elevates us because our surrender is voluntary, *willing*. Your dom accepts your power and the responsibility that goes with it; he cares for you and about you. By acknowledging and respecting limits, and building a new foundation of trust and communication, you can safely explore the outer reaches of the dark garden and the inner reaches of your erotic mind. He believes in your beauty as a submissive, and you become all the more beautiful because of his belief and acceptance of you.

Appendix A:
The Pillow-Talk Thesaurus

The Pillow-Talk Thesaurus is compiled from lists composed by Claudia Varrin, Kevin McCain, The Two Michelles, Soft, Sweet Mary, and San Francisco Sex Information.

Clitoris/Vagina:
beaver
bottom (U.K.)
box
bush
cherry
clam
cleft
clit
crack
crevasse
cunny
cunt
cunthole
cupid's door
fanny (U.K.)
flower
front door
G-spot
ginger snap
hole
honey pot
honey spot
kootch
jade gate

labia
lips, pink lips
love button
man in the boat
mound
muff
nether lips
oyster
peach
pearl
pearly gates
poonani
poontang
pussy
quim (U.K.)
sacred spot
secret flesh
secret garden
slit
snapper
snatch
swelling sex
swollen flesh
tail
yoni

Breasts:
bazooms
boobs
bust
hooters
jugs
knockers
melons
nips
puppies
tetas
tits
titties

Penis/Testicles:
balls
basket
beef
big kahoona
boner
chestnuts
chubby
cock
cojones
cucumber

dick
dong
erection
family jewels
gonads/nads
hard-on
heat-seeking moisture
  missile
hose
jade stalk
johnson
joint
joystick
knob
lance
love muscle
manhood
manmeat
member
monster
night stick
nuts
one-eyed trouser snake
organ
pecker
peter
phallus
pleasure tool
pole
prick
rod
root
schlong
shaft
skin flute
snake
spear
third leg
tool
trouser snake
unit
wang

weapon
willy
woody

Anus/Buttocks:
afterhole
arse
ass
ass meat
asshole
back door
backside
booty
brown spot
bum
bunghole
buns
butt
butt hole
cheeks
derierre
fanny
hinney
rear
rear-end
rosebud opening
rump
tail
the after-opening
the back (in, up)
tush
up the ass

Ejaculation:
assault
burst
bust a nut
come, cum
come enema
cream
cunt juice
explode

flood
get your rocks off
gism, jism
joy juice
load
love juice
ooze
pearl juice
pearl necklace
pop a cork
protein moisturizer
pussy juice
satisfy
sauce
seed
shoot
shoot a load, wad
slime
spunk
squirt

Oral Sex:
BJ
blow job
cock suck
cunnilingus
cunt lap
deep throat
eat cock, dick, pussy
face-pump
face-sit
fellatio
french
give head
go down on
gobble
muff dive/diving
oral pleasures
service
suck-off
swallow
tongue

tongue bath

Intercourse Nouns:
ball
bang
bury your bone
dip your dick
dip your wick
doggie style
doing the deed
doing the nasty
get it on
get laid
get some
hide the salami or
    sausage
hump
in-and-out
jump your bones
lay/get laid
make love
mattress mambo
nookie
open to
plug
poke
pork
pump
put out
quickie
ream
score
screw
shaft
shtumpf
sleep with
spend
spread for
stick it to
stuff it
tumble
two-backed beast

wet your wick
wild thing
work

Intercourse Verbs:
bury
doing the wild thing
drive/drive into
embed
enter
explode
force
foreplay
hammer
hump
impale
invade
mount
nose
penetrate
pierce
plow
plunge
pole-dance
pound
pork
probe
prod
pummel
pump
push
ram
rape
ream
ride
rock into
roll in the hay
root around
rub
sexed, sex up
shag
shove into

slam
spear
splay
spread
stab
stroke
thrust
violate

Anal Sex:
around the world
ass-fuck
ass-licking
ass-sucking
ass-worship
back-dooring
bit o'brown
brown road
bugger
butt fuck
cornhole
greek
Sadian
sodomize
sodomy
rim job
rimming
trip to the moon
up the ass

Slave Sounds:
breathed
cries
entreaties
hiss
mewls
moans
murmurs
pant
plea
purr
scream

shriek
sigh
slave's voice
small voice
sob
visceral moans
wail
weep
whimper
whine
whisper

Miscellaneous:
acceded to
arched like a cat
bared
beaten
caned
disciplined
enlarged
flagellated
flailed
flayed
flogged
gaping open

lashed
let fly
obediently engulf
paddled
pained
performed
potential
serve
serviced
spanked
swung at
waive
whipped

Appendix B:
Feeling and Emotion Words for the Slave and Master

Appendix B is compiled from lists composed by Claudia Varrin, The Two Michelles, Soft Sweet Mary, and San Francisco Sex Information.

abandon/ment	ashamed	brazen
abase/ment	assertive	broken
abused	assured	brutal
accessible	astonished	bubbly
aching	attracted	
adept	attuned	captivated (ing)
adoring	audacious	carefree
adventurous	available	caring
affectionate	awash	charmed (ing)
afire	awed	cheerful
aflame	awkward	cherished
aglow		childlike
alive	bad	chivalrous
all-knowing	bashful	coarse
alluring	bawdy	cocky
aloof	beguiling	cold
amazed	benevolent	compliant
amused	bestial	confident
angry	bewitching	consumed
anguish	bitchy	contented
appreciative	blissful	controllable
ardent	boisterous	coquettish
ardor	bold	cosmic
aroused	bossy	cowering
arrogant	bottled up	craven

crazy
creamy
cringing
crude
cruel
cuddly

daring
debauched
decadent
defenseless
defiant
degraded
delicate
delicious
delighted
demanding
demure
desirous
desperate
dignified
dilated
dirty
disdainful
dismissive
displayed
divine
docile
dominant
dripping

eager
earthy
eccentric
eclectic
ecstatic
effeminate
electrified
elfin
embarrassed
emotional
emotionless
empathetic

empty
enchanted
energetic
enkindle
enslaved
enthralled
entranced
enthusiastic
enticing
erotic
ethereal
evil
exacting
excited
exhibited
exotic
experienced
exposed
exquisite
exuberant

fabulous
fantastic
fascinated
fatherly
fawning
fearful
fearless
feisty
feminine
fervid
filthy
firm
flattering (ed)
flirtatious
floating
flustered
forceful
foreign
free
friendly
frightened
frisky

frivolous
funky
fusticated (ion)

gallant
gaping open
generous
gentle
giddy
glad
gleeful
glowing
good
gracious
grateful
gratified
greedy
groveled (ing)
guileful
guileless
guiltless
guilty

happy
heavenly
heightened
helpless
hesitant
honest
horny
hot
humbled
humiliated
humorous
hung
hungry (for)
hurt
hypnotized

ignited
imaginative
immoral
impetuous

impish
in charge
in control
in tune
indulgent
infantile
infatuated
inflamed
ingenuous
inhibited
innocent
insatiable
insecure
inspired
intelligent
intensified
intimate
intimidating (ed)
intoxicating
inventive
involved
irrational
irreverent

jaded
jealous
jovial
joyous
juicy

keyed up
kind
kinky
kittenish
knowing

lascivious
lewd
libidinous
licentious
little

lively
lonely
longing
loose
loud
loving
low
loyal
lubricated
lustful
lusty
luxuriated

macho
mad
masculine
masterful (ly)
mature
meek
melancholy
merciless
mesmerized
mischievous
modest
mortified
motherly
mysterious
mystical

naive
nasty
naughty
nervous
nice
noisy

obediently
obliging
obsessed
on fire
open

orgasmic
ornery
out of control
outgoing
outspoken
overjoyed
overwhelmed

pampered
parental
passionate
passive
patient
peaceful
perverse
pitiless
playful
pleasant
pleased
pliant
poised
potent
powerful
powerless
pretty
prideful
prim
prissy
proper
proud
provocative
prudish
prurient
psychic
pulsating

quail
quiet
quivered (ing)

rakish
rebellious

reckless
relaxed
relinquished
relish
remorseless
remote
removed
reserved
respect (ed) (ful)
responsible
responsive
restless
retiring
revealing
reveled
reverent
rigid
rippled
rock hard
roguish
romantic
rude
ruthless

sacrifice
sad
sadistic
safe
sated
satisfied
saucy
savage
scared
secretive
secure
seductive
self-conscious
selfish
sensitive
sensual
sensuous
sentimental

serene
serious
servile
severe
sexual
sexy
shaky
shame
shivered
shocked
shy
silly
sincere
skillful
slinky
slow
small
soft
sophisticated
special
spiritual
spiteful
splendid
spontaneous
spunky
stern
stiff
stimulated
strict
strong
subdued
subjugated
sublime
submissive
submitted
subtle
succumbed
sultry
sure
surrender
sweet
sympathetic

talented
tamed
teased
temperamental
tempted
tender
tentative
terrific
terror
thankful
thoughtful
thrilled
tickled
timid
tired
titillated
tolerated
tormented
tortured
touched
tough
tractable
tranquil
trusting
turgid
turned on

unaffected
uncompromising
understanding
unfeeling
uninhibited
unpredictable
unselfish
unyielding

valued
vibrant
vicious
violated
virtuous
vital

vivacious
voluptuous
vulnerable

wacky
wallowed
wanton
warm
wet

whimsical
wholesome
wicked
wild
willing
winsome
witty
wonderful
wondrous

yearned for
yielded
young
youthful

zany
zealous

Appendix C:
SM Friendly Book Sellers and Direct-Contact Publishers

Booksellers:

A Different Light Book Review
151 West 19th Street
New York, NY 10011
212-989-4850
FAX: 212-989-2158
MO Catalog: 800-343-4002

A Different Light Book Store
8853 Santa Monica Blvd.
West Hollywood, CA 90069
310-854-6601

A Different Light Book Store
489 Castro Street
San Francisco, CA 94114
415-431-0891

Arthur Hamilton
P. O. Box 180145
Richmond Hill, NY 11418
718-441-6066

Blowfish (Mail Order)
2261 Market Street, #284
San Francisco, CA 94114
800-352-2569
website: http://www.blowfish.com/

e-mail: Blowfish @ Blowfish.com
415-252-4340
Fax: 415-252-4349

Bob's News & Books
1515 South Andrews Avenue
Ft. Lauderdale, FL 33316
954-524-4731

Body Language
11424 Lorraine Avenue
Cleveland, OH 44111
216-251-3330

Books Bohemian
P. O. Box 17218
Los Angeles, CA 90017
213-385-6761 "Bob"

Borders Books & Music
1501 4th Avenue
Seattle, WA 98101
206-622-4599

Constance Enterprises, Ltd.
P. O. Box 43079
Upper Montclair, NJ 07043
973-746-4200
973-746-4722

The Crypt (Technologies Corp.)
3132 Jefferson Street
San Diego, CA 92110
800-938-0283

The Crypt
131 Broadway
Denver, CO 80203

The Crypt Entertainment Center
139 Broadway
Denver, CO 80203

The Crypt
1310 Union Street
Long Beach, CA 90802

The Crypt on Washington
1515 Washington
San Diego, CA 92103

Good Vibrations
1210 Valencia Street
San Francisco, CA 94110
415-974-8980

Good Vibrations
2504 San Pablo
Berkeley, CA 94702
510-841-8987

Good Vibrators Direct Mail Order
938 Howard Street, Suite 101
San Francisco, CA 94103
415-974-8990

Grand Opening
318 Harvard St., Suite 32
Brookline, MA 02146
617-731-2626

The Leather Rose Gallery
2537 W. Fullerton

Chicago, IL 60647
773-665-2069

Marigny Bookstore
600 Frenchman Street
New Orleans, LA 70116
504-943-9875

North Park Adult Video
4094 30th Street
San Diego, CA 92104

Passion Flower
4 Yosemite Avenue
Oakland, CA 94611
510-601-7750

The Source Bookstore
958 Queen Street
Southington, CT 06489
860-621-6255

Spice of Life Boutique
2940 SW 30th Avenue, #2
Pembroke Park, FL 33009
954-458-5200

Tower Books
383 Lafayette Street
New York, NY 10003
212-228-5100

The Wooden Shoe Book Store
508 South 5th Street
Philadelphia, PA 19147
215-413-0999

Publishers:

Alyson Publications
40 Plympton Street
Boston, MA 02118
617-524-5679

Black Lace
332 Ladbroke Grove
London W10 5AH UK
(catalog of titles available)

Blue Moon Books
Box 1040
Cooper Station
New York, NY 10276
800-535-0000

Creation Books (Dept. V)
83 Clerkenwell Road
London EC1 UK
011 44 171 430-9878
(catalog of titles available)

Daedalus Publishing Co.
584 Castro Street

San Francisco, CA 94110
415-974-8980

Greenery Press
3739 Balboa Avenue #195
San Francisco, CA 94121

Masquerade Books
Dept. BMRH97
801 Second Avenue
Jamaica, NY 11430
800-375-2356
(Also carries titles from Rhinerocero
    Books)

Spring Publications
299 East Quassett Road
Woodstock, CT 06281
860-974-3428

Appendix D:
SM Support Groups

Arizona Power Exchange
5821 N. 67th Avenue
Suite 103-276
Glendale, AZ 85301
602-848-8737

The Black Rose
P. O. Box 11161
Arlington, VA 22210-1161

Bound by Desire
PO Box 1322
Austin, TX 78767-1322
512-764-9900

Dedicated & Safe
6417 W. Higgens Road
Chicago, IL
312-463-2178

Dr. Susan Marilyn Block
Institute of The Erotic Arts and
   Sciences
8306 Wilshire Blvd., #1047
Beverly Hills, CA 90211
800-771-7754
FAX: 310-475-3405

Gemini
P. O. Box 282719
San Francisco, CA 94128

The Human Awareness Institute
1720 South Amphlett Blvd.
   #128
San Mateo, CA 94402
415-571-5524

Institute for Advanced Study
   of Human Sexuality
1523 Franklin St.
San Francisco, CA 94109
415-928-1133

Leather Rose Society
POB 223971
Dallas, TX 75222
214-289-0619

MOB
c/o Grand Opening
318 Harvard St., Suite 32
Brookline, MA 02146
"Kim"
617-731-2626

The National Leather Association
P. O. Box 17463
Seattle, WA 98107
(main office)

The Orb and Scepter
c/o The New Visionary Press
252 Convention Center Drive, #483
Las Vegas, NV 89109
702-251-7201

PEP: Albuquerque
1113 Delemar NW
Albuquerque, NM 87107
505-764-5748

Pervert Scouts
3288 21st Street, #19
San Francisco, CA 94110
415-285-7985

San Diego Power Exchange
P. O. Box 87564

San Diego, CA 92134-7564
619-467-1745

San Francisco Sex Information
415-989-7374

Sexuality Education and Information
   Council of the United States
   (SEICUS)
130 West 42nd St., #350
New York, NY 10036-7802
212-819-9770

Society of Janus
P. O. Box 426794
San Francisco, CA 94142
415-985-7177

The TES Association
24 Bond Street
New York, NY
212-388-7022

Suggested Reading

Nonfiction Works

Amazons: Erotic Explorations of Ancient Myths by Tammy Jo Eckhart (New York: Masquerade Books, 1997). Historically correct with very entertaining extrapolations about the sexual preferences of Amazon queens—a must for women interested in dominant women down the ages.

Anal Pleasure and Health by Jack Morin, Ph.D. (San Francisco: YES Press/Down There Press, 1981). A sensitive and thoughtful guide for those wishing to learn more about anal pleasure.

The Anne Rice Reader by Katherine Ramsland (New York: Ballantine Books, 1997). Includes a critique of the dominant and submissive qualities of the love-slave Eliot Slater from *Exit to Eden* and the slave spirit to the Mayfair family of witches, Lasher.

The Art of Sensual Female Dominance: A Guide for Women by Claudia Varrin (Secaucus, N.J.: Birch Lane Press, 1998). Discusses the art of being a dominant female and gives basic how-to instructions for budding dominas.

The Bottoming Book; Or, How to Get Terrible Things Done to You by Wonderful People by C. Liszt and D. Easton (available from Lady Green, Greenery Press, 3739 Balboa Avenue, #195, San Francisco, CA 94121). Their tongue-in-cheek style works very well in getting across what these two San Francisco communicators want you to know.

The Compleat Spanker by Lady Green (San Francisco: Greenery Press). A complete introduction to the art of the reddened cheek. Friendly, humorous, and informative.

Consensual Sadomasochism: How to Talk About It and How to Do It Safely by William A. Henkin, Ph.D., and Sybil Holiday, CCSSE (San Francisco: Daedalus, 1996). Written by a lifestyle couple, this thoughtful piece helps to demythologize consensual S&M and provides an excellent safety guide for new players.

Dark Eros: The Imagination of Sadism by Thomas Moore (Woodstock, Conn.: Spring Publications, 1994). Presents the philosophies of sadism and its eroticism intelligently.

234

A Different Loving by Gloria G. Brame, William D. Brame, and Jon Jacobs (New York: Villard Books, 1995). A sympathetic, nonjudgmental treatment of SM, complete with honest and interesting interviews of lifestylists and players in the scene.

Erotic Power by Gini Graham Scott, Ph.D. (Secaucus, N.J.: Citadel Press, 1997). One of the first women writing from clinical and empirical data, her work is a must read.

The Ethical Slut by Dossie Easton and Catherine A. Liszt (San Francisco: Greenery Press). I wish this one was around when I was in high school.

Exhibitionism for the Shy by Carol Queen (San Francisco: Down There Press, 1995). Delightful, open-minded book about freeing your inner, exhibitionistic self.

Figure Training Fundamentals by Versatile Fashions (P.O. Box 6273, Orange, CA 92863). A must for the budding corseteer.

Free Wealin': A Hitch-hiker's Guide to the London Scene by Ishmael Skyes (available from the author at The Academy Club and from Ishmael Skyes, P.O. Box 135, Hereford HR2 UK). A fun read from a scene player in London will give you a humorous look at SM across the pond.

Learning the Ropes by Race Bannon (San Francisco: Daedalus, 1992). A concise, taut how-to, successfully comparing SM play to Erotic Theater.

The Loving Dominant by John Warren, Ph.D. (New York: Masquerade Books, 1994).

Masochism: A Jungian View by Lyn Cowan (Woodstock, Conn.: Spring Publications, 1985, 1998). The author has a deep understanding of the spirituality of masochism and ancient Greek mythology as it relates to psychology.

Miss Abernathy's Concise Slave Training Manual by Christine Abernathy (available from Greenery Press, 3739 Balboa Avenue, #195, San Francisco, CA 94121).

Screw the Roses, Send Me the Thorns by Philip Miller and Molly Devon, Mystic Rose Books (available from the authors at P.O. Box 1036/SMS, Fairfield, CT 06432). Written by a lifestyle couple, male dom/fem sub, this book will give you topping from a man's point of view with interspersed comments and writings from the lady.

Sensuous Magic: A Guide for Adventurous Couples by Pat Califia (New York: Masquerade Books, 1993). A sensitive and intelligent start-up guide for couples, which includes fantasy scenarios submitted by real couples.

The Sexually Dominant Woman: A Workbook for Nervous Beginners by Lady Green (available from the author at 3739 Balboa Avenue, #195, San Francisco, CA 94121). Highly recommended for the budding dominant.

SM101: A Realistic Introduction by Jay Wiseman (available from the author, P.O. Box 1261, Berkeley, CA 94701). All the information you could ever possibly want and then some. Excellent anatomy dissertations but way too much information for the beginner; digest slowly. Geared more toward dominant males.

Soul Mates by Thomas Moore (New York: Harper Perennial, 1994). Companion piece to *Dark Eros*.

The Topping Book; Or, How to Get Terrible Things Done to You by Wonderful People by Dossie Easton and Catherine List (available from Lady Green, Greenery Press, 3739 Balboa Avenue, #195, San Francisco, CA 94121). Entertaining and informative, in their usual inimitable style. The bookend piece for *The Bottoming Book*.

An Unquiet Mind by Kay Redfield Jamison (New York: Vintage Books, 1995). A woman's search for love and security through the moods and madness of manic depression.

Women on Top by Nancy Friday (New York: Pocket Star Books, 1991). Women's dominant fantasies.

Fiction

The Ages of Lulu by Almudena Grandes (New York: Grove Press, translation copyright 1993 by Sonia Sotto).

The Amulet by Lisette Allen (Black Lace, 332 Ladbroke Grove, London W10 5AH, England, 1995, catalog of titles available).

Belinda by Anne Rice writing as Anne Rampling (New York: Jove, 1986).

The Beauty Trilogy by Anne Rice, writing as A. N. Roquelaure (New York: Plume Press): *The Claiming of Sleeping Beauty*, 1983; *Beauty's Punishment*, 1984; and *Beauty's Release*, 1985.

The Captive, The Captive II, The Captive III, The Captive IV, by Anonymous (New York: Blue Moon Books, 1991).

The Captive Flesh by Cleo Cordell (Black Lace, 332 Ladbroke, London W10 5AH England, 1993, catalog of titles available).

Delta of Venus by Anais Nin (New York: Harcourt Brace Jovanovich, 1969).

Exit to Eden by Anne Rice, writing as Ann Rampling (New York: Dell Publishing, 1985).

Jewel of Xanadu by Roxanne Carr (Black Lace, 332 Ladbroke, London W10 5AH England, 1995, catalog of titles available).

Juliet Rising by Cleo Cordell (Black Lace, 332 Ladbroke, London W10 5AH England, 1994, catalog of titles available).

Justine, Philosophies in the Bedroom and Other Writings by Marquis de Sade (New York: Grove Weidenfeld, copyright 1965 by Richard Seaver and Austryn Wainhouse).

The Last Temptation of Christ by Nikos Kazantzakis (New York: Touchstone Books, 1960).

The Marketplace by Laura Antoniou, writing as Sara Adamson (New York: Masquerade Books, 1994).

My Darling Dominatrix by Grant Andrews (New York: Masquerade Books, 1997).

Nine and a Half Weeks by Elizabeth MacNeill (New York: Henry Robbins Books, E. P. Dutton, 1978).

One Hundred and Twenty Days of Sodom by Marquis de Sade (New York: Grove Weidenfeld, copyright 1966 by Richard Seaver and Austryn Wainhouse).

The Slave by Laura Antoniou writing as Sara Adamson (New York: Masquerade Books, 1994).

The Story of "O" by Pauline Reage (New York: Ballantine Books, copyright 1965 by Grove Press, First Ballantine Books edition, 1973).

The Story of the Eye by Lord Auch by Georges Bataille, translated by Joachim Neugroschel (San Francisco: City Lights Books).

The Trainer by Laura Antoniou, writing as Sara Adamson (New York: Masquerade Books, 1995).

The Whip Angels by Anonymous (Velvet 5, Creation Books, 83 Clerkenwell Road, London EC1 England).

Venus in Furs by Leopold von Sacher-Masoch (New York: Blast Books, 1989).

Magazines

The Sandmutopian Guardian
The Utopian Network
P.O. Box 1146
New York, NY 10156
    Informative and often humorous rather than titillating, this is the longest standing pan-sexual SM magazine in the United States. It is filled with practical and factual information for novice and advanced players. New owners Gillian Blum and Mitch Kessler are the proprietors of Adam's Sensual Toys and Gillian's Whips.

Prometheus
TES
P.O. Box 2783
New York, NY 20263
    The Quarterly of the TES Association, formerly the Eulenspiegel Society, which is the oldest SM society in the country. More male dom oriented.

The Art of Fetish, Fantasy and Fun
171 Pier Avenue #308
Santa Monica, CA 90405
    Slick and pretty, loaded with very sexy, fetish-y pictures.

SECRET
P.O. Box 1400
1000 Brussels 1 Belgium
    Beautiful glossy black-and-white magazine devoted to SM in all its glory. Intelligent articles by lifestyle writers and published SM authors are informative and sexy, and the photography is very beautiful and erotic. An excellent publication.

Skin Two
For subscriptions:
Tim Woodward Publishing Ltd.
Unit 63
Abbey Business Centre
Ingate Place
London SW8 3NS England

or contact them on the Internet: web-site: www.skintwo.co.uk

The granddaddy of fetish publications, this is the one all others aspire to. High-quality paper, sexy and fun photos, amusing and intelligent articles take you through the London scene. If you follow each issue, the faces there will become like old friends. These people don't have their finger on the pulse of the SM scene—they *are* the scene.

Glossary

There are terms listed here that may not have been used in this book but you may hear them or come across them elsewhere, and I'd like you to be as informed as you can be. You will not find this glossary to be just a list of definitions but rather a feeling, an expression of SM.

abrasion: rubbing of the skin to heighten sensation.

advanced techniques: techniques that require special training from an experienced teacher.

age-play/authority figure: acting or treating another as if they were younger for the purpose of erotic role-playing.

anal (or ass) play: sexual activity such as intercourse, rimming, and fisting that involves the anus.

animal play: the practice of acting (or treating someone) like an animal (e.g., a pony) or pampered pet (e.g., lap dog) for erotic enjoyment or training.

BDSM: traditional initials that denote the triple components of bondage and discipline, dominance and submission, and sadomasochism.

body modification: practices that reshape or decorate the body for erotic purposes or to signify ownership by the top. Common practices are piercing, tattooing, and corset training.

body worship: the physical adoration, loving, or caring for the top as an object of devotion; allowing the bottom to touch or stimulate parts of the top's body for sexual gratification, to express submission, or to experience humiliation.

bondage: any form of restraint applied to the body to restrict movement, including ropes, handcuffs, shackles, hoods, gags, spreader bars, harnesses, plastic wrap, and suspension.

bottom: submissive or romantically masochistic person in a relationship.

breast torture (also tit torture): intense stimulation of the breasts and nipples.

breath control: the control by the dominant of the submissive's access to air by covering the mouth, nose, or both, to heighten sensation or for other erotic purposes. This is a very advanced technique and an extremely risky and dangerous activity.

brown showers: using scat (feces) for erotic purposes. For reasons of health, physical and psychological, this is NOT a novice game.

cane: instrument made of rattan used for discipline or corporal punishment.

cat o'nine tails: any multilashed flogger.

collar: a band of leather, metal, rubber, or cloth such as lace or velvet cord that encircles the neck of the bottom. It is a common signal that a bottom is in a relationship with a top. The gift of a collar to the bottom from the top often signifies the commencement of a committed relationship.

condition (v): to develop a reflex or behavior pattern or to cause to become accustomed to. Much of slave training in SM relies on conditioning techniques.

consenting to the nonconsensual: a consensual scenario where the bottom has agreed to allow the top to pretend to force nonconsensual actions, such as rape or interrogation, upon her.

corporal punishment: punishment inflicted directly on the body, such as whipping, caning, or spanking.

cunt torture: activities that concentration on the female genitals with the intention of producing intense sensations in the clitoris, inner and outer lips, and vagina. This is "torture" in the most playful sense: This area is very sensitive and delicate so a little goes a long way.

dark side: the shadow land of the mind where SM fantasies originate.

discipline: punishment or correction, or the method of training a submissive.

do-me-queen: a bottom that gives nothing back to the top, whose sole interest lies in receiving attention.

dominant, dom: male exercising authority or control, ruling, prevailing, the one who prefers to be on "top."

edge play: role-play near the edge of submissive's or dominant's physical or psychological limits.

endorphins: a group of morphinelike hormones secreted by the brain when the body is under unusual or extreme stress or in pain. When stimulated, these chemicals produce pain killers and tranquilizers to induce a sort of euphoria, a natural high, or pleasure-ecstacy.

exhibitionism: act of publicly exposing parts of one's body that are conventionally covered, especially in seeking sexual gratification or stimulation.

fantasy divergence: a turn of events where your fantasy takes one path and his takes another.

fetish: if originating in childhood or the teenage years, it is a devotion to a nonsexual object or activity, like the foot or leather, that excites erotic feelings. If the fetish is developed later in life, the object need not be nonsexual but can be a breast, buttock, or other traditionally sexual body part.

fetishism: in psychology, it identifies the concept of devotion of desires; a condition in which erotic feelings are aroused by a sexual or nonsexual object which involves the use of the object itself, or at times the use of the object with a sexual partner.

Fetterati: one level of kook-a-maniacs, these SMers are deeply involved in SM but unlike Perverati, Fetterati usually prefer to keep their SM practices and games behind closed doors.

fisting (also called handballing): inserting the entire hand into the vagina or anus for erotic pleasure. For some, this will always remain in the realm of hot fantasy. It is also an advanced technique and requires training from an expert.

flogger: any multilashed whip.

flying or floating: a state of well-being induced by endorphin euphoria; a rare and special transcendent state of consciousness achieved during an SM scene.

going under: the gradual achieving of the submissive state; the emotional process by which the slave becomes immersed in fantasy (not as deep as *flying* or *floating*).

golden showers: urinating on another person for erotic gratification.

head games: manipulating a person's psychological state for erotic purposes. This is domination where the focus is mental, as in humiliation, or the use of fear, anxiety, or embarrassment to intensify control. (This is friendly and not to be confused with a mind-fuck.)

high colonics: a series of enemas to flush all waste matter from the large intestine. Done as a preparation for extensive anal play and/or fisting, as an act of control over, and humiliation of, the bottom by the top, or for purely erotic sensation.

humiliation: playfully humbling or teasing the bottom about her sexual desires, ranging from mild embarrassment to shame to degradation. This can be done by lowering her status from that of a human to something of lesser value, like a cat or an orifice for sex. This is the deliberate reduction of the ego for erotic purposes and is not to lower or injure self-esteem.

interrogation: consensual, playful resistance games where the top questions the bottom using "torture" to get secret information and push the bottom's limits. The information could be the safe-word, the bottom's name, anything.

Kegels: an exercise to improve control over the pubococcygeus (PC) muscle and enhance orgasm. To do Kegels, locate the PC muscle by pretending you are urinating, then contract the muscles to stop the flow of urine. Once you locate this muscle, practice contracting and relaxing it. The first Kegel exercise is to inhale deeply and contract the PC muscle as tightly as you can. Hold your breath and the muscle for a few seconds, then relax and exhale completely. In the second Kegel, inhale deeply and contract the muscles as quickly as you can for about ten contractions. Then exhale and completely relax.

Kook-a-mania: affectionate term for SM games.

latex: rubberlike material used in making tight, or restrictive, fetish clothing, often a fetish object in itself.

leather master: a dominant who prefers to dress in leather.

limits: boundaries the dominant and submissive set for each other during the talk-it-over stage regarding dos and don'ts using the scene; point where something that was fun, isn't anymore.

masochist: one who gets erotic pleasure from physical or psychological pain or intense sensation, either inflicted by others or self-inflicted; one who can accept pain and turn it into pleasure, making it an erotic event.

master: male dominant partner in an SM relationship.

mental bondage: assuming a bondage position on command and "holding it" as if tied in ropes.

military scene: fantasies involving wearing uniforms, adopting rank, and using imaginary military settings as part of SM play.

mummification: intense form of complete bondage where the sub is totally swathed in ace bandages, plastic wrap, cloth and tape, or some other material, making her look like a mummy.

"O" ring: a style of ring made popular as a gift from the master to the slave in *The Story of O.* The ring is a plain band with a ring hanging from it, similar to the rings used to restrain the slaves at Roissy. Like a collar, the giver can ask for the ring back when the relationship has ended.

over-the-knee (OTK): classic spanking position.

paddle: a rigid, flat implement made of wood or leather used to smack a bottom.

pain slut: slang for a masochist who derives pleasure from physical pain.

Perverati: the hierarchy of the Kook-a-maniacs, Perverati are driven by their sexuality. This SM group has incorporated SM techniques into their lovemaking on a regular basis, in private and in public.

pet: a bottom who gives up physical and psychological control, and through submission and service to the master is treated as a prized possession.

player: person participating in an SM scene or activity.

playing: engaging in an SM scene or activity.

position training: process of teaching the submissive to assume certain positions on command.

power exchange: the temporary, consensual transfer of control for the duration of the scene.

property: the bottom who feels that she is owned like chattel, or controlled, either fully or partially by the top. Written contracts often spell out the exact terms of these relationships.

punishment scene: fantasy where the top pretends or intends to correct the bottom for improper behavior.

rim job or rimming: slang term for anal-oral sex.

ritual: a ceremony of acceptance, as in kissing a collar or leash or other actions that give a ceremonial air to the proceedings.

role-playing: enactment of a prearranged scene wherein the two players assume characters different from their own to better play out the fantasy.

sadist: one who gets sexual pleasure from consensually and romantically mistreating others, or who gets pleasure from inflicting consensual emotional or physical pain on others; one who can turn what would otherwise be an unpleasant experience into an erotic event.

safe-word or safe-signal: word or action used by the submissive to stop or slow down the action.

sensation slut: one who gets erotic pleasure and satisfaction from experiencing different types of sensation, such as from hot wax, ice cubes, feather tickling, wartenberg wheel; also known as a slave of sensation.

sensory deprivation: the taking away of one or more of the submissive's senses to heighten her awareness of the others.

service: in the SM context, doing for the other as an expression of love, devotion, obedience, submission, and so on or performing sexual acts upon command for the master, as in "servicing the master."

service-oriented top: a top who achieves gratification by fulfilling the bottom's specific fantasy or scenario; a top who expects, enjoys, and graciously accepts services rendered to him by the bottom, such as cooking, cleaning, laundry, boot polishing, and so on.

slave: human being who, in a fantasy, is owned as property by another and is absolutely subject to his will; a person who is completely dominated by some outside influence, habit, or another person. This was once a generic term for a bottom but now it is impolite to assume that someone is a slave merely because she is submissive or a masochist.

slave training: the process of teaching a submissive to serve the dominant.

SM: abbreviation of the new-age term "SexMagick" or "Sensual Magic." There is a movement afoot, here and overseas, to make SM the general term for our erotic techniques.

SM orgasm: full-body release of emotional, physical, and spiritual energy often accompanied by tremors and shivers, quivers and spasms. The genitals are not necessarily involved in this mind and body earthquake.

S&M: traditional term for sadomasochistic sexual terms, now fallen out of favor because of its connotations with abuse, pornography, and serial killers.

spanking: good old-fashioned hand walloping delivered to the sub's bottom.

speculum: originally a piece of medical equipment, it is designed to hold the vagina or anus open for examination. In SM, it is used to display the bottom, or to hold her open to expedite stuffing an orifice.

Spicers: those who incorporate SM techniques into their lovemaking on an occasional basis.

spreader bar: strong bar of wood, metal, or other material, with rings and cuffs attached to keep the sub's arms or legs apart.

submissive (adj): having a tendency to submit without resistance; docile; yielding.

submissive (n): someone who surrenders control to the dominant in a prearranged scene, slang "sub."

surrender: the mental, physical and emotional state of sensual submission; the willing relinquishing of control and/or power.

switch: to change roles during the SM scene, or one who can change roles during the scene or alternates between being a top and a bottom.

temperature play: using hot or cold, or alternating the use of hot or cold, to stimulate sensation.

topping from the bottom: when the submissive partner is more experienced than the top, the bottom will control the action with the top's permission; otherwise, it is taking control of a scene by the submissive person without attempting to preserve the illusion that the dom is in charge.

vampire glove: leather glove that has sharp metal tines or tacks lining the palms.

vanilla sex: term used by players for the sexual habits of non-SM players.

verbal humiliation: the use of disparaging language, or dirty words, to scold, insult, chastise, or humiliate the bottom for erotic pleasure.

Victorian scene: a fantasy that takes place in an imaginary Victorian setting such as a school or a bordello. Corsets, caning, and role-playing as lord or maid may be included, among other props, pastimes, and passions.

water sports: sex play involving enemas and golden showers.

Index